Echoes of Emerson

STUDIES IN AMERICAN LITERARY REALISM AND NATURALISM

Echoes of Emerson

RETHINKING REALISM IN TWAIN, JAMES, WHARTON, AND CATHER

DIANA HOPE POLLEY

THE UNIVERSITY OF ALABAMA PRESS
Tuscaloosa

The University of Alabama Press
Tuscaloosa, Alabama 35487-0380
uapress.ua.edu

Hardcover edition published 2017.
Paperback edition published 2019.
eBook edition published 2017.

Typeface: Garamond Pro

Cover image: A. A. Mills, *Man Strolling in Wooded Landscape*,
mid-nineteenth century
Cover design: David Nees

Paperback ISBN: 978-0-8173-5971-3

A previous edition of this book has been catalogued by the Library of Congress
as follows:
Library of Congress Cataloging-in-Publication Data
Names: Polley, Diana Hope, 1970– author.
Title: Echoes of Emerson : rethinking realism in Twain, James, Wharton, and
Cather / Diana Hope Polley.
Description: Tuscaloosa : The University of Alabama Press, 2017. | Series: Studies
in American literary realism and naturalism | Includes bibliographical references
and index.
Identifiers: LCCN 2017007703 | ISBN 9780817319564 (cloth) | ISBN
9780817391393 (e book)
Subjects: LCSH: Realism in literature. | American fiction—19th century—
History and criticism.
Classification: LCC PS374.R37   P55 2017 | DDC 813/.409—dc23
LC record available at https://lccn.loc.gov/2017007703

For my family

Contents

Acknowledgments

Echoes of Emerson has come to fruition through the invaluable support of family, friends, and colleagues. I am indebted to the many outstanding faculty members at the Graduate Center of the City University of New York (CUNY) —most notably William Kelly, Morris Dickstein, and David Reynolds—who fostered my growth as a scholar and taught me how to be a better writer. Among a host of talented and unique individuals I met at CUNY, Andrea Knutson, Samuel Cohen, Kimberly Engber, and Tanya Radford inspired me then and continue to show me what it means to be an academic and a friend.

I am also indebted to all of my colleagues—past and present—at Southern New Hampshire University (SNHU). I have been privileged to be a part of a community of dedicated faculty who care deeply about teaching and scholarship and who never forget how to balance work with the pleasures of food, drink, friendship, and fantasy football. I am fortunate enough to have too many wonderful colleagues to thank all individually, but special thanks must go to Andrew Martino, Ken Nivison, Megan Paddack, Brooke Gilmore, Liz Henley, David Swain, Susan Youngs, Allison Cummings, and Elise Pepin for being my sounding board and motivating me to do everything I do, better. Susan Cook, my tireless research partner at SNHU, has been particularly instrumental to this project, reading every line of my manuscript at least three times and providing vital feedback—sometimes painful, always indispensable. In addition, the project was supported by SNHU in the form of generous summer grants, which gave me the time and space to complete the book.

Several organizations have helped promote the development and publication of this book. Many years ago, I took part in a dynamic and stimulating

NEH Summer Seminar on Emerson in Albuquerque, New Mexico, with Russell Goodman, Stanley Cavell, and Barbara Packer; that seminar propelled me to continue my work on Emerson and the realists. Nynke Dorhout was especially accommodating in providing me access to the library at "The Mount," Edith Wharton's home; there, I had the unique pleasure of perusing Wharton's personal collection of Emerson's writings, which helped inform my chapter on *The House of Mirth*. I would also like to thank Dan Waterman and Gary Scharnhorst at the University of Alabama Press as well as the manuscript's two reviewers, whose thoughtful and thorough suggestions went a long way toward making this a better book. A condensed version of my chapter on Willa Cather's *My Ántonia* was previously published in the *Willa Cather Newsletter & Review* (Winter–Spring 2006) and subsequently reprinted in *Bloom's Modern Critical Interpretations: Willa Cather's "My Ántonia"* (2008); I appreciate their permission to include a revised version of that material in my book.

To all of my friends and family outside academia, I am grateful for your steadfast support. I am particularly indebted to Cathy La Forge, Leilany Brenes, Karina Fassett, Chris Holbrook, and Brad Weaver: you have all been my greatest cheerleaders, even when my work as a professor and scholar may have seemed mystifying. Finally, I dedicate this book to my family, who instilled in me the importance of education and taught me the limitless rewards of culture, history, and inquiry. I have been so fortunate—as a daughter, granddaughter, sister, aunt, niece, and cousin (as well as a "mom" to a little wheaten terrier named Dash)—to be inundated with your unconditional love, patience, and boundless encouragement. I owe an enormous debt of gratitude, in particular, to my parents, who have always been my most ardent supporters. Without my family, this book would not have been possible.

Echoes of Emerson

Introduction

One may say that the Civil War marks an era in the history of the American mind. It introduced into the national consciousness a certain sense of proportion and relation, of the world being a more complicated place than it had hitherto seemed, the future more treacherous, success more difficult. . . . The good American, in days to come, will be a more critical person than his complacent and confident grandfather. He has eaten of the tree of knowledge. He will not, I think, be a sceptic, and still less, of course, a cynic; but he will be, without discredit to his well-known capacity for action, an observer.

—Henry James, *Hawthorne*

On September 12, 2001, news agencies around the world were quick to label September 11, 2001, "the day the world changed" ("Day" 13). 9/11 became a major pinnacle, a new epoch in national, international, and even "civilizational" history (Hertzberg 27). The September 12 *New York Times* editorial page described the day as "one of those moments in which history splits, and we define the world as 'before' and 'after.' . . . We look back at sunrise yesterday through pillars of smoke and dust, down streets snowed under the atomized debris of the skyline, and we understand that everything has changed" ("War"). In a *Washington Post* article, George F. Will observed that just "when American political debate had reached a nadir of frivolousness, . . . the nation's decade-long holiday from history came to a shattering end." In *Newsweek*, Fareed Zakaria proclaimed: "We are struck silent by honest-to-goodness history. Or History. This is surely the End of the End of History." This tragic event was no longer simply about "history," the narratives read by schoolchildren in textbooks; this was about "History," long dormant, waiting for its next apocryphal moment.[1]

There is little question why these writers saw 9/11 as a watershed moment. The sheer number of casualties was unimaginable; according to William Safire it was "the worst bloodbath on our territory since Antietam Creek's waters ran red." Moreover, visual representations of death and destruction surpassed any of those previously witnessed by Americans. Eight million New Yorkers saw the smoke and felt the ashes for weeks after the attacks. For those who did not witness the events firsthand, images were forever seared into memory by live feeds, endless media montages, slow-motion replays, and minutely detailed timelines. The baseball season stalled, Disney World closed its doors, national air travel froze, regular television programming paused, and for over ninety commercial-free hours "three broadcast networks . . . covered one news event for more consecutive hours than any previous event in American history" (Carter and Rutenberg). Perhaps most shocking of all was that the unexpected had happened. The possibility of something like 9/11, of a foreign attack on national soil, had been seemingly absent from the national consciousness. A formidable, long-held myth of American security—both physical and economic—suddenly collapsed.

Critical fallout predicted a restructuring of the American psyche, one not unlike Henry James's vision in *Hawthorne* regarding the Civil War. The feeling was that the world had, yet again, become "a more complicated place than it had hitherto seemed." Pundits' reactions reflected a similar sense that the post-9/11 American had "eaten of the tree of knowledge," that "in days to come, [he would] . . . be a more critical person than his complacent and confident grandfather" (114). Roger Simon of *US News and World Report* declared: "In just one chilling hour, America joined the ranks of the lost innocents. . . . Life as we know it in these United States ended Tuesday morning." Roger Rosenblatt of *Time* declared that the tragic events "could spell the end of the age of irony"; Americans, he claimed, would now cease to think that "nothing is real."

Post-9/11 narratives constructed by these writers were, in a sense, fictions. History had never ended, America was no less innocent, and irony was alive and well. The terrorists had been planning these attacks for years; September 10 was as "real" as September 12, and the world was certainly no more dangerous than it had previously been. Rather, news analysts and critics confirmed Frank Kermode's theory of narrative, of man's need for "sense-making" through crisis, his need to give meaning to lives by constructing concrete beginnings and ends (3). Kermode writes in *The Sense of an Ending* that "we thrive on epochs" (7), and it is precisely this "need to live by the pattern rather than the fact" that seemed to drive so many readings of 9/11 (11). Instead of a force that is continuously active, continuously in motion, these narratives constructed history as fragments, bound by critical moments of time into a decisive sense of before and after.

This twenty-first-century historical event helps readers grasp how late-nineteenth-century Americans such as Henry James might have envisioned the seemingly radical change in America after the Civil War. While the particulars of 9/11 and the Civil War may appear disparate—not only in terms of the events themselves but also in terms of their geopolitical ramifications—what resonates in each of these events is the perception of historical magnitude and its concomitant effects on national consciousness.[2] In both historical moments, Americans experienced a type of sublime connection to traumatic events, where the relationship between the subject and the objective world collapsed, and transcendental detachment seemed to become impossible. This relationship was most evident during the early days of the Civil War: on July 21, 1861, during the First Battle of Bull Run, civilians from all over the Washington area gathered to picnic and watch the eagerly anticipated battle unfold; convinced of a quick and bloodless Union victory, these naive citizens instead encountered frightened, fleeing soldiers, gory injuries, and mass fatalities. This breakdown of consciousness, this disruption of a solidified romantic vision, would continue throughout the war as soldiers returned with missing limbs and Mathew Brady published his widely disseminated photographs of mutilated corpses on battlefields. As with 9/11, the publicized events of the Civil War exceeded imaginative possibility, dispelled myths of American stability, and invoked ideas of a new historical moment in which everything had changed.[3]

In the days, months, and years since 9/11, American culture has begun to respond to the historical magnitude of this event, yet critics are only just starting to make sense of its cultural ramifications.[4] The shift in American culture after the Civil War, however, is far more evident. In literary history, 1865—the year the Civil War ended—marks the unofficial start of American realism: that cultural movement founded upon a growing distrust of romance. Of course, the Civil War was not realism's only historical influence. In 1859, for example, Charles Darwin published *On the Origin of Species*, a text that would forever reconfigure notions of the individual and his relationship to the environment. New evolutionary theories were compounded by revolutionary technologies and inventions; the transcontinental railroad, completed in 1869, stands out among them as the major historical development. This technological progress, along with the Civil War and its economic fallout, resulted in rapid industrial growth and territorial expansion. In 1893, Frederick Jackson Turner told America that "the frontier has gone, and with its going has closed the first period of American history" (38). These historical components converged to create the impression of a new era, one that Mark Twain and Charles Dudley Warner would dub the "Gilded Age." American realism, as so many critics contend, emerged from the notion that it was time to "face facts."

David E. Shi writes that "realists of all sorts—scientists, philosophers, writers, artists, architects, and tastemakers—muscled their way onto center stage of American culture and brusquely pushed aside the genteel timidities, romantic excesses, and transcendental idealism then governing affairs of the mind" (3). Critics such as Shi understand literary realism as a rejection of earlier American romantic philosophy and a commitment to recognizing a new postbellum ideology. William Dean Howells, who helped define and promote the realist movement, argued that the writer's "soul is exalted, not by vain shows and shadows and ideals, but by realities, in which alone the truth lives" (*Criticism* 15). In *On Native Grounds*, Alfred Kazin explains that after the Civil War romantic writers such as Ralph Waldo Emerson "seemed to speak from another world" (18).

While this study assumes an intrinsic relationship between history and literature, it proceeds from a general distrust of such clear, definable historical markers.[5] When one reads through Henry James's adamant assertions in *Hawthorne* against the illusions and complacency of an earlier generation of romantic writers, one recognizes an almost forced insistence on difference, on establishing a fundamental break with the American past. As much as realism may have overtly made these claims, however, its philosophy does not easily account for the literature of the period. There exists an alternative voice in the texts, another layer of historical consciousness that denies such adamant assertions of difference. Thus, while realist texts—such as Mark Twain's *Adventures of Huckleberry Finn*, Henry James's *The Portrait of a Lady*, Edith Wharton's *The House of Mirth*, and Willa Cather's *My Ántonia*—clearly reflect the emerging desire to "face facts," amid this historical consciousness the novels also reveal a competing discourse, a specific brand of Emersonian romance that struggles to be heard. *Echoes of Emerson* examines these conflicting voices within American realism.

In *Marxism and Literature*, Raymond Williams outlines a theory that helps explain these conflicting voices. Williams notes that the "complexity of a culture is to be found not only in its variable processes and their social definitions—traditions, institutions, and formations—but also in the dynamic interrelations, at every point in the process, of historically varied and variable elements" (121). He defines these "dynamic interrelations" in terms of dominant cultural movements, their residual antecedents, and emergent hegemonic structures. Of that residual culture, Williams states: "The residual, by definition, has been effectively formed in the past, but is still active in the cultural process, not only and often not at all as an element of the past, but as an effective element of the present. Thus, certain experiences, meanings, and values which cannot be expressed or substantially verified in terms of the dominant culture are nevertheless lived and practiced on the basis of the residue—cultural as well as social—of some previous social and cultural institution or formation" (122). His definition of residual culture, as a force that is still "active in the [dominant] cultural process," accounts for competing discourses within realist literature. His argument implies that, despite our overt declarations regarding major historical shifts and our persevering "need to live by the pattern rather than the fact," any given period is, in fact, much more "dynamic" than our absolute readings of history and insistence on finite endings suggest. What comes before, Williams tells us, remains a persistent force within what follows.

M. M. Bakhtin's theory of heteroglossia, specifically outlined in *The Dialogic Imagination*, complements Williams's discussion of culture and suggests how these "historically varied and variable elements" get expressed within the literature itself. Bakhtin's argument is based on the premise that language incorporates the immense diversity of social, political, and cultural experience. Verbal discourse, he asserts, "is a social phenomenon," and, as a result, language and experience, text and context, are inherently blurred (259). According to Bakhtin, the novel is the literary form that best reflects this heteroglossia: "The novel must represent all the social and ideological voices of its era, that is, all the era's languages that have any claim to being significant; the novel must be a microcosm of heteroglossia. . . . Every language in the novel is a point of view, a socio-ideological conceptual system of real social groups and their embodied representatives" (411). Just as Williams locates within *history* the residual, dominant, and emergent cultures, so Bakhtin locates within the *novel* those "varied and variable" cultural discourses (Williams 121). Language, culture, and history, these writers explain, are both dynamic and dialogic.

Echoes of Emerson employs the theories of Williams and Bakhtin in order to explain the dialogic relationship between residual, dominant, and emergent cultures within the realist novel. I argue that, even as these realist texts by Twain, James, Wharton, and Cather write against an earlier discourse of "genteel timidities, romantic excesses, and transcendental idealism," they also embrace the ideas, and often idealisms, of that residual romantic tradition (Shi 3). More specifically, the double-voiced discourse gets expressed within realist literature through a fraught dialogue between postbellum history and the antebellum transcendental philosophies of Ralph Waldo Emerson. Emerson becomes that significant residual "social and ideological voice" in late-nineteenth-century American culture, and it is through his language that readers discover the major source of heteroglossia in the realist novel (Bakhtin 411). While the realist writers treated here make clear concessions to realism, to facing facts and acknowledging history, they nevertheless maintain a persistent and undeniable allegiance to Emerson's romantic ideas of nature, self-reliance, and spiritual individualism.

Although my book addresses the role of Emersonian transcendentalism in realist literature, my argument distinguishes itself from the myth and symbol school that dominated American criticism in the mid-twentieth century. The primary goal of such critics—most notably Richard Chase in *The American Novel and Its Tradition* and R. W. B. Lewis in *The American Adam*—was to carve out a space for American literature in the canon by celebrating the American romance and linking subsequent American literature to this superior and inimitable form. Their criticism was, itself, a project of nation building. As Amy Kaplan explains in *The Social Construction of American Realism*, this "romance thesis" substitutes metaphor and myth for history in its analysis of American literature (Kaplan 1) as a way of negotiating what James calls "the absent things in American life" (*Hawthorne* 35). In doing so, such early examinations of American realism overlooked critical issues of postbellum historical and social change—war, technology, economics, science, Reconstruction, the rise of the New Woman—that deeply affected the culture of the period. For this reason, the romance thesis has generally lost its currency in contemporary literary studies. Despite their problematic lack of historical analysis and their tendency to oversimplify and idealize American literary culture (and, broadly speaking, America), many of these works continue to provide a critical backdrop for American studies and, as such, are invoked sporadically throughout my study. The book as a whole, however, situates itself within a critical discourse that recognizes the complex and inextricable relationship between culture and history. In fact, it is precisely this relationship, I argue, that characterizes the realists' struggle between their cultural inheritance of Emerson's seemingly ahistorical philosophies and a growing commitment to the sociohistorical realities of postbellum America.

The critics that envisioned the American literary canon as primarily romantic and mythic stripped American literature of its historical context; by contrast, an early brand of twentieth-century historical critics, such as Alfred Kazin and Warner Berthoff, often treated American realism as a stubborn and unqualified rejection of the romantic. They tended to define realism according to its historical markers (post-Civil War to World War I) and read the period not so much in terms of what it represented but rather what it reacted against. Berthoff sums up this interpretive approach: "One can more readily say what kinds of writing the new American realists were in revolt against than what exactly they wanted to create" (1). Some readings from this period were not quite so black and white. In "Realism as Disinheritance: Twain, Howells and James," for example, Roger B. Salomon investigates the complex and occasionally fraught process of historical and literary disinheritance in the three realists' work. Ultimately, however, Salomon's analysis still settles on the conclusion that realism "was both a response and a solution to the problem of the past" (537). These early studies established the prevailing vision of American realism, the vision that defines literary history according to before and after. While any critic of realism cannot easily escape such historical demarcations (American realism will always, to some extent, be defined by such divisions), I read the historical relationship between American realism and its literary past—which the realists, according to Berthoff, were so clearly "in revolt against"—as far more nuanced than the prevailing historical criticism has allowed.

The texts that have most broadly informed my work are those by more recent literary and cultural critics who locate conflict and ambiguity within the period and, furthermore, read the period's literature as the space in which that conflict is worked out. Often involving interdisciplinary approaches and building off developments in literary theory and cultural studies, the critics who have proven most influential for my study—such as T. J. Jackson Lears, Michael Davitt Bell, and Amy Kaplan—focus on establishing and scrutinizing fundamental tensions and disruptions within cultural history. Amy Kaplan's *The Social Construction of American Realism*, in particular, has provided an important foundation. Kaplan shares with Lears and Bell an interest in examining the anxieties and contradictions in the period, but she takes her reading one step further by arguing that American realists not only negotiate such tensions but "actively create and criticize the meanings, representations, and ideologies of their own changing culture" (7). The realist novel becomes a "production of the real as an arena in which the novelist struggles to represent reality against contradictory representations" (7). Her premise has helped shape my own reading of American realism. I similarly argue that the ubiquitous invocations of Emerson in the realist novel are not simply passive reflections, either of realists' yearning for a romantic past or their unqualified repudiation of a naive and outdated philosophy. Rather, the realist novel becomes the space through which these authors confront and test residual cultural influences in light of dominant historical forces.

My argument, however, diverges from Kaplan's not only in terms of focus—she concentrates on class conflict and the rise of mass culture—but more importantly in her often adamant insistence that American realism distances itself from the American romance. Kaplan understands realism as "an aggressive and a defensive literary stance . . . against the residual forms of the romance" (15–16). Furthermore, in her extended introduction on the history of American literary criticism she insinuates that any analysis that gives credence to the influence of residual romantic culture within realism—whether by those 1950s critics who employed the romance thesis or by more contemporary critics influenced by literary theory—undermines critical discourse on the period. I would suggest that her argument actually opens the door to revisit such an association. Kaplan maintains that "realistic narratives enact this search [for reality] not by fleeing into the imagination or into nostalgia for a lost past but by actively constructing the coherent social world they represent" (9). I contend that, far from "fleeing into the imagination" or invoking "nostalgia for a lost past," such narrative invocations of Emersonian romance are precisely how American realists "actively create and criticize the meanings, representations, and ideologies of their own changing culture" (7). *Echoes of Emerson* therefore differs from ahistorical interpretations by acknowledging history as central to American realism but also departs from traditional historical interpretations by reading history as neither neatly linear nor monologic. While American realism engages in a dialogue with its literary past, it is not simply a return to that past or a reaction against that past; rather its active struggle with the residual past is exactly what characterizes the nature of its historicism.

In this way, *Echoes of Emerson* aligns itself more closely with recent literary criticism that interprets American realism in terms of its fundamental engagement with residual literary trends.[6] For example, in *Writers in Retrospect: The Rise of American Literary History, 1875–1910*, Claudia Stokes analyzes realism's relationship with the American past by chronicling the emergence of the literary historian during that time period. In particular, she addresses an interesting contradiction, perhaps even paradox, in the period, namely that—despite "its advocacy of present-oriented fiction" (29)—the period was particularly "sympathetic to literary retrospection" (25) and saw the "emergence of literary history" (23) as a cultural and academic practice. In *Contesting the Past, Reconstructing the Nation: American Literature and Culture in the Gilded Age, 1876–1893*, Benjamin A. Railton also recognizes the complex relationship between American realism and its national past. Railton reasons that during this period, while American cultural history promoted a unified, monologic construction of its past, works of historical literature often raised critical social issues that challenged such monologic views with their own "dialogic alternative narratives" (x). Like Stokes, Railton examines realism through a very different lens than my own study. Nonetheless, both recent texts recognize the presence of historical retrospective within the period. Moreover, this tendency toward historical retrospective in realism, we seem to agree, is far more interactive than previously established by critics.

While critics such as Stokes and Railton have considered realism's dynamic relationship to its cultural and historical past, there are no book-length studies outlining this specific relationship between American realism and Emerson's transcendental vision. In his 1956 book *American Literary Naturalism, a Divided Stream*, Charles Child Walcutt writes that "naturalism is the offspring of transcendentalism," but he concentrates solely on naturalism and, in the tradition of earlier ahistorical readings, sees naturalism primarily as a continuation of transcendentalism (vii). More recently, in his 1997 study *The Emerson Museum*, Lee Rust Brown acknowledges that there is "unexplored common ground between fictional realism and Emerson's 'transcendental' writing project" (141). He situates this "common ground" specifically within "pre-Darwinian natural history" (142), focuses his own study on Emerson rather than American realists, and invites future critics to investigate the connections between American realism and Emerson. Since the publication of *The Emerson Museum*, critics have not fully explored or explained such connections.[7] Although *Echoes of Emerson* does not focus on "pre-Darwinian natural history," it does begin where Brown leaves off, with the idea that "even though the lines of affiliation have become by nature hard to see, American realism, like so much else, starts with Emerson" (142).

Despite Emerson's prominence as a romantic writer, his connection to the American realists makes sense. Emerson was the most eminent and admired philosopher of nineteenth-century America and by the mid-1860s had become, as Robert D. Richardson Jr. explains, "an inescapable part—a fixture—of American public life" (551). He was, as Charles E. Mitchell remarks, a "glorified cultural icon" (13), and, according to Andrew Taylor, his celebration of "sturdy self-reliance . . . continued to influence hegemonic national self-definition" into the early twentieth century (5). There is certainly vast evidence that, among other realist writers, Mark Twain, Henry James, Edith Wharton, and Willa Cather all read and greatly admired his work. *Echoes of Emerson*, however, is less concerned with issues of direct *influence* than with the idea of literary *inheritance*. Emerson figured as an objective correlative for a specific variety of nineteenth-century romantic American ideology, one realists saw as untainted by the complications of late-nineteenth-century American history and, instead, characterized by a "posture of hopeful expectancy" (James, "Ralph" 245). Emerson's writing came to represent an entire constellation of romantic ideas surrounding the importance of spiritual individualism; in this way, he offered writers such as Twain, James, Wharton, and Cather a critical language through which to express their conflicted allegiance to both self and society.

Because these realist writers associated Emerson with a particular epistemology of romance (one located in the first half of the nineteenth century), this study focuses first and foremost on the ideas found in Emerson's earlier works, such as *Nature* (1836), "The American Scholar" (1837), "The Divinity School Address" (1838), and "Self-Reliance" (1841). There is no doubt that Emerson's philosophy changed throughout his life and that his later works begin to reflect this change; Emerson was as much subject to shifting critical traditions as his literary successors.[8] James himself acknowledged this shift. He writes in *Hawthorne*, for example, how the Civil War affected the writer and his literary circle: "Their illusions were rudely dispelled, and they saw the best of all possible republics given over to fratricidal carnage. This affair had no place in their scheme, and nothing was left for them but to hang their heads and close their eyes" (114). James saw that by the middle of the 1860s romantic writers such as Emerson were, themselves, already giving way to a new emerging culture. Like James, I recognize that Emerson's views developed over the course of his career, but for the purposes of this study I am most concerned with Emerson's more traditional legacy, the legacy James outlines and adopts in *Hawthorne*: "He was the Transcendentalist *par excellence*. Emerson expressed . . . the value and importance of the individual, the duty of making the most of one's self, of living by one's own personal light and carrying out one's own disposition" (67). In examining how Emerson's voice figures in the realist novel, *Echoes of Emerson* therefore refers primarily to the earlier texts, which best reflect antebellum romantic ideology.

Bakhtin contends that multiple socio-ideological voices enter the novel by a number of means, such as "authorial speech, the speeches of narrators, inserted genres, [and] the speech of characters" (263). *Echoes of Emerson* locates the major source of dialogic discourse in the relationship between plot and character. As discussed above, one central premise of American realism was that postbellum American culture had a responsibility to address historical truth. The realist novel articulates this need by placing contemporary experience at the forefront of its texts. Its heroes and heroines are caught up in postbellum worlds of Gilded Age materialism and corruption; their plots become the driving forces of the novels. And yet, the heroes and heroines themselves are undeniably romantic and thoroughly Emersonian. Against the weight of history, these characters question social conformity and desperately cling to the possibility of spiritual individualism. In spite of their plots, they maintain a fierce allegiance to Emerson's "republic of the spirit" philosophy.[9]

The relationship between character and plot in these novels is best described through the language of Georg Lukács. In *The Theory of the Novel*, Lukács argues that the novel is an expression of "transcendental homelessness" (41), characterized by an "inadequate relation between soul and reality" (112). Although his theory seems too broad as a grand narrative of the novel form, the phrase "transcendental homelessness" is a useful expression to explain that "inadequate relation between" character and plot in the realist novel. He describes one type of transcendental homelessness as "the inadequacy that is due to the soul's being wider and larger than the destinies which life has to offer it"; in this scenario, a character whose "interior reality . . . is full of content and more or less complete in itself enters into competition with the reality of the outside world" (112). This type of competition between dual realities is precisely what one finds in the realist novel. In each of the texts discussed—*Adventures of Huckleberry Finn*, *The Portrait of a Lady*, *The House of Mirth*, and *My Ántonia*—an Emersonian hero/ine confronts "the reality of the outside world," and readers watch as this character searches for individuation in a historical moment that can seemingly no longer contain that "wide" and "large" unconventional spirit.

Critics who recognize Emerson's presence in these texts tend to argue that the novels employ his romantic language precisely to undermine it, to demonstrate, according to Millicent Bell, "the *weakness* of Emerson's idealism" (90; emphasis added). *Echoes of Emerson*, however, argues against such assumptions and proposes an alternate reading, one that accepts the conflicting mandates in realist literature. In the final lines of *The Great Gatsby*, F. Scott Fitzgerald suggests a critical paradox in the relationship between individual desire and historical forces: "Gatsby believed in the green light, the orgastic future that year by year recedes before us. It eluded us then, but that's no matter—tomorrow we will run faster, stretch out our arms farther. . . . And one fine morning— So we beat on, boats against the current, borne back ceaselessly into the past" (189). Fitzgerald describes a potentially futile but nonetheless insistent pursuit: we row against a tide that will, perhaps, get us nowhere, but we beat on anyway; the quest is still celebrated despite the fact that history may have rendered our ideals inaccessible. These words from *The Great Gatsby* serve as a poignant metaphor for the realist novel, where character heroically struggles against the historical forces of plot. Although the novels discussed here recognize that postbellum breach between character and plot, they do not condemn the Emersonian character. The most important facet of the hero/ine's quest is that it does not simply culminate in a disillusionment with or disavowal of Emersonian individualism, nor does it naively idealize those values. The texts portray their characters' transcendental homelessness but still fully "believe in the green light"; they acknowledge objective reality but do not yield to it. Emerson is not, therefore, easily dismissed as an irresponsible visionary. Instead, voices of both romance and realism exist together as a paradox, a type of irony that cannot be resolved. This paradox ultimately accounts for why, as Amy Kaplan notes, "realistic novels in general have such trouble ending" (159). The novels never finalize the struggle between the Emersonian character and his plot, between philosophical and historical truth. Until the end, the conflict between residual and dominant cultures remains.[10]

Echoes of Emerson focuses on Mark Twain's *Adventures of Huckleberry Finn*, Henry James's *The Portrait of a Lady*, Edith Wharton's *The House of Mirth*, and Willa Cather's *My Ántonia* primarily because the four novels most closely address the fundamental debate between antebellum romantic philosophy and postbellum history. Nonetheless, my critical theme is not limited to the four realist novels discussed here; many other realist texts—in particular, Louisa May Alcott's *Work*, Mark Twain's *Life on the Mississippi*, Hamlin Garland's *Main-Travelled Roads*, Sarah Orne Jewett's *The Country of the Pointed Firs*, Kate Chopin's *The Awakening*, Henry James's *The Ambassadors* and *The Bostonians*, and Sherwood Anderson's *Winesburg, Ohio*—might have been included in my study, as they all highlight, in various forms, what I read as the central conflict inherent in American realism. In attempting to rethink the movement itself, however, I focused my analysis on those novels that critics have traditionally considered canonical representatives of American realism—whether regional, social, or psychological—in both form and theme.[11]

One obvious question remains: why is the fiction of William Dean Howells absent from this discussion of American realism? Howells was, after all, perhaps the most important spokesperson for the movement and is certainly considered a canonical realist writer. Amy Kaplan, for example, notes that "American realism emerges in literary history in bellicose terms—as a war, a struggle, a campaign—and William Dean Howells appears as the leader of the charge" (15). There is no doubt that Howells, as critic and commentator, helped dictate and define American realism. And yet, it is precisely those "bellicose" assertions that seem to disqualify his novels as natural representatives of the movement he helped found. As critic, Howells was so intent on defining an emerging literary movement that his novels—in their insistence on translating this philosophy into fiction—appear as self-conscious accounts of his own literary criticism. As a result, they do not represent that movement as organically as the other realist novels discussed in my book. This may, in fact, account for why writers such as Frank Norris and Willa Cather spoke disparagingly about his literature, complaining specifically of what they saw as his stilted and limiting plots. Even his great admirer Henry James, in an 1888 letter to Howells, complains: "[You] insist more upon the restrictions & limitations, the *a priori* formulas & interdictions, of our common art, than upon that priceless freedom which is to me *the* thing that makes it worth practicing" (qtd. in Davidson 86). Taking James's lead, I would argue that Howells's three canonical novels—*A Modern Instance*, *The Rise of Silas Lapham*, and *A Hazard of New Fortunes*—work so hard to execute the philosophies of American realism (thus, "a modern instance") that they consciously prohibit the residual, dialogic voice of Emersonian romance found in other literature of the period. For this reason, while I present his criticism as the dominant cultural voice of the period, a proxy for the realist movement, in this study I have chosen to focus on other literary representations of that movement.

In order to highlight the dialogism inherent not only in the novels of Twain, James, Wharton, and Cather but in the period itself, I start each chapter by placing the novels in a larger cultural and autobiographical context, specifically working to establish the author's dialogic connection to the Emersonian tradition. Chapter 1, for example, begins with an extended discussion of an infamous joke Mark Twain told at an 1877 celebration dinner for John Greenleaf Whittier's seventieth birthday and the twentieth anniversary of the *Atlantic Monthly*, which I incorporate as a way to understand both the growing chasm between these two generations of writers as well as the deep ambivalence American realists such as Twain felt about their relationship to their literary predecessors. Chapter 2 opens with an in-depth analysis of Henry James's *Hawthorne*, focusing on James's conflicted perspective on nineteenth-century American romantic writers such as Hawthorne and Emerson, as well as his complex understanding of nineteenth-century American history, particularly the Civil War and its effect on American culture. I frame chapter 3 through a discussion of Edith Wharton's autobiographical *A Backward Glance*, identifying Wharton's interest in questions of individual identity and, more specifically, her profound concern with the individual caught between transcendental desire and historical and material necessity. And, finally, given Willa Cather's contentious role in American literary history—alternately as a realist, a naturalist, a modernist, an impressionist, and a regionalist—chapter 4 discusses the elusive cultural and historical mystique of her literature, works to identify her role within the larger cultural context of the other novels discussed, and ultimately establishes *My Ántonia* as a cultural product of late American realism. I follow each of these introductory discussions with a close reading of the respective novels—*Adventures of Huckleberry Finn*, *The Portrait of a Lady*, *The House of Mirth*, and *My Ántonia*—to illustrate exactly how and where the central conflict of and ambivalence inherent in American realism find their ways into the literature of the period.

Because my goal in this book is to present the texts as a continuing historical dialogue between two cultural moments, the readings are generally placed in chronological order according to dates of publication. Chapter 1, however, begins with Mark Twain's *Adventures of Huckleberry Finn*—published in 1885, four years after *The Portrait of a Lady*—for one primary reason. While Twain published *Huck Finn* in 1885, he set the story "forty to fifty years" earlier, before the Civil War. This temporal gap between the text's 1840s antebellum historical setting and its 1885 postbellum authorial voice highlights the double-voiced discourse with which my project is engaged and, as a result, provides an ideal starting point. Chapters 2 and 3, on Henry James's *The Portrait of a Lady* and Edith Wharton's *The House of Mirth*, illustrate the heart of the period's literary culture and reflect two representative perspectives: psychological and social realism. The book concludes by examining Willa Cather's *My Ántonia*, an example of late American realism. Cather's *My Ántonia* offers a valuable endpoint in much the same way that Twain's *Huck Finn* provides an ideal starting point. In fact, its publication/setting dichotomy mirrors that of *Huck Finn*. Cather published *My Ántonia* in 1918, but, like Twain, she set her narrative during an earlier historical period (in 1885, the same year *Huck Finn* was published). As such, *My Ántonia* is inscribed within the realist tradition, yet it simultaneously responds to that tradition and begins to reflect a new emerging culture. Thus, while *Echoes of Emerson* is first and foremost about American realism, it also speaks more broadly to the ongoing relationship between history and culture. Historical narratives—particularly those generated by epic events such as the Civil War or 9/11—provide us with critical markers of before and after, but these four realist novels illustrate how and why such narratives mask the cultural conflict that exists in every historical moment.

I

Mark Twain's

Adventures of Huckleberry Finn

It is easy in the world to live after the world's opinion; it is easy in
solitude to live after our own; but the great man is he who in the midst
of the crowd keeps with perfect sweetness the independence of solitude.
—Ralph Waldo Emerson, "Self-Reliance," *Essays*

I

On December 17, 1877, at the Hotel Brunswick in Boston, Mark Twain spoke
at a dinner celebration commemorating both the seventieth birthday of John
Greenleaf Whittier and the twentieth anniversary of the *Atlantic Monthly*.
Among the sixty guests were three leading American literary figures: Ralph
Waldo Emerson, Henry Wadsworth Longfellow, and Oliver Wendell Holmes.
The short speech given by Twain and directed at these three eminent figures
would haunt the comic genius for years to come. He would later write in his
autobiography: "When I sat down [from speaking] it was with a heart which
had long ceased to beat. I shall never be as dead again as I was then. I shall
never be as miserable again as I was then" (266).

William Dean Howells had begun by introducing Twain as "a humorist
who never makes you blush to have enjoyed his joke" (qtd. in Smith 151). The
"humorist" then proceeded to spin a yarn about his encounter with a middle-
aged miner thirteen years earlier, during an "inspection tramp through the
southern mines of California" (Twain, *Autobiography* 261). Twain's story may
be summarized as follows: the year is 1864, and it is early evening when Twain
knocks "at a miner's lonely log cabin in the foot-hills of the Sierras" (261). A
weary, barefoot man answers the door and looks particularly depressed when
he hears the visitor introduce himself with his nom de plume, "Mark Twain."
The frustrated older man informs his young visitor: "You're the fourth . . . littery man that's been here in twenty-four hours—I'm a-going to move." The
miner continues to explain that three rough and drunken "littery" men by

the names of Mr. Emerson, Mr. Longfellow, and Mr. Holmes dropped by the evening before, much as Twain has just done. The miner complains that these men ate his food, drank his liquor, gambled, and stole his boots:

They came here just at dark yesterday evening, and I let them in of course. Said they were going to Yosemite. They were a rough lot . . . . Mr. Emerson was a seedy little bit of a chap, red headed. Mr. Holmes was as fat as a balloon . . . . Mr. Longfellow was built like a prize fighter. . . . They had been drinking; I could see that. And what queer talk they used! Mr. Holmes inspected this cabin, then he took me by the buttonhole, and says he—

"Through the deep caves of thought
      I hear a voice that sings;
Build thee more stately mansions,
      O my Soul!"

Says I, "I can't afford it, Mr. Holmes, and moreover I don't want to." Blamed if I liked it pretty well, either, coming from a stranger, that way. However, I started to get out my bacon and beans, when Mr. Emerson came and looked on a while, and then *he* takes me aside by the buttonhole and says—

"Give me agates for my meat;
Give me cantharides to eat;
From air and ocean bring me foods,
From all zones and altitudes."

Says I, "Mr. Emerson, if you'll excuse me, this ain't no hotel." . . . When I woke at seven, they were leaving, thank goodness, and Mr. Longfellow had my only boots on, and his own under his arm. Says I, "Hold on there, Evangeline, what are you going to do with *them?*" He says: "Going to make tracks with 'em, because—

Lives of great men all remind us
      We can make our lives sublime;
And, departing, leave behind us
      Footprints on the sands of Time."

As I said, Mr. Twain, you are the fourth in twenty-four hours—and I'm a-going to move; I ain't suited to a littery atmosphere.

When Mr. Twain suggests that, perhaps, these men were impostors, the miner pauses and replies: "Ah! impostors, were they? are *you?*" (261–64).[1]

Despite the comic brilliance of his speech, Twain proved Howells wrong: he later recalled that the faces of those in the audience not only blushed but "turned to a sort of black frost. . . . It was the sort of expression that faces would have worn if I had been making these remarks about the Deity and the rest of the Trinity; there is no milder way in which to describe the petrified condition and the ghastly expression of those people" (265–66). As for the honorees, Henry Nash Smith says that "Emerson paid little attention to it. Whittier, Longfellow, and Holmes seemed politely amused, but were slightly baffled and uncomfortable" (155). Newspaper accounts differed as to the extent of the damage, but most agreed that the joke had failed.[2] Twain himself later reported, with his trademark satirical humor: "All Boston shuddered for several days. All gaieties ceased, all festivities; even the funerals were without animation" (*Autobiography* 267). Twain knew, in the words of Ron Powers, that he had made a "shining . . . ass of himself" (409). For the next thirty years, Twain would waver on whether this "unhappy episode" had been caused by bad delivery, poor taste, or an unappreciative audience (*Autobiography* 264).

While critics often mention this incident in passing, few emphasize the symbolic importance of the speech and its reception.[3] The dinner celebration and the Twain speech that accompanied it, however, represent a pivotal moment of transition between American realism and its romantic literary predecessor. Twain's joke brilliantly reveals, both within the tale itself and within the realm of its delivery and reception, the growing chasm between the burgeoning author and three aging literary sages. Just as the miner is unable to understand the romantic metaphors (the "queer talk") of his rude "littery" guests, so Emerson, Longfellow, and Holmes, in their "baffled" response to the joke, cannot seem to make sense of Twain's own "queer talk."[4] By 1877 American literary sensibilities were shifting. Twain's joke reflects this emerging interpretive gap.[5]

In many ways, the miner represents the new philosophy of American realism. First, he symbolizes Howells's idea of the aesthetic of the common. Far from the genteel elite of New England, this working-class miner from the West does not represent "the romantic, the bizarre, the heroic, the distinguished," but rather speaks to Howells's call that the "arts . . . become democratic" (*Criticism* 67); he is a photographic portrait of an expanding, transforming nation. Second, the miner does not understand romantic metaphors, only literal truths. He is tricked because he is incapable of fully understanding the poets' abstruse language. In a sense, Emerson, Longfellow, and Holmes have succeeded in using romantic poetry to manipulate the miner—or, in the words of Kimberly W. Benston, to "trope-a-dope" (qtd. in Gates 52). Richard S. Lowry points out that Twain's joke inverts "the vernacular paradigm, in which literary texts commonly highlight the rich strangeness of colloquial speech. Instead, it is poetry that intrudes as fragments of an inscrutable and ultimately irrelevant world" (34). In ways quite similar to his realistic use of vernacular in *Adventures of Huckleberry Finn*, Twain uses the miner's language as the linguistic norm, against which the romantic maxims of Emerson, Longfellow, and Holmes appear foreign and alienating. Finally, the miner's central concerns in this tale are those ordinary needs the realists viewed as primary, specifically those of mundane daily concerns. The miner cares little for "stately mansions" or "footprints on the sands of Time," but he does care for the food on his plate, the whiskey in his glass, and the boots on his feet.

Inherent in this linguistic conflict is a clear stab at Emerson and his romantic associates, a stab not only at their language but also at their values. In spite of its seeming light humor, the joke mocks both the poets' arrogance and their distance from the "real" issues of their fellow countrymen. Lawrence Buell maintains that after the Civil War Emerson began to replace Washington Irving as the "father of Anglo-American literature" (142). This claim is supported by early postbellum writers such as Rebecca Harding Davis, who describes Emerson in her autobiography as "the first of living men. He was the modern Moses who had talked with God apart and could interpret Him to us" (42). Twain was ridiculing men who, according to Davis, were not only national heroes but were regarded as divine mediators. His joke implied that these godly writers had forgotten the common man and that their message no longer resonated with many Americans, now ready to embrace that more prosaic and gritty reality. Although Twain may not have intended it, his joke spoke for a new generation of writers, who criticized the romantic bombast of their literary predecessors and expressed a willingness to create a new language, a new literature.

To stop here, however, is to miss the struggle embodied in this literary shift. Twain may have acted as a saboteur that evening, but his actions were conflicted and reluctant at best. One obvious conflict involves Twain's own self-mockery. After all, his jab is not only directed at the three romantic poets but also at the miner and at "Mr. Twain" himself. The poets trick the miner with their romantic language; as such, the miner is presented as simple and naive. Yet, the miner gets the last laugh by suggesting that "Mr. Twain" may be as much an impostor as his three "littery" visitors. The miner's last words implicate Twain in the offenses of the earlier intruders, place him in that same subject position, and deny him the removed literary position that he assumes. Given that Twain and Howells were dining that evening with the so-called "impostors," in mutual celebration, the miner's rhetorical question seems particularly apt. Although realists sought to repudiate romantic forms by embracing the aesthetic of the common, the joke's ending ironically questions the cultural distance between these two "littery" trends.

The irony seeps beyond the level of the story and the outer frame of its reception to the dinner as a whole. Twain's job that night was to celebrate not only Whittier but also the *Atlantic Monthly*. The celebration thus honored both literary movements: the life of one of America's most important romantic cultural figures and the literary accomplishments of a leading American magazine that—with the introduction of Howells in 1871 as editor—had helped foster the birth of American realism. Twain was simultaneously celebrating a passing and an emerging cultural moment; while he poked fun at those earlier American literary giants, he also revered them.

In fact, the most extreme reactions to the tale came from Howells—who called it "the ghastliest funeral since the Crucifixion"—and from Twain himself, two central representatives of this nascent literary trend (qtd. in Everett Emerson 110). Despite even the cruelest newspaper accounts of the event, such as those by the *Republican*, Twain's response to his speech seems a bit melodramatic. Later that year, he wrote to Howells: "My sense of disgrace does not abate. It grows. I see that it is going to add itself to my list of permanencies—a list of humiliations that extends back to when I was seven years old. . . . I must have been insane when I wrote that speech & saw no harm in it, no disrespect toward those men whom I reverenced so much" (qtd. in Bush, "Mythic" 58). Twain looked back at the *Atlantic Monthly* dinner as a low point in his literary career. And Howells, even as late as the 1910 publication of *My Mark Twain*, still called the moment "the amazing mistake, the bewildering blunder, the cruel catastrophe" (51). Clearly, Howells and Twain viewed these romantic poets and New England sages as untouchable, beyond the grasp of such biting humor.

It is difficult to fathom the dialogic extremes involved in the joke and its aftermath. How can one attempt to make sense of the crisp humor of Twain's joke and the elaborate self-abuse that followed? Such a question may seem poised for deconstruction, but this conflict never actually reaches any logical impasse. Instead, the cultural conflict is best understood through the lens of Bakhtin. Here the binary threads of critique and worship, and—on a larger scale—the residual and emerging literary trends of romance and realism, come together to form a "double-voiced discourse." The threads, Bakhtin contends, are "dialogically interrelated . . . ; it is as if they actually hold a conversation with each other" (324). Such dialogic discourse is what helps to define American realism. As with Twain's celebratory dinner speech, the American realists insist on addressing what David E. Shi labels "the concrete facts and visible realities" of a changing America, but they do so almost reluctantly, not quite willing to let go of the values of an older, more romantic tradition (3).

Huck Finn is an extension of this duality. In particular, the novel represents a troubling late-nineteenth-century conflict between American philosophy and experience. With the introduction of Mathew Brady's photographs of Civil War battlefield casualties, Darwin's new scientific theories, and industrialism's growing claim on Americans' daily lives, it became more and more difficult for literature to avoid the literal, tangible truths that Americans witnessed. Howells's philosophy of American realism emanated from these facts. He argued that it was time for writers to record life not simply according to their ideals but as they saw it: "what is unpretentious and what is true is always beautiful and good, and nothing else is so" (*Criticism* 9–10). In many ways, Twain's novel is representative of Howells's philosophy. Yet, while the text supports Howells's claims, it also pays tribute to Emerson's earlier transcendental philosophy. As with Twain's joke at the *Atlantic Monthly* dinner, both historical-literary models exist simultaneously.

Twain offers a fascinating narrative experiment: *Adventures of Huckleberry Finn* becomes the story of an Emersonian character who sets out to confront the empirical world. Huck Finn is Emerson's self-reliant "little boy" who now struggles to find a home where, "in the midst of the crowd" (Emerson, "Self-Reliance" 261), he can keep "with perfect sweetness the independence of solitude" (263). Huck comes to embody Georg Lukács's notion of "transcendental homelessness," defined as the "inadequacy that is due to the soul's being wider and larger than the destinies which life has to offer it" (112). According to Lukács, it is a "legitimate desire" for writers to "create, by purely artistic means, a reality which corresponds to this . . . utopian longing of the soul." He nonetheless calls such a fictional reality "an illusory solution" and questions "whether the ability to imagine a better world can be ethically justified" (115). It is precisely this ethical problem that *Huck Finn* (and, indeed, all of the realist novels discussed in my book) attempts to address: Twain invents a unique, vibrant, and authentic Emersonian hero but also refuses to "create, by purely artistic means, a reality which corresponds to" his protagonist's spirit.

II

In *Life on the Mississippi*, Twain fiercely criticizes Walter Scott, condemning his brand of "girly-girly romance" (303) as "in great measure responsible for the [Civil War]" (304). He defends his hyperbolic assertion by highlighting the ruinous influence Scott's literature had on antebellum Southern culture; he blames Scott for setting "the world in love with dreams and phantoms . . . with the sillinesses and emptinesses, sham grandeurs, sham gauds, and sham chivalries of a brainless and worthless long-vanished society. He did measureless harm; more real and lasting harm, perhaps, than any other individual that ever wrote" (303–4). Twain berates Scott's literary sentimentality, which he claims irresponsibly avoids reality in order to construct "fantastic heroes and their grotesque 'chivalry' doings and romantic juvenilities" (270). According to Twain, Scott dangerously filled the minds of antebellum Southerners with false ideas and abandoned empirical fact for the sake of fantasy. Most of all, Twain reinforces the responsibility of writers to tell the truth.

His quips on Scott are complemented by his criticism of James Fenimore Cooper. In his 1895 essay titled "Fenimore Cooper's Literary Offenses," Twain claims that Cooper, in his novel *The Deerslayer*, violates eighteen "rules governing literary art."[6] Among these "rules" are the necessity to "*say* what he [the author] is proposing to say, not merely come near it," to "use the right word, not its second cousin," and to "employ a simple and straightforward style" (671). In addition to his biting analysis of Cooper's style, Twain incorporates a rather severe attack on Cooper's treatment of nature: "If Cooper had any real knowledge of Nature's ways of doing things, he had a most delicate art in concealing the fact. For instance: one of his acute Indian experts, Chingachgook (pronounced Chicago, I think), has lost the trail of a person he is tracking through the forest. Apparently that trail is hopelessly lost. Neither you nor I could ever have guessed out the way to find it. It was very different with Chicago. Chicago was not stumped for long. He turned a running stream out of its course, and there, in the slush in its old bed, were that person's moccasin tracks. The current did not wash them away, as it would have done in all other like cases—no, even the eternal laws of Nature have to vacate when Cooper wants to put up a delicate job of woodcraft on the reader" (672). Although a brilliant jest on Cooper's literary blunder, Twain's tone is clearly disparaging, and his humor only thinly veils the rather deep offense he takes at Cooper's violation of these "eternal laws of Nature."

What is at stake in Twain's anger? What is it about Scott's and Cooper's romantic writings that provokes this unapologetic, unilateral distaste for their art? After all, Twain's own literature shares certain commonalities with Cooper's Leatherstocking Tales; in many ways, both *The Adventures of Tom Sawyer* and *Adventures of Huckleberry Finn* reproduce Cooper's nostalgic celebration of youth and nature. The answer to these questions seems partially embedded in the hyperbole of Twain's statements, particularly those regarding Scott and the Civil War. A fundamental element of realism was its commitment to forging new connections between history and literature. When Twain blames Scott—a Scottish writer with no direct ties to America—for the Civil War, he does so figuratively, expressing the general irresponsibility of romance and its detachment from historical truth. Though Scott writes historical fiction, his novels are set in what Twain labels "worthless long-vanished" societies; rather than facing facts, rather than engaging in local and relevant historical issues, Scott "sets the world in love with dreams and phantoms." In examining Scott's place in literary history, Twain treats the power of literature as more than simply a reflection of and reaction to history. He implies that literature has the power to *shape* history, to dictate social politics, and to affect America's future. His anger reveals his frustration with romantic writers who disregard their literary obligations, conceal the facts, and avoid even the most basic truths (such as moccasin tracks) to accommodate fantasy. Twain does not, therefore, facilely reject romance. In many ways, his literature actually reflects a deep desire to hold onto romantic tradition, specifically the romantic ideas of American transcendentalism, but his dedication to the ideas behind realism meant that he would have to negotiate historical truths that writers such as Scott and Cooper seemed to overlook.

Twain's response to Scott and Cooper is clearly expressed in his first book about Mississippi river life. *Life on the Mississippi*, published two years before *Huck Finn*, is Twain's account of his experience as a cub pilot on the Mississippi River. As a pilot, Twain's awareness of and adherence to empirical reality becomes a physical necessity. Mr. Bixby, his mentor, instructs the young cub: "My boy, you've got to know the *shape* of the river perfectly. It is all there is left to steer by on a very dark night. Everything else is blotted and gone. . . . You only learn *the* shape of the river; and you learn it with such absolute certainty that you can always steer by the shape that's *in your head*, and never mind the one that's before your eyes" (53–54). Mr. Bixby maintains the absolute importance of empiricism, where even the pilot's senses, primarily his vision, can belie the true shape of the river. He teaches young Clemens the value of science and experience in ascertaining truth: if a pilot should veer even slightly off course, he could "destroy a quarter of a million dollars' worth of steamboat and cargo in five minutes, and maybe a hundred and fifty human lives into the bargain" (*Life* 52). Because steamboat travel in the mid-1800s was so notoriously dangerous, facing facts for a pilot such as Twain would have become a matter of life and death.

Inherent in this rigid empiricism, however, is Twain's sad realization of all that is lost in such an undertaking. Twain reflects on his new river expertise: "No, the romance and the beauty were all gone from the river. All the value any feature of it had for me now was the amount of usefulness it could furnish toward compassing the safe piloting of a steamboat" (66). Here Twain expresses the spiritual sacrifice offered in exchange for his commitment to realism. While Twain denounces Scott and mocks Cooper—both easy, exaggerated targets for Twain's attack on romance—this brief passage from *Life on the Mississippi* accounts for his frustration and expresses his divided loyalty and dual appreciation for the real and romantic, for scientific facts and the beauty of the unknown.

Huck Finn reflects Twain's conflicted allegiances. On the one hand, the novel is steeped in the emerging philosophy of artistic verisimilitude. For the

most part, Twain's masterpiece radically departs from earlier romantic literature in both content and style. Where Howells writes that the writer's "soul is
exalted not by vain shows and shadows and ideals, but by realities, in which
alone the truth lives," Twain translates this idea into the realistic and even gritty
tale of an orphan boy and a runaway slave (*Criticism* 15). Yet, unlike Harriett
Beecher Stowe's 1852 book *Uncle Tom's Cabin*, to which the text has often been
compared, Twain's realist novel is not set in the mode of melodramatic propa-
ganda (with its "vain shows and shadows and ideals") but is ironically more
threatening for its *lack* of sentimentality and idealization.[7] Justin Kaplan, for
example, notes that "early readers found Mark Twain's great novel objection-
able because it violated genteel standards of literary and social decorum. Instead of refined language, an exemplary hero, and an elevating moral they encountered a narrative written in the idiom of a shiftless, unlettered boy from
the lowest class of Southern white society" (354). The narrator's youth, class,
and naive simplicity exclude him from the refined world of "shadows and ideals" found in earlier romantic novels.

   In place of such "genteel standards of literary and social decorum," Twain
presents a new type of narrator and a new type of language, a vernacular that
Ralph Ellison would later credit as "a medium of uniquely American literary
expression" (140). Sherwood Cummings reiterates this idea when he asserts
that "Mark Twain's discovery of Huck's voice helped change American literature, turning it away from idealism and fantasy to realism, from the legend-
ary past to the here and now, from 'literary' expression to the vernacular" (2).
Twain introduces his new vernacular in a prenarrative "explanatory" note: "In
this book a number of dialects are used, to wit. . . . The shadings have not
been done in a hap-hazard fashion, or by guess-work; but pains-takingly, and
with the trustworthy guidance and support of personal familiarity with these
several forms of speech." Twain's comment, while brief, works to establish the
novel's dedication to verisimilitude. He anticipates his subsequent 1895 essay by
contending that in *Huck Finn* he will not duplicate "Fenimore Cooper's Literary Offenses." Instead, he will "*say* what he is proposing to say, not merely
come close to it," will "use the right word, not its second cousin," and will
"employ a simple and straightforward style" (671). Before he hands the story
off to his protagonist—who, as narrator, will soon take the reins without authorial interference—Twain insists on legitimizing Huck's tale.

   Twain plays with the idea of authenticity as early as the first page, where
he introduces his untutored narrator: "You don't know about me, without you
have read a book by the name of 'The Adventures of Tom Sawyer,' but that ain't
no matter. That book was made by Mr. Mark Twain, and he told the truth,
mainly. There was things which he stretched, but mainly he told the truth"
(13). Here Twain pushes realism to its ironic extreme by attempting to posi-

tion the fictional narrator as more "real" than his creator. As Joseph Sawicki explains, "in effect, Huck takes the authority for the narrative that follows away from Twain" (694). In a sense, Twain reverses the literary paradigm discussed and critiqued by Henry James in "The Art of Fiction": "In a digression, a parenthesis or an aside, he [Trollope] concedes to the reader that he and this trusting friend are only 'making believe.' He admits that the events he narrates have not really happened . . . . Such a betrayal of a sacred office seems to me, I confess, a terrible crime; . . . It implies that the novelist is less occupied in looking for the truth . . . than the historian" (46–47). In his opening to *Huck Finn*, Twain becomes, like the historian, a novelist "looking for the truth." Although he joins Trollope in breaking down the fourth wall, in this instance he does so not to undermine but rather to *validate* Huck's story. Far from "making believe," Twain incorporates the humorous narrative transgression as a way to collapse the boundaries between narrator and author and promote the text as autobiography. In *Huck Finn*, Twain refuses to mediate the reality his narrator-protagonist represents. Instead, he establishes himself, as Joyce would later write, "like the God of creation . . . invisible, refined out of existence, indifferent, paring his fingernails" (156–57). Huck not only speaks but also remains the central eye, the focalizer, throughout the novel's entirety; readers know only what Huck the character knows, no more and no less, and they witness the unfolding events through his adolescent perspective.

Like Twain, Huck the narrator is himself a realist, a pragmatic observer and processor of facts. He is precisely the kind of narrator that Howells endorsed in his own philosophy of realism. In *Criticism and Fiction*, for instance, Howells uses the analogy of a grasshopper to discuss what he deems appropriate, realistic literary description. He mocks the romantic readers— "some sweet elderly lady or excellent gentleman whose youth was pastured on the literature of thirty or forty years ago"—who prefer the idealized "wire and card-board [grasshopper], very prettily painted in a conventional tint"; instead, Howells calls for the artist as well as "the common, average man" to "reject the ideal grasshopper" and embrace the real grasshopper "found in the grass," the "simple, honest, and natural grasshopper" (13). Huck's own narrative techniques embody this literary method. His descriptions forego the symbolic landscape of romance for the more practical world of literal representation. Such narrative precision appears early in Huck and Jim's adventures when they come across a frame house floating in the river. Huck describes his experience with a rare level of detail that moves beyond narrative necessity and toward encyclopedic realism:

There was heaps of old greasy cards scattered around over the floor, and old whisky bottles, and a couple of masks made out of black cloth; and all over the walls was the ignorantest kind of words and pictures, made with charcoal. There was two old dirty calico dresses, and a sun-bonnet, and some women's under-clothes, hanging against the wall, and some men's clothing, too. We put the lot into the canoe; it might come good. There was a boy's old speckled straw hat on the floor; I took that too. And there was a bottle that had had milk in it; and it had a rag stopper for a baby to suck. We would a took the bottle, but it was broke. There was a seedy old chest, and an old hair trunk with the hinges broke. They stood open, but there warn't nothing left in them that was any account. The way things was scattered about, we reckoned the people left in a hurry and warn't fixed so as to carry off most of their stuff. (62)

Huck doesn't stop there. He continues for an additional half page to describe exactly what other treasures they found and collected. Even the smallest details are presented, down to the value of the "bran-new Barlow knife" and the thickness of the fish-line, which Huck explains is "as thick as . . . [his] little finger" (62). Huck's ability to take stock of the empirical world around him would have made Mr. Bixby proud.

Huck not only dismisses but simply cannot understand the very different narrative strategies of his romantic contrast, Tom Sawyer. While Huck is playful, his form of play exists in the tangible world around him; he literally cannot grasp the Walter Scott-esque world of adventure that extends beyond his own empirical vision. For example, when Tom tells Huck that "he had got secret news by his spies that next day a whole parcel of Spanish merchants and rich A-rabs was a going to camp in Cave Hollow with two hundred elephants, and six hundred camels, and over a thousand 'sumter' mules, all loaded down with di'monds," Huck, who wants to "see the camels and elephants," goes along. He is disappointed to find—in the place of Spaniards, A-rabs, camels, and elephants—only "a Sunday-school picnic": "I didn't see no di'monds, and I told Tom Sawyer so. He said there was loads of them there, anyway; and he said there was A-rabs there, too, and elephants and things. I said, why couldn't we see them, then? He said if I warn't so ignorant, but had read a book called 'Don Quixote,' I would know without asking" (24–25). The ironic distance between Tom's romantic imagination and Huck's realistic vision accounts for the scene's humor and establishes the opposing natures of these two characters. While Huck represents Twain's own sense of literary realism, Tom represents the problematic romanticism against which Twain rebelled.

And yet, even as *Huck Finn* helped secure Twain's position as an American realist, even as the text reinforces his allegiance to the realist literary philosophy, it also incorporates fundamental elements of earlier American writing. Critics—primarily but not limited to those of the early-to-mid-twentieth century—consistently describe the novel in romantic terms, as a mythic vision of America. Bernard DeVoto, for example, celebrates the text as a romantic homage to America: "It is a passage through the structure of the nation. . . . It is the restlessness of the young democracy borne southward on the river—the energy, the lawlessness, the groping ardor of the flux perfectly comprehended in a fragment of lumber raft drifting on the June flood. In a worn phrase— it is God's plenty" (10). Like DeVoto, Richard Chase ties *Huck Finn* to a national romantic sensibility: "That life on the raft is idyllic and that *Huckleberry Finn* is a pastoral fiction that looks back nostalgically to an earlier and simpler America—this does not need arguing" (148). Both critics associate the novel with basic American literary tropes: the connection between man and nature, the glory of the American pioneer, and the freedom of uncharted territory. William Lyon Phelps sums up this type of romantic reading when he declares that "*Huckleberry Finn* is not only the great American novel. It is America" (qtd. in Budd 4).

Although the content and form of *Huck Finn* clearly place the novel within the tradition of American realism, the text's romantic elements are prominent and, as the critics above contend, cannot be ignored. The issue with these earlier readings is that they fail to account for the historical context that shapes the novel; instead, they persist in linking *Huck Finn* to an ahistorical, mythic vision of the American Adam. At stake in these ahistorical readings, as Jonathan Arac has argued, is the politically wrought hypercanonization of American literature, the attempt to allegorize literature as a way to nationalize it ("Nationalism" 18). So while the arguments of critics like DeVoto and Chase still resonate, they should be recast: rather than read the text as a timeless portrayal of a "true America," *Huck Finn* should be understood as a direct conversation with a specific residual romantic tradition, one grounded in a specific historical moment ("Nationalism" 19). Despite Huck's realistic narrative vision, his character is best defined by Emersonian romance. Huck becomes the living embodiment of Emerson's early philosophies of nature, self-reliance, and spiritual transcendence. In the most general sense, Huck's narrative is about one boy's quest to free himself from the grip of society (what he calls "sivilization"), to live independently in both the physical and spiritual sense. What makes Huck particularly Emersonian is that he does all of this unconsciously, innately. He is neither a philosopher nor a proselytizer. He is instead Emerson's "boy" who "gives an independent, genuine verdict." He is the "formidable" youth "who can thus avoid all pledges, and having observed, observe again from the same unaffected, unbiased, unbribable, unaffrighted innocence" (Emerson, "Self-Reliance" 261).

Huck is a romantic, but he is not a romantic in the sense of Tom Sawyer; he does not substitute fantasy for empirical reality. Tom Sawyer enjoys the comforts of society because he creates a fantastical world that obscures its banalities; he covers up mundane truth with camels and elephants. He forsakes reality for illusion, and this is exactly the type of failure that Twain condemned in the figures of Walter Scott and James Fenimore Cooper. By contrast, Huck's romance emanates from his experience. While Tom *romanticizes* experience, Huck *experiences* romance. Huck embraces the imagination, but he does not transform a Sunday-school picnic into a "whole parcel of Spanish merchants and rich A-rabs" (Twain, *Adventures* 24). Rather, his romantic imagination is unearthed in his interaction with and absorption in the natural world. Readers see this in chapter 1, for example, when Huck describes the view from his bedroom window: "The stars was shining, and the leaves rustled in the woods ever so mournful; and I heard an owl, away off, who-whooing about somebody that was dead, and a whippowill and a dog crying about somebody that was going to die; and the wind was trying to whisper something to me and I couldn't make out what it was, and so it made the cold shivers run over me. Then away out in the woods I heard that kind of a sound that a ghost makes when it wants to tell about something that's on its mind and can't make itself understood, and so can't rest easy in its grave and has to go about that way every night grieving" (16). Unlike Tom, who sees elephants in place of school children, or even Cooper's Chingachgook, who according to Twain violates the laws of nature, Huck looks to the mysterious phenomena of nature as a way to interpret the world around him. He experiences nature as a romantic metaphor for reality.

Huck's romantic relationship to nature is coupled with an Emersonian relationship to the past. In his introduction to *Nature*, Emerson tells readers not to "grope among the dry bones of the past," but rather to embrace the present, to acknowledge that the "sun shines to-day also" (7). Huck lives, in this way, primarily in the moment. He flees his past by running away from the widow Douglas, Miss Watson, and Pap. The money Judge Thatcher holds for him signifies both his past and his potential future; as a result, Huck sees it merely as a burden. And, in what amounts to a symbolic gesture of rebirth, Huck fakes his own death, effectively killing himself off and separating himself from "the dry bones of the past" in order to enjoy that "original relation to the universe" on the river with Jim (Emerson, *Nature* 7). Huck rarely focuses on what has been or may be. Instead, he allows the river, and therefore nature, to dictate his narrative.

Huck's most salient Emersonian feature is his moral and spiritual self-reliance. This trait does not come easily to Twain's hero: throughout the text, he struggles with his attachment to social customs and religion. Yet, during those moments when Huck wrestles with the moral implications of Jim as a runaway slave, he ultimately favors "the integrity of ... [his] own mind" over his socially constructed consciousness (Emerson, "Self-Reliance" 261). Huck displays his unconventional attitude in one of the novel's more famous scenes, when he tears up his letter to Miss Watson revealing Jim's whereabouts and chooses to "*go* to hell" rather than turn Jim in (Twain, *Adventures* 223). Huck, to be certain, lacks the *social* consciousness to understand that his decision is in fact the ethical one, but the irony of the moment highlights—all the more—his organic, *internal* moral sense. His loyalty to his spirit, his ability to embrace nature over society, and his religion of the self all make him one of the most Emersonian characters in American literature.

Several other critics have linked Huck Finn to Emerson. In *A World Elsewhere*, Richard Poirier, for example, connects Huck to Emerson, but he qualifies the connection by acknowledging Huck's dislike of solitude and loneliness, both seemingly un-Emersonian traits.[8] Poirier writes that "any Emersonian detachment from society for the companionship of the 'stars' would never satisfy Huck . . . for very long" (184). It seems shortsighted, however, to dismiss Huck's occasional loneliness or desire for companionship as incompatible with Emerson's philosophy. It is true that Emerson felt that solitude was the *safest*, the most secure way to guarantee self-reliance, but he also claims that it is the "great man" who can locate the "independence of solitude" in the "midst of the crowd" (Emerson, "Self-Reliance" 263). Even as he acknowledges the difficulty, Emerson praises the desire and attempt to accommodate love and friendship into one's personal philosophy of self-reliance. His essay "Friendship" amounts to an almost romantic homage to friendship, which, he says, like the "immortality of the soul, is too good to be believed" (343). He qualifies his belief in solitude with the comment: "I chide society, I embrace solitude, and yet I am not so ungrateful as not to see the wise, the lovely, and the noble-minded, as from time to time they pass my gate" (342). Like Emerson, Huck may express feelings of loneliness and temporarily enjoy the company of those who "pass his gate," but he always seems relieved to return to that "lonesome" but magical river. As Huck declares, "We said there warn't no home like a raft, after all. Other places do seem so cramped up and smothery, but a raft don't. You feel mighty free and easy and comfortable on a raft" (Twain, *Adventures* 134). While one might say that Emerson's philosophy exists in the hypothetical, Huck becomes a fictional embodiment of Emersonian possibility.

III

Huck Finn's narrative, however, immediately and continually demonstrates the precarious nature of this Emersonian possibility. Although elements of realism and romance coexist in Huck's character, the balance is unstable. Twain must have wondered, when he started writing the novel in 1876, how to produce a believable character like Huckleberry Finn, how to maintain a sense of realism while celebrating Huck's romantic spirit. How does one create a realistic narrative and conceive of an environment that allows for a hero to float down the Mississippi River in a raft with a runaway slave in a quest for physical and spiritual freedom? What conditions permit such a quest? Furthermore, how does one accomplish this task in the tradition of realism without sinking into the melodrama of *Uncle Tom's Cabin*?

In *The Nature of Narrative*, Robert Scholes, James Phelan, and Robert Kellogg argue that for a text like *Huck Finn* to maintain its connection to representational realism, it must "convey a total and convincing impression of the real world" (84) and adhere to "historical, psychological, or sociological truth" (88). Feminist critics such as Nina Baym and Nancy A. Walker maintain that Huck's gender is the central "sociological truth" that allows for his "dream of escape to freedom" (Walker 487).[9] The fact that Huck is male is obviously pivotal in his ability to "light out"; women in the text clearly do not share Huck's mobility. Nevertheless, gender is not the only factor in the novel that conveys "a total and convincing impression of the real world." In order to understand how Huck's story maintains credibility, readers have to move beyond gender and explore all of the ways in which Twain qualifies Huck's social circumstances. Huck's physical and spiritual adventure is made possible by a number of additional environmental factors that temper his parasitic relationship to society and connect his quest more closely to "historical, psychological, or sociological truth."

The single most important condition that liberates Huck is his position as a young orphan. This quality may, in fact, be the closest sociological link that ties Huck Finn to the other Emersonian hero/ines discussed in this book. Like Huck, Isabel Archer, Lily Bart, and Jim Burden are all orphans; in *Huck Finn*, *The Portrait of a Lady*, *The House of Mirth*, and *My Ántonia*, family continually proves a major impediment to the possibility of spiritual individualism. Almost immediately when *Huck Finn* opens, the narrator hints that both of his parents are dead and reveals that he is under the care of the maternal widow Douglas and her Bible-toting, slaveholding sister, Miss Watson. Although the reader learns that the widow Douglas "took . . . [Huck] for her son," there is little allegiance between the two characters, either legal or emotional (13). Huck has only recently come under the widow's care, and the widow and her sister are described primarily as two-dimensional characters who repress Huck's true nature. As a result, Huck is allowed a type of narrative freedom not readily available to young adolescent characters, male or female, who maintain strong family connections.

When Pap actually returns, not dead after all, readers learn just how imprisoning family can be. Pap impedes Huck's narrative quest, literally incarcerating him in a cabin across the Mississippi River in Illinois. In these early chapters, he proves to be a degenerate drunk (incapable of fulfilling his promises to Judge Thatcher to sober up), a thief (regularly taking money from Huck), a kidnapper, a child beater, and a bigot (as readers discover through his racist tirade against the government). Even for those more pious or conservative readers who consider the widow to be a suitable caretaker, Huck's confinement and physical danger give him both sociological and psychological cause to "light out" on his river quest to freedom.

Even Huck's role as an orphan, however, is not sufficient for Twain to confirm the needed "historical, psychological, or sociological truth." In order to secure his safety from Pap and his independence from the widow, Huck must, in an act of self-defense, fake his own death; he explains that this is the only way that Pap and the widow "won't bother no more" about him (46). After an elaborate scheme, readers find him at last safe in his canoe "a-spinning down stream soft but quick in the shade of the bank" (47). This plot turn implies, in effect, that Huck must die to live, that he must execute his own death to ensure his self-reliance. Thus, even before Huck's true river "adventures" begin, the text illustrates how difficult it is to be free and self-reliant in Emerson's terms. In order to align his fictional tale with reality, in order to create that element of historical, psychological, and sociological truth, Twain must effectively kill off his narrator. It is not enough that Huck simply be male or orphaned. From Twain's perspective of postbellum America, death becomes the central plot prerequisite for Huck's quest, the only way for Huck to escape the dangers of social conformity.

Of course, once he reaches Jackson Island, Huck's plot takes a new twist. His subsequent flight down river with Jim puts his anonymity at risk; even if the townspeople stop searching for him, they will certainly continue to look for a runaway slave. This element might seem to negate the effects of Huck's fictional death and endanger his search for independence, but at the same time it gives Huck's quest a level of both moral and ethical responsibility. By the time Twain published the novel in 1885, slavery, the Civil War, and the failure of Reconstruction had become a stain on American history. Even if racial equality was far from realized, the North had won the war and Lincoln had become the great martyr of emancipation. In addition to the historical perspective offered by his twenty-year remove, Twain emphasizes the evils of slavery by clearly associating the slaveholders in his text with the hypocritical Miss Watson, who speaks of religious virtue but treats Jim "pooty rough" and makes a deal to sell her slave "down to Orleans" despite her promises to the contrary (55). Against this background, Huck Finn retains a sound heart and stands apart from the morally culpable. As such, Huck's new partnership with Jim helps ennoble both his character and his romantic quest. Alone, Huck may turn into a potential wayward tramp; with Jim, he aligns his own spiritual expansion with a visionary political pursuit. His desire for self-reliance is now more closely connected to Emerson's complementary sense of moral responsibility.

And yet, regardless of this moral justification, Huck and Jim achieve freedom only by virtue of their continual transience. As many critics have noted, the river in *Huck Finn* acts as an essential spiritual metaphor for freedom; on a literal level, it also allows them movement and anonymity. The river represents one of the last spaces—even in Huck's fictional antebellum America—where society will not catch up with the two drifters, where they can maintain an unfettered relation to self and nature. The problem, of course, is that Huck and Jim cannot live on the river indefinitely. As discussed below, Huck and Jim's river adventure is marred by a series of events that impede their Emersonian narrative; society continually frustrates their plot. In addition, as Walter Blair has established in his book *Mark Twain and Huck Finn*, such narrative hindrances are mirrored by Twain's own troubled attempts to write the book. Twain penned the novel in fits and starts over a period of about seven years.[10] He continually ran into narrative snags, replicating the same narrative frustration found in the text itself. The textual history of the novel, therefore, reflects Twain's own inability to conceive of a plot that would allow for the perpetuation of Emersonian freedom. It is as if Emerson's vision, so pronounced and celebrated within Huck's character, is repeatedly halted by historical truth.

This historical truth is accentuated by the gap in time between author and plot—between 1885, when Twain published the book, and those "forty to fifty years" earlier, when Huck lives it. Historical accuracy required that the novel take place in antebellum America, prior to the Gilded Age. In addition to the obvious fact that the text tells the story of a runaway slave, Huck's voyage would have been radically altered by the "forty to fifty years" of historical change that separate the internal and external narrative contexts. The railroad—a symbol of industrialism and ensuing technological development—represents the most self-evident change. In his 1854 book *Walden*, for example, Henry David Thoreau protests this modern intrusion: "The whistle of the locomotive penetrates my woods summer and winter, sounding like the scream of a hawk sailing over some farmer's yard" (414). After 1862, when Lincoln signed the Pacific Railway Act authorizing the construction of the first transcontinental railroad, Huck would have heard the whistle of technology's beckoning calls. In effect, the railroad symbolically deadened the romantic, Edenic vision of river travel.

In *Life on the Mississippi*, Twain recounts his 1882 return to the river of his youth: "The absence of the pervading and jocund steamboatman from the billiard-saloon was explained. He was absent because he is no more. . . . The towboat and the railroad had done their work, and done it well and completely" (159). By 1885, the railroad had altogether altered the landscape and man's relationship to nature. Instead of the steamboat with its open decks, travel now took place in enclosed railcars, where glass constantly encapsulated man and separated him from his environment. In addition, the man-made rails virtually controlled the machine's course; gone were the days when cub pilots had to contend with nature's changing channels.[11] By placing Huck's plot in 1840s America, Twain is able to bridge that gap between romance and realism. His Emersonian vision can be sustained without the intrusion of postbellum reality.

The finite negotiations that Twain makes with character, story, space, and time all reflect the extremely tenuous nature of Huck's narrative. To locate "historical, psychological, or sociological truth"—in essence, to keep the romance real—Twain maneuvers a multitude of environmental factors. Huck's character must be male; he must be young; he must be orphaned and even presumed dead; he must be free of responsibility and yet morally responsible; he must constantly travel and never settle; and he must go back in time, to an antebellum preindustrial America. It is only with these factors that Huck's self-reliance and spiritual quest for freedom can be deemed realistic, can uphold a connection between the fictional and real worlds. Each of these preconditions allows Huck the potential to put into practice Emerson's central philosophical ideals and to experience an "original relationship to the universe" (Emerson, *Nature* 7).

IV

Twain's attempts to negotiate the text's setting and circumstance should not, however, be read—as so many early critics contend—as a nostalgic longing for America's romantic past. After all, *Huck Finn* addresses one of the darkest facts of American antebellum history: slavery. Although Huck's life on the raft may serve as romantic escape, Huck's world is certainly not idyllic. For the realists, it is not simply that romantic possibility was once an intrinsic part of antebellum American life and then quickly vanished after the Civil War. Rather, realists such as Twain suggest that the romantic writers who dominated American literature in the first half of the nineteenth century—those Americans Henry James called overly "complacent and confident"—never properly and fully confronted the historical truths before them (*Hawthorne* 114).

Inherent in Emerson's idea of an "original relationship to the universe," for example, is the notion that one can and should try to escape tradition and history.[12] Emerson addresses this issue throughout many of his early works but particularly in "Self-Reliance": "History is an impertinence and an injury, if it be any thing more than a cheerful apologue or parable of my being and becoming" (270). Huck's escape from family, from society, and even from forty to fifty years of American history reflects this Emersonian vision; the hero must abandon his past to "be" and "become." The problem, of course, is that history continually impedes Huck's narrative. Twain's novel insists on the power of history as a force that cannot be suppressed, even by the power of Huck's romantic vision.

History specifically filters into the novel through a dialogic system of textual voices. In "Discourse in the Novel," Bakhtin explains that "the living utterance, having taken meaning and shape at a particular historical moment in a socially specific environment, cannot fail to brush up against thousands of living dialogic threads, woven by socio-ideological consciousness around the given object of an utterance" (276). The "dialogic threads" in *Adventures of Huckleberry Finn* are expressed on a number of different levels. Primarily, two historical voices occur in every moment of the text. Each utterance exists within the dual contexts of Twain's own postbellum America and Huck Finn's antebellum world.[13] The utterance is spoken at one "particular historical moment" and in one "socially specific environment," but it is located in a different historical and social moment.

This dialogism manifests itself most clearly within the novel's many subplots. Huck and Jim's voyage down river is defined by several troubling encounters with a variety of antagonists, among them the Grangerfords, Colonel Sherburn and Boggs, the Duke and the King, the Wilkses, the Phelps, and Tom Sawyer himself. Although each personality carries its own socio-historical critique, the characters symbolically fall into two historical categories: those who represent a slaveholding, Walter Scott-reading Southern world, and those who embody the dangerous traits of postbellum industrial America. Twain clearly enjoys satirizing his characters across this historical spectrum; in his typical democratic fashion, Twain manages to expose the flaws in each personality. The characters who symbolize postbellum America, however, are not only satirized in their own right but tend to become more threatening to the survival of the narrative itself. Those who represent the antebellum world tend to self-destruct: the Grangerfords kill themselves off, and the Wilkses ensure their own ruin. Huck Finn becomes a voyeur in these scenes of self-destruction; they may bother him ethically or psychologically, but they never impair his Emersonian quest. By contrast, the characters who represent postbellum America (specifically the Duke, the King, and Tom Sawyer) actually impede Huck's plot. Their danger lies in their ability to ensnare Huck into their own plots, into Gilded Age schemes of personal gain and self-interest.

During their first adventure after leaving Jackson Island, Huck and Jim encounter "a steamboat that had killed herself on a rock" (76). In *Huck Finn*, the steamboat plays an interesting role as a linchpin between the premodern and modern worlds. In one sense, the steamboat is associated with antebellum Southern culture. As mentioned above, Twain observes in *Life on the Mississippi* that the Civil War "annihilated the steamboat industry"; the war halted river commerce, and the tugboat and railroad would later displace the steamboat as the industrial standard (115). In keeping with this notion, Huck's observation of three thieves—Bill, Jake, and the tied-up Jim Turner—aboard the dilapidated, sinking ship provides an important symbolic reference to prewar culture. That this steamboat, as Huck later discovers, has been named the "Walter Scott" is particularly suggestive. The association of Walter Scott with the thieves' lawlessness and with a sinking ship indicates the archaic nature of this antebellum Southern world. Like the collapsed steamboat that has "killed herself," the South—through its inability to move beyond medieval concepts of fantasy and chivalry—has self-destructed.

In keeping with the dialogic nature of the text, the steamboat not only symbolizes Southern self-destruction but, at the same time, offers a prescient image of the dangers of ensuing industrialism. When Huck climbs aboard the *Walter Scott*, he acts as a voyeur; he watches the thieves and steals their boat but manages to escape before the steamboat sinks and the men can discover or harm him. While Huck remains an observer in the *Walter Scott* scene, in other sections of the text the steamboat signifies an important symbolic threat to Huck's river quest. This threat is evident, for example, when Huck observes "up-bound steamboats fight[ing] the big river in the middle" (*Adventures* 74). The suggestion here is that the steamboat literally and figuratively opposes an Arcadian vision of nature that the boy and the river typify.

Indeed, shortly after Huck and Jim float past Cairo, the steamboat quite literally ruptures their raft, the symbolic representation of their quest. Huck describes the destruction of the raft: "all of a sudden she [the steamboat] bulged out, big and scary, with a long row of wide-open furnace doors shining like red-hot teeth, and her monstrous bows and guards hanging right over us. . . . As Jim went overboard on one side and I on the other, she come smashing straight through the raft" (115). Huck personifies the steamboat as a wild, destructive animal, its blazing mouth ready to swallow Huck and Jim's raft. This symbol of technology consumes Twain's hero and halts his travels. Huck's forced eviction from the river is mirrored by Twain's own literary struggles. Shortly after writing this scene in 1876, Twain put aside the manuscript for three years (Reif). It is as if the steamboat impedes the novel's quest both on a metaphorical level (interrupting the author's purpose) and on a literal level (affecting his character's intended plot). The Emersonian vision is momentarily jarred. The steamboat now propels Huck back to land and, consequently, back to an intricate social and historical plot that, thus far, the river has allowed him to evade.

Huck is cast ashore on the property of the Grangerfords, a family that will come to embody all that is most menacing about the antebellum South. On the most superficial level, the Grangerfords are mocked for their ornamental house, sentimental women, and chivalric men. Huck appreciates the decor, calling it a "mighty nice house," but his narration belies this assertion (120); the scene's humor primarily arises from the distance between narrator and author. Huck describes the house in terms that, in fact, suggest extreme garishness: "Well, there was a big outlandish parrot on each side of the clock, made out of something like chalk, and painted up gaudy. By one of the parrots was a cat made of crockery, and a crockery dog by the other; and when you pressed down on them they squeaked, but didn't open their mouths nor look different nor interested. . . . On a table in the middle of the room was a kind of a lovely crockery basket that had apples and oranges and peaches and grapes piled up in it which was much redder and yellower and prettier than real ones is, but they warn't real because you could see where pieces had got chipped off and showed the white chalk or whatever it was, underneath" (120). This description of the house and its "sham grandeurs" (*Life* 304) smacks of all that Twain criticized about Walter Scott, in particular the image of "materials all ungenuine within and without, pretending to be what they are not" (*Life* 271). Each object in the Grangerford house is purely decorative and lacks use value: the chalk parrots cannot speak, the fake cats and dogs squeak with disinterest, and the chipped fruit is inedible.

These kinds of "windy humbuggeries" say much about the type of people that live in the house (*Life* 270). The feud between the Grangerfords and the Shepherdsons, in particular, comes to represent Twain's strongest critique of antebellum Southern life. When readers first meet the Grangerfords, the scene is one of paranoia; the Colonel has set his dogs on Huck, three "big men" point guns at him, and thirteen-year-old Buck arrives downstairs, half awake, "dragging a gun along" as he would a teddy bear or blanket (119). Young Buck's innocence accentuates the meaninglessness of the feud. When Huck asks him what a feud is, Buck responds: "a feud is this way. A man has a quarrel with another man, and kills him; then that other man's brother kills him; then the other brothers, on both sides, goes for one another; then the *cousins* chip in—and by and by everybody's killed off, and there ain't no more feud" (128). Buck's nonchalance reflects Twain's affinity for dark humor: the innocent child unknowingly becomes the victim of his meretricious family. That Buck cannot respond to any of Huck's follow-up questions about what or who started the feud emphasizes this evil. Ultimately, the denouement of the feud—the slaughter of Buck and his entire family—becomes the most nightmarish scene in *Huck Finn*, where humor quickly halts in the face of tragedy.

While the horror of Buck's death cannot be underestimated, it is important to recognize that Huck never gets caught in any crossfire or deeply ensnared in the feud itself. Once the family discovers that Huck is not a Shepherdson, they welcome him into their home, offer him a bed, and feed him well. In fact, it is one of the Grangerfords' slaves, Jack, who leads him back to Jim, the restored raft, and his river pilgrimage. On the day of the final battle, when Huck complains that Buck has left to face the Shepherdsons without waking him up, Jack tells him: "Dey warn't gwyne to mix you up in it" (132). Huck watches the final battle from a tree and is never in immediate danger. Obviously, what he witnesses greatly affects him, so much so that he has difficulty "talk[ing] much about the next day" and later admits to having bad dreams (132). Nevertheless, this event has the consoling effect of returning him to Jim, the raft, and the river. In the antebellum world of the Grangerfords and Shepherdsons, Huck remains an observer. He witnesses the thoughtless, medieval clan through the eyes of a young critic. The feud itself does not depend upon Huck for its existence. Huck's role is simply to watch, to report, and to illustrate the ironies of antebellum Southern aristocratic culture without getting caught up in its depravity.

The same is not the case with Huck and Jim's next river adventure. Shortly after returning to the "free and easy and comfortable" raft, they meet the Duke and the King (134). From the start, these men prove to be tricksters entrenched not in antebellum "humbuggeries" but rather in Gilded Age corruption. They stand in stark historical contrast to the Grangerfords and help highlight the various "living dialogic threads" in the novel (Bakhtin 276). As Walter Blair remarks in *Mark Twain and Huck Finn*: "This pair . . . were products of the life which their creator was living when he wrote of them. The author's picturing of them was shaped by experiences in the world of business which increasingly absorbed his attention and his energies" (259). With the introduction of the Duke and the King, Twain's own historical moment permeates the text; more specifically, figures that represent the most debased form of 1880s capitalism invade the novel. The King, for example, describes his profession as follows: "I've done considerable in the doctoring way in my time. . . . And I k'n tell a fortune pretty good, when I've got somebody along to find out the facts for me. Preachin's my line, too; and workin' camp-meetin's; and missionaryin' around" (139). The King divulges much about himself in these lines, primarily his role as an itinerant quack who preys upon others' weaknesses. His schemes are matched by those of the Duke, who proclaims that he does "most anything that comes handy, so it ain't work" (139). It is telling that the Duke does not associate making money with work. Perhaps most importantly, the first time readers see the Duke and the King they are both carrying "big fat ratty-looking carpet-bags" (137). This rather anachronistic reference clearly alludes to the postbellum term "carpetbagger," used as a pejorative to describe Northerners who moved South during Reconstruction to take advantage of

financial opportunities. The Duke and the King exemplify postbellum specu-
lators, get-rich-quick schemers who seek to gain capital without labor.

Their greed is matched by their desire for power, another Gilded Age trait.
They are impostors whose lack of a consistent identity allows them to maintain
their power over others. The Duke creates his own royal past, and the King
misappropriates history to assume a superior rank as "the late Dauphin" (141).
The titles that they claim for themselves are employed primarily as a means of
control, over each other and over Huck and Jim. Huck lists the demands that
the King sets for them: "he said it often made him feel easier and better for a
while if people treated him according to his rights, and got down on one knee
to speak to him, and always called him 'Your Majesty,' and waited him first at
meals, and didn't set down in his presence till he asked them" (141–42). The
Duke and the King both assume aristocratic identities, though not out of any
antebellum sense of pride or chivalry; unlike the Grangerfords, they have no
strong sense of historical identity. In fact, they have no fixed identity at all.
Rather, they occupy chameleon roles as a means to acquire power and capital.

Without any ties to other people or to their environment, they enter into
an itinerant course of exploitation, acting and cheating their way through the
South. In a sense, they mirror the postbellum westward expansion that treated
the land and its people as a capitalist opportunity. They pervert Huck and
Jim's river raft trip, transforming it from a voyage of spiritual freedom to one
of lawless marauding. Through their antics, Twain succeeds in critiquing both
antebellum Southern society and the postbellum society of the Duke and the
King. While the Duke and the King represent the emotional detachment and
immorality of 1880s capitalism, those Southerners who become their dupes
prove themselves guilty of either bad judgment or sheer stupidity. The Wilks
sisters, who welcome the frauds into their home as family, are one such culpable party; in their home, the Duke and the King become literal gold dig-
gers, descending into the Wilks's basement to round up and count Mr. Wilks's
coins. The impostors' actions become especially destructive when they put the
house up for auction and sell the slaves. Their utter inability to feel compassion sets them apart from the Wilks sisters; while the latter are excessively sentimental, the former are morally sterile.

Most importantly, the Duke and the King now manage to ensnare Huck
and Jim into their own mischievous plots. In every other episode thus far—on
the sinking *Walter Scott*, at the Grangerfords, at the Royal Nonesuch, during
the Sherburn and Boggs affair—Huck has been able to remain a voyeur. By
contrast, during the Wilks episode, the Duke and the King enmesh Huck in
their scam and force him to act as their accomplice. Perhaps worst of all, they
implicate Huck in their most callous schemes involving Jim. The issue of racism has been paramount in critical discussions of Twain's novel and is often

tied to Twain's arguably blithe treatment of slavery in the text; ironically, how-ever, it is the Duke, the King, and Tom—precisely the characters who reso-nate more with *postbellum* Gilded Age culture than with antebellum Southern slave culture—who display the most virulent racism.[14] For example, the Duke and the King are the characters who suggest keeping Jim chained to the raft all day and concoct the childlike, degrading disguise of the "sick Arab." The most horrific example of their heartless indifference to others is when they sell Jim for forty dollars. Through an act of utter disregard for human life, these Gilded Age villains reenslave Jim and terminate Huck's spiritual journey.

In the final episode of the text—often referred to as the evasion chapters—Tom Sawyer, like the Duke and the King, characterizes the more corrupt facets of 1880s America. In many ways, Tom represents the antithesis of Huck Finn. As discussed above, Tom, unlike Huck, does not *experience* romance; rather, he *performs* romance and, as such, requires an audience to verify and validate his importance. His motives reflect a deep reliance on society; this is why, early in the novel, Tom only allows Huck to be in his band of robbers if he will "go back to the widow and be respectable" (14). Tom relies on society as much as Huck tries to escape from it. It could be argued that Tom's sense of romance establishes him more as a figure of Walter Scott-esque chivalry than of Gilded Age capitalism. Yet, Tom remains particularly distinct from such antebellum representatives as the Grangerfords. The latter do not appreciate their actions as romantic, and they are dangerous precisely because they are blinded by their own ideology. Tom, on the other hand, remains fully con-scious of his romantic games and their literary roots; for Tom, romanticism offers relief from the boredom of society. As Brander Matthews notes in his 1885 review of *Huck Finn*, Tom's philosophy emanates from the idea that "if you want to get fun out of this life, you must never hesitate to make be-lieve very hard" (331). Tom's need to relieve the boredom of his conventional, middle-class life is a product of a postindustrial age. John S. Whitley affirms that "Tom is the hero of Twain's Gilded Age, an era which Twain had already described as false and possessing an almost Jonsonian capacity for corrupt-ing the truth" (163). In short, Tom's romanticism is what James M. Cox calls "bourgeois romanticism," a pernicious reaction to modernity (145).

Jim becomes Tom's main victim in his search for romantic entertainment. In a symbolic sense, Tom attempts to escape the ennui of postbellum America by erasing history and rewinding time. He reenslaves Jim as the final and most injurious outlet for his restlessness. Despite his claims to the contrary, Tom's desire is not to set Jim free but to put that off for as long as possible; as he tells Huck, "there ain't no hurry" (243). When Huck comes up with a direct, expedient plan to free Jim, for example, Tom complains that "it's too blame' simple. . . . What's the good of a plan that ain't no more trouble than that?"

(242). In his fear of facing reality, Tom works to satisfy his own needs and, like the Duke and the King, has little regard for anyone other than himself. Again, while Huck and Jim become hesitant participants in Tom's game, it is Tom who precipitates most of the racism in this scene. Jim becomes the melodramatic victim of Tom's romance novel. He subjects Jim to painful rock inscriptions, tear-inducing onions, rattlesnakes, rats, spiders, and, of course, the perpetual anxiety of captivity, all in order to accentuate his role as a fictional romantic hero. Perhaps the most insulting blow comes when, after Jim discovers that Miss Watson has already freed him in her will, Tom offers Jim forty dollars for his willing participation as prisoner; he literally pays for Jim's performance in his own slave narrative. Forty dollars is, of course, the same amount that the Duke and the King have grossed from selling Jim. Tom uses money as a "means of moral reparation," but at the root of both episodes is a primary emphasis on the business transaction (McMahan 9). The evasion, therefore, becomes Tom's *in*vasion, where the modern capitalist values of Twain's world collide with Huck's plot.

V

Many other critics have discussed the multifaceted issues inherent in the evasion episode. Paramount in most of these discussions is the question of artistic failure, the question of whether the ending marks, as Leo Marx contends, Twain's "failure of nerve" ("Mr. Eliot" 305). Critical history of the text offers little disagreement with Hemingway's line from *Green Hills of Africa*: "If you read it [*Huckleberry Finn*] you must stop where the Nigger Jim is stolen from the boys. This is the real end. The rest is cheating" (22).[15] This is the moment in the novel, at least, where one would *like* the text to end, where Huck's quest would achieve a greater unity. But, despite the reader's desires, the text continues, leading Huck and Jim to an alternate plot. It is therefore easier for critics to examine the ending as a formal failure, because such a reading allows one to justify and negotiate the unsettling contradictions in the text. It is more difficult to acknowledge the ending not as a formal failure but as a reflection of historical contradictions—of the competing forces of antebellum and postbellum America—that occur not only at the end but throughout the text. Like Lukács's spiritually homeless figure who suffers a "rift between 'inside' and 'outside,' . . . between the self and the world" (29), Huck Finn's quest becomes the attempt to find a home for his Emersonian spirit. His search is continually halted by permutations of the Gilded Age, which, in the form of the Duke, the King, and Tom, emerge as representatives of the dominant historical modes of the 1880s. Objective reality regularly threatens to subvert Huck's romantic spirit; the latter is celebrated, but the former continually intrudes. Huck preserves his Emersonian ethos but remains in a perpetual state of transcendental homelessness.

In the final lines of the text, Tom Sawyer proposes that they "get an outfit" and "go for howling adventures amongst the Injuns, over in the Territory, for a couple of weeks or two" (295). Once again, Tom hopes to use the land and its people for temporary sport. His proposal is portentous and evokes the ensuing evils of westward expansion. In Huck's most famous lines, he declares that he's "got to light out for the Territory ahead of the rest" (296). Beneath the calm humor of the young boy lies a sense of fear and anxiety, a suggestion that he will always have to stay one step ahead of society in order to hold onto that "same unaffected, unbiased, unbribable, unaffrighted innocence" (Emerson, "Self-Reliance" 261). Of course, by 1885 most readers would have known that "the Territory" had already been occupied, that Huck's plot could only become smaller and smaller. The "midst of the crowd" had become almost impossible to avoid (Emerson 263).

From his "notice"—where he states that "persons attempting to find a plot . . . will be shot"—Twain would have readers believe that the text is more of a picaresque, an episodic narrative without a beginning or end. The implication is that one can live without plot and above the telic forces of history. Emerson himself offers a similar idea in his essay on "Self-Reliance": "He cannot be happy and strong until he too lives with nature in the present, *above* time. This should be plain enough" (270; emphasis added). Although *Adventures of Huckleberry Finn* becomes the celebration of one boy's attempt to live outside of plot—"with nature in the present, above time"—the text illustrates the inevitability of plot and, ultimately, history. Just as Twain, at the *Atlantic Monthly* dinner, may have played the role of reluctant saboteur in his stab at Emerson, he now seems reluctant to carry Huck toward this opposing end, the ambiguous but clearly less propitious ending. But he does, because while the realistic ending may be the more disturbing ending, it is also the more honest ending. And Twain's disapproval of Walter Scott suggests that this is exactly the type of ending that he would refuse to avoid. When we as readers close the book, we may in fact—much like Hemingway—feel cheated. Unsure of where we have been left and where we are going, we sense both possibility *and* defeat, manifested as a backward glance at Emerson's romantic philosophy and a forward nod to historical reality. The two seemingly contradictory notions exist, simultaneously and intact.

2

Henry James's

The Portrait of a Lady

Nothing is at last sacred but the integrity of your own mind.
            —Ralph Waldo Emerson, "Self-Reliance," *Essays*

I

In 1879, around the same year he began writing *The Portrait of a Lady*, Henry James published *Hawthorne*, a biography that remains both a representative document of American realism and an instructive preface to *Portrait*.[1] The text not only communicates James's vision of Nathaniel Hawthorne but also reveals his perspective on nineteenth-century American culture and, more broadly, on literature, history, and nation. What emanates most clearly from *Hawthorne* is ultimately a sense of contradiction and conflict—between James's conscious and often patronizing attempts to distance himself from the seemingly antiquated work of his literary predecessor and, alternately, his enduring attraction to antebellum, romantic literary culture. *Hawthorne* uncovers James's struggle to negotiate the binaries of romance and realism, a struggle that will eventually inform *Portrait*.

On the surface, James's biography is an insulting, hyperbolic dismissal of the American romantic tradition—what Richard H. Brodhead refers to as a "systematic reduction" (135). For this reason, the book was not well received by the American public. As Dan McCall points out in his foreword to the text, American readers asked: "Who was this traitor to his native land, this expatriate snob who had 'gone British' and thumbed his London nose at his predecessor's achievements?" (viii). Sheldon M. Novick observes that "for an American to say these things was terrible, a contravention of the national creed, as James knew perfectly well" (*Young Master* 406). Even William Dean Howells recognized in the text a note of "high treason" (Review of *Hawthorne* 143).

In a letter James wrote in early 1880, he reacts to the biography's vitriolic reception: "The hubbub produced by my poor little *Hawthorne* is most ridiculous; my father has sent me a great many notices, each one more abusive & more abject than the others. The vulgarity, ignorance, rabid vanity & general idiocy of them all is truly incredible" (qtd. in Monteiro 153). Although James's letter reveals little in the way of contrition, much like Mark Twain's literary offense two years earlier at the *Atlantic Monthly* dinner, James's discussion of Hawthorne clearly seemed a great affront not only to his literary subject but to America's entire literary heritage.

This affront comes through first and foremost in the barrage of patronizing language he uses to describe Hawthorne's legacy. Critics, starting with Howells's review in 1880, tend to fixate on James's superfluous and insulting use of the word "provincial," a word that occurs around a dozen times in the text and, as Howells complains, "strikes us as somewhat over-insisted upon" (Review of *Hawthorne* 143). Perhaps more interesting and far more telling is James's excessive use of words such as "pretty," "delicate," and, in particular, "little," a word James uses 157 times. Given that the text is only around 145 pages long, and that the word "Hawthorne" itself only shows up around 320 times, the overwhelming presence of the adjective "little" is especially noteworthy. James invariably deploys the word to qualify any of Hawthorne's successes, referring to his "little tales" (8), "little masterpieces" (25), and—in the span of one page—his "little paper," "little work," and "little descriptive effusions" (31). James's hyperbolic belittling and ultimate emasculation of Hawthorne is summed up in his discussion of the "little attempts, little sketches, a little world" of *Twice-Told Tales*, comparing them to "delicate, dusky flowers" (44); Hawthorne's work is characterized as a "modest nosegay" with the "rarest and sweetest fragrance."[2] Such language works to relegate Hawthorne to a more feminine American romantic tradition that is "subtle and slender and unpretending" (2).[3]

James's "systematic reduction" of his subject is cast not only in belittling, often feminine terms but also in terms of absence. He begins the biography, for example, by noting not what Hawthorne represented but rather what he lacked: "He was not a man with a literary theory . . . . He had certainly not proposed to himself to give an account of the social idiosyncrasies of his fellow-citizens . . . , he has none of the apparatus of an historian, and his shadowy style of portraiture never suggests a rigid standard of accuracy" (3–4). Using an abundance of negatives, James defines Hawthorne's style, and the American romance in general, in terms of absence. He observes that even where these writers were "exquisite," they redeemed their otherwise barren prose by being "intensely and vividly local," by focusing on that small "crevice" (3) of New England or what James insultingly refers to as "that little clod of Western earth" (135). The problem with romance, for James, is in part a problem of deficiency, of a "general vacancy in the field of vision" (35).

Almost immediately, James ties this vacancy to a national and cultural condition. He complains that "the flower of art blooms only where the soil is deep, that it takes a great deal of history to produce a little literature, that it needs a complex social machinery to set a writer in motion" (2). In a now-infamous quote, James describes America in terms of what it lacks: "No sovereign, no court, no personal loyalty, no aristocracy, no church, no clergy, no army, no diplomatic service, no country gentlemen, no palaces, no castles, nor manors, nor old country-houses, nor parsonages, nor thatched cottages, no ivied ruins; no cathedrals, nor abbeys, nor little Norman churches; no great Universities nor public schools—no Oxford, nor Eton, nor Harrow; no literature, no novels, no museums, no pictures, no political society, no sporting class—no Epsom nor Ascot!" (34). This quotation draws up, as James himself says, the "absent things in American life" (35). According to James, America is a country that lacks a historical narrative: of class, religion, architecture, education, or culture. In one of his more arrogant remarks on America's "crude and simple society," he concedes that "if Hawthorne had been a young Englishman, or a young Frenchman of the same degree of genius, the same cast of mind, the same habits, his consciousness of the world around him would have been a very different affair" (34). Hawthorne's successes were marred, it seems, by an accident of birth.

Although it is difficult to overlook this blatant dismissal of his mother country, James does in fact focus his attack on a particular moment in American history. He quickly qualifies his hyperbolic statement by specifying its connection to "the American life of forty years ago" (35). Furthermore, and quite humorously, he declares later in the work that "an American of equal value with Hawthorne, an American of equal genius . . . is now almost inevitably more cultivated, and, as a matter of course, more Europeanised in advance, more cosmopolitan" (128). In other words, another writer of Hawthorne's "genius" (such as Henry James) would be—in *postbellum* America—inherently more sophisticated and worldly, perhaps even more manly, than Hawthorne had been. James therefore blames that "general vacancy in the field of vision" as much on history as on nation. While the affront to American culture remains, it belies his larger intent in the text: to create a fundamental distinction between the American romantic and realist periods, to declare the former a "modest nosegay" and the latter a more cultivated, more "Europeanised" literary form. Given that James was writing primarily for an English audience, this distinction would have been particularly important. As Gordon Fraser has argued: "The book . . . provides a model to which British readers can look as they judge the talent of a future cosmopolitan U.S. writer—namely,

Henry James himself" (2). Despite the fact that he had moved to London a decade earlier, James was still considered an American writer, and—not un-like Twain, Howells, and other up-and-coming realists in the late nineteenth century—he wanted to carve out a new literary space and distinguish him-self from what he saw as America's unsophisticated literary heritage. His dis-missal of nineteenth-century American culture, in particular his association of America with absence, worked toward this end.

For James, the crucial historical moment in America—the moment that separated romanticism from realism and developed the necessary "social ma-chinery" to produce a substantive and more refined literary culture—was the Civil War. He asserts that the "Civil War marks an era in the history of the American mind," that the postbellum American will be "a more critical person than his complacent and confident grandfather. He has eaten of the tree of knowledge" (114). He maintains that, in their later years, his romantic liter-ary predecessors felt this great shift; with the outbreak of civil war, "their il-lusions were rudely dispelled, and they saw the best of all possible republics given over to fratricidal carnage. This affair had no place in their scheme, and nothing was left for them but to hang their heads and close their eyes" (114). James proposes a full stop here, a period in the syntax of American literary history. In this way, he offers the American writer a place to begin anew and succeeds in carving out space for the up-and-coming realist who, unlike his "complacent and confident grandfather," now knows better. *Hawthorne*, Brod-head tells us, "is the work of a recently emerged author bent on putting the tutors of his youth behind him" (138).

James's commentary on Hawthorne and romanticism in general is so pa-tronizing, at times even humorously so, that it becomes easy to miss a subtler tone in the text, a tone that counters such brazen criticism. Throughout his biography, James venerates the Hawthorne tradition of American romanticism even as he critiques it. Regardless of his equivocations, he shows a deep respect for Hawthorne. First and foremost, the text itself acts as its own celebration of Hawthorne's life. McCall explains that "James wrote the book for the En-glish Men of Letters series; he was the only American contributor, Hawthorne the only American subject" (vii). James honors Hawthorne as *the* American "man of letters," as a man of "genius and . . . eminence," as a "master of ex-pression" (1–2). Hawthorne becomes James's representative American, emblem-atic of the nation's literary promise. He admits, for example, that Hawthorne "has the importance of being the most beautiful and most eminent represen-tative of a literature" (2), emphasizes his birth on the Fourth of July, and as-sociates him with "the clearest Puritan strain" (4–5). Before *Hawthorne*, few texts had been written about American authors; as such, James was promot-ing a new national literature.

In addition to his praise of Hawthorne, one is particularly struck by James's admiration, almost veneration, of Emerson. James incorporates an entire chapter on Brook Farm and Concord. While the section on Brook Farm relates directly to Hawthorne's *The Blithedale Romance* and is therefore apt, his section on Concord seems somewhat extraneous. One might argue that James includes commentary on Concord simply in order to dismiss the entire transcendental movement. This argument certainly has its merits; in the chapter, James labels the movement a "little epoch of fermentation" (66) and rudely dispels Thoreau as "worse than provincial—he was parochial" (76). His section on "the admirable and exquisite Emerson," however, not only flatters but honors the romantic philosopher:

> He was the Transcendentalist *par excellence*. Emerson expressed . . . the value and importance of the individual, the duty of making the most of one's self, of living by one's own personal light, and carrying out one's own disposition. . . . He talked about the beauty and dignity of life, and about every one who is born into the world being born to the whole, having an interest and stake in the whole. . . . He insisted upon sincerity and independence and spontaneity, upon acting in harmony with one's nature, and not conforming and compromising for the sake of being more comfortable. He urged that a man should await his call, his finding the thing to do which he should really believe in doing, and not be urged by the world's opinion to simply do the world's work. (66–67)

James extols Emerson for another page before concluding: "There were faulty parts in the Emersonian philosophy; but the general tone was magnificent; and I can easily believe that, coming when it did and where it did, it should have been drunk in by a great many fine moral appetites with a sense of intoxication" (68).[4] What James tries to mask, by qualifying and historicizing Emerson's success, is his *own* intoxication with that "exquisite" figure. His use of stylistic repetition—"Emerson expressed," "he talked," "he insisted," "he urged"—emphasizes Emerson's genius and reflects his personal enchantment with the philosopher and his rhetoric. His section on Emerson represents a major tonal shift in the text and becomes a stunning eulogy; it illustrates a moment where James sheds his aloof air and instead embraces this romantic figure and American romanticism in general. As much as James may have been trying to cordon off these figures and relegate them to an extinct past, Emerson seems to escape James here, proving a persistent presence in the young realist's life.

Another factor contributes to this reading. While condescending words such as "provincial," "delicate," and "little" are prolific in his narrative, James readily employs another word to describe nineteenth-century American culture: "natural." James's use of the word "natural" is particularly instructive, as it promotes an alternate reading of American romanticism. "Provincial"—defined by the *OED* as "parochial or narrow-minded; lacking in education, culture, or sophistication"—is rarely viewed as a complimentary adjective, except in its occasional association with the questionable term "quaint." "Natural," on the other hand, offers a rival interpretation of the same subject, where what may initially have seemed provincial now becomes redefined as unpretentious, inherent, organic. It is exactly in this light that James so frequently describes Hawthorne and the transcendentalists. In speaking of Hawthorne's character, for example, he refers to his "natural shyness and reserve" (21), his "easy and natural feeling about all his unconventional fellow-mortals" (37), and his "beautiful, natural, original genius" (144). His writing is described as "charming and natural" (32), as having "purity and spontaneity and naturalness of fancy" (45), and as revealing "a sort of straightness and naturalness of execution" (95). In his discussion of Thoreau, among an otherwise unflattering description, James's one kind word is his admission of the philosopher's "extreme natural charm" (76). Finally, James ties the genius of these writers to their natural surroundings, praising the "magnificently natural character" and "natural resources" (14) of Maine in 1818, where Hawthorne then lived, and noting the overall "state of things" in New England as "extremely natural" (23). Against the facade of provincialism, James paints a very different picture of these writers. They possessed, he implies, a pristine, spontaneous relationship with their environment, the type of relationship that Emerson clearly promotes in his own writing.

It is, ironically, the hyperbolic nature of his critique that most starkly exposes James's veneration of Hawthorne. Numerous critics have noticed James's "anxiety of influence," which resonates in the biography. I would go so far as to say that *Hawthorne* reads like an anachronistic homage to Harold Bloom's theory.[5] James unflinchingly describes Hawthorne and the entire antebellum period with an aggregate of belittling adjectives—"tranquil," "uneventful," "deficient," "simpler," "unagitated," "limited," "modest," "delicate," "subtle," "slender," "unpretending" (and this from the biography's first paragraph alone)—so hypertrophic that the text begins to sound like a study in reaction formation (1–2). In his exaggerated attempt to diminish the American romance, James paradoxically points to its importance by employing a similar romantic discourse. He begins the text, for example, with the following aside: "It will be necessary, for several reasons, to give this short sketch the form rather of a critical essay than of a biography" (1). Yet, as Charles Caramello has shown, James's *Hawthorne* becomes more of "a biographical romance" than a "work of critical realism" (53). Richard Ruland, likewise, observes that much of James's "argument turns on the qualities of romance he has identified with Hawthorne" (106). And Matthew Peters recognizes that "James's immersion in his subject led him to adopt characteristically Hawthornean constructions" (314n32). As these critics contend, *Hawthorne* is ultimately infused with the very essence of American romance it seems intent on discrediting.

In a particularly melancholy passage toward the end of his biography, James reasserts the Civil War's role as America's major historical marker, as the critical demarcation between the romantic and the real. For James, the Civil War not only alters the national consciousness but allows the American writer to escape the "provincial" and become a more critical, rational, and sophisticated thinker. As much as James seems to welcome this historical shift, however, there remains a distinct sense of romantic longing in the passage, a sense that history has replaced the natural "state of things" with something far less organic:

> Our hero was an American of the earlier and simpler type . . . . The generation to which he belonged, that generation which grew up with the century, witnessed . . . the immense, uninterrupted material development of the young Republic; and when one thinks of the scale on which it took place, of the prosperity that walked in its train and waited on its course, of the hopes it fostered and the blessings it conferred—of the broad morning sunshine, in a word, in which it all went forward— there seems to be little room for surprise that it should have implanted a kind of superstitious faith in the grandeur of the country, its duration, its immunity from the usual troubles of earthly empires. This faith was a simple and uncritical one, enlivened with an element of genial optimism, in the light of which it appeared that the great American state was not as other human institutions are, that a special Providence watched over it, that it would go on joyously forever. . . . From this conception of the American future the sense of its having problems to solve was blissfully absent; there were no difficulties in the programme, no looming complications, no rocks ahead. (112)

James pegs the innocent nature of "our hero" as somewhat tragic; he is described as a figure who would soon fold under the weight of "fratricidal carnage" (114). In critiquing Hawthorne's naive vision of history, however, James also struggles with the downside of history: its "problems," "difficulties," and "complications."

To the end, James appears to relish his authoritative tone, his ability to "put his predecessor in his place" (Brodhead 134). Even in the last line of the biography, James remains equivocal about Hawthorne's success: "Man's conscience was his theme, but he saw it in the light of a creative fancy which added . . . ,

I may almost say, an importance" (145; emphasis added). In this delicious final jab at his subject, James stops just short of acknowledging Hawthorne's legacy. And yet, in the process of dismissing Hawthorne, he continually slips, and the "anxiety of influence" gives way to open admiration, even yearning. In his synecdochic connection of Hawthorne with American romanticism and antebellum America, James reveals a deeply romantic appreciation for this earlier literary period, when the thin deposit of history lay over the "hard substratum of nature," and the writer could embrace the illusory as the real (10).

II

The conflict between romance and realism, between residual and emerging American literary cultures, is evident in James's own life. When Brodhead says that James was "bent on putting the tutors of his youth behind him," he is not just speaking figuratively. From birth, Henry James Jr. was immersed in the culture of transcendentalism. James's father was a transcendentalist, had an intellectual fascination with Charles Fourier, and agreed with the French philosopher's belief that evil was "the constraints which civilization put upon the individual" (Edel 9). Most importantly, Henry James Sr. was a close personal friend of Ralph Waldo Emerson, who often stayed with the James family during his trips to New York (Fred Kaplan 11).[6] In *Notes of a Son and Brother*, James nostalgically recalls his childhood memory of Emerson: "I 'visualise' at any rate the winter firelight of our back-parlour at dusk and the great Emerson—I knew he was great, greater than any of our friends—sitting in it between my parents, before the lamps had been lighted . . . , and affecting me the more as an apparition sinuously and, I held, elegantly slim, benevolently aquiline, and commanding a tone alien, beautifully alien, to any we heard roundabout, that he bent this benignity upon me by an invitation to draw nearer to him, off the hearth-rug, and know myself as never yet, as I was not indeed to know myself again for years, in touch with the wonder of Boston. The wonder of Boston was above all just then and there for me in the sweetness of the voice and the finish of the speech" (204). In this passage, James offers an idyllic image of Emerson, a portrait of a supernatural, ethereal being. James grew up both physically and mentally entrenched in Emersonian ideology, and he regarded Emerson as an almost mystical presence in his young life.

As much as James was rooted in the Emersonian tradition, however, he was just as insistent upon distancing himself from it, not only in his literature but also in his life. Even as a young man, James tried to create his own distinct literary identity. In the mid-1860s, shortly after the end of the Civil War, James made the acquaintance of another up-and-coming realist, William Dean Howells; they quickly became friends and collaborators, examining literary culture and pursuing what Michael Gorra calls a "distinctively American realism" (25). Although James seems to have retained a genuine fondness for Emerson throughout his life, after touring the Louvre with Emerson in 1872 he wrote a letter home in which he complained that the romantic philosopher's "perception of art is not, I think, naturally keen"; he condescendingly reported to his family that "Concord can't have done much to quicken it" (qtd. in Edel 135–36).[7] His 1879 biography of Hawthorne gave James the chance to announce publicly the distance he was adamant on professing in his personal and professional life. The text allowed him to rebel against his romantic heritage and proclaim his position both as an important literary critic and as a prominent, successful American realist.

Critics most commonly read James's turn—both physical and cultural—from America to Europe in the late 1860s as part of this rebellion, specifically as his attempt to move away from American romance toward a land more ripe for realism. We tend to take James at his word when he says in *Hawthorne* that "art blooms only where the soil is deep" (2). Fred Kaplan, for example, argues that James became an expatriate because he felt "his ambitions as a writer could be furthered better by more exposure to Europe than by staying at home" (80). In other words, James left America because he needed a more "complex social machinery to set a writer in motion" (*Hawthorne* 2). Gorra similarly remarks that James "needed the thickened air of history. He needed its baggage and furniture, he wanted its Louis Quinze, and in his own overvaluation of Europe he associated history itself with abroad, as something America couldn't give him" (36). In order to become an American realist, James ironically had to leave America.

Given James's remarks in *Hawthorne*, particularly those denouncing the cultural limitations of his native country, the idea that James left America for Europe primarily to trade the parochial for the urbane is certainly valid; that said, it does not adequately acknowledge James's highly complex relationship to such divergent cultures. One might argue that James's expatriation was not simply an attempt to trade the romantic ideology of his youth for the "thickened air of history." Despite James's own contention that "history, as yet, has left in the United States but so thin and impalpable a deposit," perhaps American history had, instead, become too palpable, too *real*, too overwhelming for James. To continue his own metaphor, the soil had become *too* deep (*Hawthorne* 10).[8] In this reading, James left America not because he yearned for but rather because he wanted to escape from reality.

Much of what has been said of James's own involvement in the Civil War might best be summed up in Gorra's epigrammatic quote: "Henry had a peculiar war" (18). James was eighteen years old when the war began; although his two younger brothers enlisted, he chose not to participate. Most critics and biographers like to point to the writer's own justification for avoiding service, the "obscure hurt" (Edel 57) he suffered from a Newport fire in 1861, but this mysterious injury seems less important than the fact that James was, as Leon Edel says, "temperamentally unsuited for soldiering, unable to endure violence," and that he "had long ago substituted close observation of life for active participation" (57). Although James often rejoiced in his alternative temperament, justifying it as ripe for an intellectual writer, there is a fair amount of evidence indicating that the war, and his lack of participation in it, greatly affected him, even enough to cause certain vague psychosomatic symptoms.

Such psychosomatic symptoms, according to Edel, were directly linked to James's insecurities regarding his masculinity: "Henry found himself a prey to anxieties over the fact that he might be called a malingerer, and had a feeling that he was deficient in the masculinity being displayed by others of his generation on the battlefield" (61).[9] In recent years, increasing attention has been paid to James's gender and sexual identity. Whether because of his mysterious "obscure hurt" in 1861 or on account of the characters and plots of his fictional texts, critics tend to agree with Eric Haralson, in *Henry James and Queer Modernity*, that Henry James struggled "to articulate a modern manhood—apart from the normative script of a fixed national identity, a vulgarizing, homogenizing career in business and commerce, a middle-class philistinism and puritanical asceticism in the reception of beauty, and crucially, a mature life of heterosexual performance as suitor, spouse, physical partner, and paterfamilias" (3).[10] What seems most compelling about Haralson's claim is not only what it says about James's complex sexual identity but, more broadly, what it says about his tortured relationship with the world around him. In 1860s America, James witnessed a bloody and violent war; he attempted to face his own insecurities as a young man too infirm to fight in that war; he struggled, as Haralson contends, to "articulate a modern manhood"; and according to Fred Kaplan, he was heavily burdened by "his debilitating family environment" (83). As such, James's expatriation in the late 1860s seems more in line with his desire to avoid rather than embrace the figurative "baggage and furniture" of history. In *Hawthorne*, James appears to openly relish the fact that the Civil War made the American "a more critical person than his complacent and confident grandfather"; his life, however, reveals a troubled relationship with the harsh realities of postbellum America.

In this sense, one may interpret James's departure from America as a romantic, Emersonian quest to discover "a poetry and philosophy of insight and not of tradition" (Emerson, *Nature* 7). As one reads through his biographies, one is continually struck by the fact that, while he attributed his move to the "thinness" of American culture, James was also escaping a place where the American individual, through the mounting realities of personal and national history, had actually lost some of his "wonder" and "mystery" (*Hawthorne* 40). Edel hints at this reading when he notes that James's turn away from American culture was a turn away from what James calls "the hard reality of things" (qtd. in Edel 130). Edel maintains that "he would stay abroad as long as he could, to show whether his pen could accomplish in Europe what it had failed to do in America—give him freedom and independence" (130). For James, the distinction between romance and realism was not as straightforward as so many have claimed. Beneath his easy mockery of Hawthorne's provincial America, James was conflicted about American culture; though he criticized American romance, he was simultaneously ambivalent about the changing reality of nineteenth-century America.

Above all, what one finds in James's life is a sense of physical and spiritual homelessness, a continual search for that "freedom and independence" that he could not locate in Cambridge (Edel 130). As Earl Rovit explains: "James's life was a long methodical search for his own place" (436). Rebecca West, in her 1916 biography of James, summarizes his paradoxical quest when she labels James a man who "could never feel at home until he was in exile" (9). In reading about James's life, one witnesses the incredible restlessness of a man who "liked to move about" and never felt comfortable or at home in any one place (Edel 594). Even when he gave up his American passport and became a British subject, an act read by his contemporaries and future critics as a great snub at America, James was not necessarily attempting to make a political statement; he once again wanted to "move about," and World War I had made it difficult to do so without a British passport (Edel 703). In 1915, near death, James was often incoherent and forgot where he was. He told his secretary: "This place in which I find myself is the strangest mixture of Edinburgh and Dublin and New York and some other place that I don't know" (qtd. in Edel 708). Edel states that he was "shuttling in his confused memory between the cities of his pilgrimages—the Ireland of his father and grandfather, the London, Rome, Edinburgh, of his own experience—he had a sense of being in two places at once" (709). In his travels through Europe, James was not simply trying to create an alternate plot, one that would replace American provincialism with experience. Rather, his homelessness signifies his attempt to avoid active participation in life and plot altogether, to escape those "problems," "difficulties," and "looming complications" of American history that James describes in *Hawthorne*. His life suggests that, as much as he was a new realist bent on embracing objective truth and leaving the illusions of his predecessors behind, he also maintained a highly complex and contradictory relationship to American romance and to what he saw as the "blissfully" naive world of Hawthorne (*Hawthorne* 112).

III

These cultural contradictions dominate James's 1881 masterpiece, *The Portrait of a Lady*.[11] As *Hawthorne* made its way into bookstalls, James sat down to compose the tale of his most romantic Emersonian figure, Isabel Archer, "affronting her destiny" (Preface 8). James explains in his preface that he started writing the novel "not at all in any conceit of a 'plot,'" but "altogether in the sense of a single character . . . to which all the usual elements of a 'subject,' certainly of a setting, were to need to be super-added" (4). In this way, one might read Isabel's plot as analogous to Huck's. Like Mark Twain in *Huck Finn*, James uses Isabel's plot as an organic narrative experiment: to see what happens when an Emersonian character comes into contact with those "difficulties in the programme" and "looming complications" that he had earlier envisioned as "the American future" (*Hawthorne* 112). *Portrait* becomes the story of an antebellum, romantic subject who leaves her library of books to search for postbellum history and what James refers to as "the complications of existence" (Preface 5). Ralph Touchett's own query figures as the central question of the text: "She was intelligent and generous; it was a fine free nature; but what was she going to do with herself?" (*Portrait* 64). What does the plot of an Emersonian character "affronting her destiny" look like? What possibilities lie in store for the romantic figure who tries to live out her ideals?

That Isabel is, in fact, an Emersonian character is not only undebated but has become a somewhat hackneyed claim in literary criticism. Whether she is labeled "a daughter of the transcendental afterglow" (Matthiessen 584), a "young lady of an Emersonian cast of mind" (Rahv 141), "authentically Emersonian" (Poirier, *Comic Sense* 219), or a character "imbued with Emersonian idealism" (Taylor 100), descriptions of her inevitably return to Emerson, so much so that Isabel becomes an almost allegorical figure. As Gorra notes: "In truth, there's nothing easier than to find Emersonian tags for Isabel's self-conception" (114). The more contested issue involves what happens to her character throughout the narrative and what her story ultimately says about James's own position on Emerson and, more largely, transcendentalism. The most common reading is that *Portrait* depicts Emerson's romantic vision as both problematic and potentially tragic. James scholars often insist upon the danger inherent in Isabel's transcendental quest. Leon Edel claims that the text is a "critique of American 'self-reliance'" (259); Richard Poirier argues that Isabel's "dilemma is a comment on the efficiency of . . . Emersonianism" (*Comic Sense*

235); Millicent Bell contends that Isabel's "search for expression of her bound-less self is doomed" and that James "shows the weakness of Emerson's ide-alism" (90); Annette Niemtzow holds that the novel "mocks . . . transcen-dental innocence" (377); and M. Giulia Fabi explains that Isabel is "defeated as an Emersonian free agent" (6). Rarely do scholars even qualify what they read as James's utter dismissal of Emerson; instead, Isabel's story becomes the failure of transcendentalism, its absolute incompatibility with reality, and its potentially self-destructive nature. These critics agree, in essence, that James employs the values of Emersonian transcendentalism only in order to under-mine them. Thus, Edwin H. Cady writes that in *Portrait* James was "engaged in the realist's joyous game of shooting down romantic balloons, piercing them through to let the gassy hot air out and drop them back to earth" (58).

What these readings underestimate, however, is the complex relationship in *Portrait* between the competing forces of romance and realism. Far from unilat-erally denouncing transcendentalism, the novel highlights an intense struggle between those opposing forces, a struggle that is acknowledged and yet left primarily unresolved. At the end of the novel, Isabel Archer is not simply a doomed and disillusioned woman, beaten down by the power of history. De-spite her plot, she retains fundamental elements of Emersonian transcenden-talism, in particular a proud insistence on self-reliance and the knowledge that "nothing is at last sacred but the integrity of your own mind" (Emerson, "Self-Reliance" 263). Through her experience she has become conscious of history and the pitfalls of plot, but she is also determined not to submit to them. In fact, the novel's decidedly open ending indicates the possibility of a new plot, one that is unwritten and uncertain but that allows for a poten-tial, albeit difficult, synthesis of romance and realism. At the very least, James leaves readers as he started: by insisting that character—in this case the roman-tic character—is primary and that the rest is "super-added," even incidental.

One significant element of *Portrait* remains uncontested: the novel is a quin-tessential work of American realism. James is one of the most eminent fig-ures of this cultural movement, and his novel is generally considered its rep-resentative. John W. Crowley summarizes the "rudiments of realism as James and Howells would define it": "Realism eschews the devices of romance, es-pecially reliance on melodrama and exotic backgrounds. Realism seeks sub-tly to raise the taste of an unrefined audience while appealing to 'initiated' readers capable of detecting artfulness, however 'lurking.' Realism depends on character rather than story for its effects. Realism values the particularity of ordinary life. Realism is ultimately a matter of *seeing* the world accurately" (120). In *Portrait*, James closely follows these "rudiments of realism," begin-ning his novel, for example, with the assertion that, far from melodrama, his tale is "a simple history" (17). He employs additional devices of realism: attempting to avoid all traces of "artfulness," skipping scenes for which "no report has remained" (38), and labeling himself not an author or even a narrator but "our heroine's biographer" (101). Furthermore, his novel goes beyond "depend[ing] on character rather than story for its effects"; it openly insists that plot is entirely secondary. James ultimately makes realism his central subject by painting a portrait of a lady steeped in romance who—according to most critics—learns to face reality and see "the world accurately." One could write an entire book dedicated to James's use of realism; such books have, in fact, been written.[12] I openly accept the novel's place in literary history: *Portrait* is a crucial part of the literary movement known as American realism. Nevertheless, I also contend that two distinct voices—the voice of realism and the voice of romance—exist within this movement and more specifically within this novel, and that American romanticism not only maintains an important presence but struggles to be recognized as *equally* important.

As discussed, the novel's romantic elements are embedded primarily in Isabel Archer's character, which is most accurately linked to Emerson's philosophy of transcendentalism. Isabel is first described—through a telegram from her aunt, Mrs. Touchett—in two words: "quite independent" (24). When her aunt meets Isabel, she is sitting in the office of her Albany home "trudging over the sandy plains of a history of German Thought" (34). In his reference to romantic German philosophy, James makes a clear connection between Isabel and Emerson, whose philosophy was founded on that same "German Thought."[13] The connection only begins here. When the narrator relates that "her solitude did not press upon her; for her love of knowledge had a fertilising quality and her imagination was strong" (*Portrait* 31), it recalls Emerson's lines from *Nature*: "I am not solitary whilst I read and write, though nobody is with me" (9). As someone who wants to "leave the past behind her" and "begin afresh" (*Portrait* 39), Isabel is cast as the Emersonian figure who distrusts conventional wisdom and instead "believe[s], always, in seeing for one's self" (35).

Isabel recognizes her own philosophic leanings. Early on, the narrator provides just enough access to the workings of her consciousness to expose her self-prescribed spiritual sensibilities: "Her nature had, in her conceit, a certain garden-like quality, a suggestion of perfume and murmuring boughs, of shady bowers and lengthening vistas, which made her feel that introspection was, after all, an exercise in the open air, and that a visit to the recesses of one's spirit was harmless when one returned from it with a lapful of roses" (56). Isabel displays pride ("in her conceit") not only in her "garden-like" nature and exercise of "introspection" but in her spiritual independence, which "she never called . . . the state of solitude, much less of singleness; she thought such descriptions weak" (55). Instead, she celebrates her independence, telling Caspar Goodwood: "I try to judge things for myself; to judge wrong, I think, is more honourable than not to judge at all. I don't wish to be a mere sheep in the flock; I wish to choose my fate and know something of human affairs beyond what other people think it compatible with propriety to tell me" (143). Isabel, an educated woman, is cognizant, and even boastful, of her Emersonian qualities. In this way she is an Emersonian character, but not quite in the same mold as a Huck Finn; rather than an unread child of nature, she openly identifies as a self-proclaimed, self-reliant individual, eager to affirm her transcendental ideals.

What Isabel does *not* see is the potential conflict between her transcendental introspection and her fascination with the world around her. Readers learn early in the text that, despite her desire "to feel the continuity between the movements of her own soul and the agitations of the world," Isabel avoids the realities that cast doubt on her spiritual leanings (41). As the narrator explains: "she had a natural shrinking from raising curtains and looking into unlighted corners. The love of knowledge coexisted in her mind with the finest capacity for ignorance" (173). This "capacity for ignorance" comes from her contradictory predilections to observe the world and yet ignore its darker side. She remarks to Ralph, "I don't wish to touch the cup of experience. It's a poisoned drink! I only want to see for myself" (134). Isabel's problem is that, while she prides herself in aligning "her own soul" with the "agitations of the world," her romantic sensibility remains completely theoretical, and her sense of reality lies entirely in her imagination.

The novel seems to blame her "ridiculously active" imagination and youthful ignorance on her upbringing: "She had had the best of everything, and in a world in which the circumstances of so many people made them unenviable it was an advantage never to have known anything particularly unpleasant. . . . Her father had kept it away from her—her handsome, much-loved father, who always had such an aversion to it" (39). Isabel's sheltered childhood and her library of books provide her with a warped and remote sense of reality, one that seems almost romantic in its elusive quality. With the arrival of the Civil War, the moment James acknowledged as so critical and tragic in American history, readers find a young Isabel "in a state of almost passionate excitement, in which she felt herself at times (to her extreme confusion) stirred almost indiscriminately by the valour of either army" (41). In short, readers learn that Isabel's "thoughts were a tangle of vague outlines which had never been corrected by the judgment of people speaking with authority. In matters of opinion she had had her own way, and it had led her into a thousand ridiculous zigzags" (53). The novel paints a portrait of a lady who is deliciously quaint but also woefully naive.

For this reason, critics tend to read the text as James's personal critique of self-reliance, mockery of transcendentalism, and open ridicule of Emerson; yet, in doing so, they overlook an important distinction between Isabel and transcendentalism. In *Hawthorne*, James takes aim at American transcendentalism for failing to fully account for history in its vision, for proposing romance at the expense of reality. James does not imply, however, that Emerson was *ignorant* of history, only that he mistakenly thought it could be circumvented. Emerson's philosophy emphasized the principle that civilization is a powerful social construct that could and should be avoided. "History," Emerson declares, "is an impertinence and an injury, if it be any thing more than a cheerful apologue or parable of my being and becoming" (Emerson, "Self-Reliance" 270). Emerson's metaphor of the "transparent eye-ball" reinforces this notion: one must actively avoid the "joint-stock company" called society and instead become "part and particle" of a larger, ahistorical "Universal Being" (Emerson, *Nature* 10). Both the Brook Farm and Walden Pond experiments were based on the assumption that one could bypass history and construct an alternate reality in which the individual could be free from dangerous social constraints.

The important difference, therefore, between Isabel and Emerson is that Isabel has no interest in evading history. While she senses its danger and understands experience as a "poisoned drink," she also wants to charge into history blindly. As she explains to Henrietta Stackpole, her idea of happiness is a "swift carriage, of a dark night, rattling with four horses over roads that one can't see" (146). Emerson recognized the dangers of those "roads that one can't see" and knew that if one wanted to merge one's soul with the outside world, one would literally have to transcend it; it is only "the great man," he understood, "who in the midst of the crowd keeps with perfect sweetness the independence of solitude" (Emerson, "Self-Reliance" 263). Isabel does not yet understand this distinction. In her eager "determination to see, to try, to know," she maintains a vulnerable naivete that Emerson sidesteps (*Portrait* 54). Isabel becomes an anachronistic figure: a young woman with a spiritual connection to antebellum transcendental philosophy and simultaneously an ingenuous faith in history and experience, a desire to "eat . . . of the tree of knowledge" that James tied to a post-Civil War sensibility.

The narrator emphasizes the danger of this union, in particular Isabel's "combination of the delicate, desultory flame-like spirit and the eager and personal creature of conditions: she would be an easy victim of scientific criticism if she were not intended to awaken on the reader's part an impulse more tender and more purely expectant" (54). Although Isabel may awaken such "tender" and "purely expectant" reactions, she does not remain free from "scientific criticism." As discussed, the text takes on Isabel's story as its own "scientific criticism," as an experiment to discover what happens to a "desultory flame-like spirit" when it comes into contact with those "complications of existence" lying beyond her Albany home (Preface 5).

IV

Against Isabel's romantic character, James offers a series of other characters, most of whom are realists with more faith in the objective than spiritual world, all of whom plot against Isabel and seek to slip her the "poisoned drink" of experience. In his preface, James subtly unveils his intentions for this cast of characters when he describes them as the "definite array of contributions to Isabel Archer's history" and the "concrete terms of . . . [his] 'plot.'" The characters will help to answer James's primary question: "'Well, what will she *do*?' Their answer seemed to be that if I could trust them they would show me. . . . They were like the group of attendants and entertainers who come down by train when people in the country give a party; they represented the contract for carrying the party on" (12). These entertainers will introduce Isabel to the "complications of existence," challenge her resolve, and help reveal the central conflict—between philosophy and experience—at the heart of the novel.

Mrs. Lydia Touchett becomes the first entertainer; she initiates Isabel's realist plot when she enters her niece's Albany house unannounced. Mrs. Touchett narrates the specific circumstances to her son, Ralph: "I found her in an old house in Albany, sitting in a dreary room on a rainy day, reading a heavy book and boring herself to death. She didn't know she was bored, but when I left her no doubt of it she seemed very grateful for the service. You may say I shouldn't have enlightened her -I should have let her alone. There's a good deal in that, but I acted conscientiously; I thought she was meant for something better. It occurred to me that it would be a kindness to take her about and introduce her to the world. She thinks she knows a great deal of it—like most American girls; but like most American girls she's ridiculously mistaken" (47). In anticipating Ralph's objections, Mrs. Touchett displays a certain presumptuousness, smug satisfaction, and even cruel delight in interrupting Isabel's seclusion and enlightening her. Not unlike the realist movement itself, she hopes to expose the naive perspective of the insular romantic. In this sense, Mrs. Touchett acts as Isabel's harbinger of reality. As James's heroine herself later acknowledges: "if her Aunt Lydia had not come that day in just that way and found her alone, everything might have been different" (472).

In removing Isabel from her family home, Mrs. Touchett leaves her niece homeless, figuratively and literally. Readers learn, for example, that Isabel's childhood home is for sale and that, as her aunt tells her, "they'll probably pull it down and make a row of shops" (35). In *Dwelling in the Text*, Marilyn R. Chandler claims that the most common "notion of the house" in American culture is "as an extension or shell of the self that 'grows up' around the inhabitant and participates in his or her attributes" (92). Because Isabel both is separated from her house and can expect its permanent destruction, she has been forced to shed her protective shell. In Lukácsian terms, she is a subject whose "purely interior reality . . . [now] enters into competition with the outside world" (112). As someone who has been exceedingly sheltered and shielded from the "outside world," Isabel leaves herself particularly vulnerable to those, like her aunt, who wish to "introduce her to the world," expose her, and test her ideals.

Isabel's first test occurs almost immediately after she moves in with her aunt. Lord Warburton's and Caspar Goodwood's sudden marriage proposals emphasize Isabel's new vulnerability, but it is her cousin Ralph who proves most interested in challenging her resolution: "She was intelligent and generous; it was a fine free nature; but what was she going to do with herself? . . . Isabel's originality was that she gave one an impression of having intentions of her own. 'Whenever she executes them,' said Ralph, 'may I be there to see!'" (64). Ralph's curiosity is the curiosity of the reader, who wonders what will happen next, but his impetus is the impetus of the author, who initiates plot. Ralph is the central schemer in the text because, by convincing his dying father to leave Isabel a fortune, he gives her the means to live out her ideals. Importantly, however, while Ralph initiates plot, he does not attempt to *shape* Isabel's plot. Rather, his interest is primarily as a voyeur, to see how this portrait of a lady will evolve. Like James, the "germ of . . . [his] idea" does not begin in any specific "conceit of a 'plot,' . . . but altogether in the sense of a single character, the character and aspect of a particular engaging young woman" (Preface 4).

In his book *Novelists in a Changing World*, Donald David Stone marks Ralph Touchett "the greatest 'villain' of *The Portrait*, because he is the least aware of Isabel's limitations and because he is the most Jamesian figure in the book" (222–23). While labeling Ralph a "villain" may be overstated, the observation is apt: as an authorial figure who initiates a narrative in order to highlight the brilliance of his subject, Ralph recalls James himself. At the same time, this connection creates a certain level of irony. If, as Stone contends, Ralph "bears the closest resemblance to James," Ralph's own ignorance of Isabel's limitations begs the question: how can this authorial figure so thoroughly misjudge his own character (223)? How can the author underestimate the potential force of his own plot? Yet, it is exactly this incongruity that I argue informs the novel. Ralph, or James for that matter, is not simply a romantic idealist, ignorant of Isabel's "limitations." Ralph is a very sick man, fully aware of the real-life "complications of existence"; at the same time, he is also a postbellum romantic philosopher, guided by the hope that Isabel may still find a home for her transcendental spirit. In short, Ralph (like James himself) embodies the struggle between romance and realism. He wants to believe that history can still accommodate the self-reliant individual, but, even if unconsciously, he questions the outcome. His project, his simultaneous interest in offering her the means and his curiosity to see the end result, affirms his uncertainty.

In contrast to Isabel (the romantic subject) and Ralph (the curious author), readers encounter a number of other plotters, all of whom are quite stark, often spiritless, American realists. Despite the relatively limited critical attention paid to them, Caspar Goodwood and Henrietta Stackpole have particularly significant roles in the text. If Isabel and Ralph represent the more spiritual and visionary side of America, Goodwood and Henrietta are fiercely practical. While Henrietta criticizes Isabel for having "too many graceful illusions," she and Goodwood, by contrast, demonstrate an unwavering dedication to reality and inability to see or feel beneath the surface of human nature (188). In *The Perverse Gaze of Sympathy*, Laura Hinton provides a fitting description of Henrietta as "a figure for the colonialist doctrine of Manifest Destiny" (128). Caspar Goodwood should be included in this description. Both characters are unforgiving nationalists who plot to reappropriate Isabel and strip her of her "graceful illusions."

Despite her role as a "light *ficelle*, not of the true agent" (Preface 13), Henrietta is a forceful presence whom James even describes as a "superabundance," a reflection of his "tendency to *overtreat*" his subject (15). Her "superabundance" comes through not in the depths of her character but rather in her often vulgar insistence on prodding others—in her determination, as she remarks to Lord Warburton, "to get some satisfaction out of" them (*Portrait* 121). She is a journalist who is committed to visual, objective truth; thus, when Mr. Bantling offers to tell her about the royal family, she insists: "all I want is that he should give me the facts" (149). She often pursues her story, however, with belligerence. Several incidents illustrate her often ruthless tenacity. When she considers writing a story about Ralph Touchett, for example, she refers to him as "the alienated American," a subject she hopes to "handle . . . severely"; when Isabel complains that Ralph would have "died" from the publicity, Henrietta retorts: "I should have liked to kill him a little" (82); and, when Ralph's father is on his deathbed, she unthinkingly tells Ralph that she "should like to commemorate the closing scene" (148). In these moments, Henrietta reveals a side of her character that is thoughtless and even cruel. Unlike Ralph, and James himself, Henrietta is interested in story at the *expense* of character.

Not only is Henrietta an aggressive reporter, but she often gets her story wrong. She claims that she comes to Europe "to see as much as possible of the inner life" (78). Yet, far from getting at the spiritual underbelly of her subjects, she judges purely on appearance. When Henrietta first visits Gardencourt, for instance, she interrupts Isabel and Lord Warburton, who have been having a profound discussion about marriage, politics, happiness, and fate. Rather than perceive the true depths of their conversation, Henrietta completely misreads the scene and assumes they have been talking about her: "Miss Archer has been warning you! . . . Isn't that why she came off alone with you here—to put you on your guard?" (121). The exchange is brief but illuminating: Henrietta is a poor reader. She judges every subject she encounters, but her judgments are often wrong.

In many ways, Henrietta symbolizes a specific phenomenon of nineteenth-century American history: American expansionism and systematic conquest. Isabel herself explains to Ralph that Henrietta is "a kind of emanation of the great democracy—of the continent, the country, the nation. I don't say that she sums it all up, that would be too much to ask of her. But she suggests it; she vividly figures it" (87). Isabel develops her metaphoric connection between woman and nation: "I like the great country stretching away beyond the rivers and across the prairies, blooming and smiling and spreading till it stops at the green Pacific! A strong, sweet, fresh odour seems to rise from it, and Henrietta—pardon my simile—has something of that odour in her garments" (88). While Isabel maintains a more natural and spiritual interest in the land, Henrietta's sense of "the great country" is more closely linked to colonial conquest. She comes to Europe to disseminate the importance and power of American culture, to reclaim American subjects, and to analyze and often mock European culture as America's inferior alternative. She reminds one of those early transcontinental railroad passengers who—shortly after the surge of nineteenth-century railroad travel—would get out in the middle of their journey to watch the natives "perform."[14] In a similar sense, Henrietta—whose "eyes lighted like great glazed railway-stations" (406)—rides across Europe treating humans as spectacles and spreading her national agenda. Henrietta's nationalism is crass and superficial, but it is also destructive. In keeping with Isabel's own simile, she represents not only "the great country stretching away beyond the rivers and across the prairies," but also the colonist who attempts to both conquer and acquire under the guise of frontier democracy.

Henrietta focuses her conquest on Isabel, whose presence in Europe she views as a national, and thus personal, affront; her main priority is to recall Isabel to America permanently. She admits to Ralph that her intentions are to rescue Isabel "from foreign parts and other unnatural places": "I wish her to form some strong American tie that will act as a preservative" (111). Henrietta envisions this "strong American tie" as a marriage union between Isabel and Caspar Goodwood, a "straight young man from Boston" (42). Goodwood's background—his education at Harvard, his strong physique, his successful cotton-mill business in Massachusetts, and his aptitude for inventions and "the mystery of mechanics" (106)—all make him the perfect candidate for Henrietta's "little plot" (149). Furthermore, like Henrietta, Goodwood also embodies an association with hard facts. Isabel recognizes this quality herself when she refers to him as "the stubbornest fact she knew" (105). If Henrietta represents a theoretical construction of aggressive American democracy, Goodwood represents a physical construction of American strength—the ingenuity, industry, and potency that Henrietta celebrates.

What makes Goodwood so strong and powerful also makes him a threat to Isabel's quest for individuation. Even his physical description denotes a troubling rigidity that is overbearing and oppressive: "He was tall, strong and somewhat stiff; he was also lean and brown. He was not romantically, he was much rather obscurely, handsome; but his physiognomy had an air of requesting your attention, which it rewarded according to the charm you found in blue eyes of remarkable fixedness, the eyes of a complexion other than his own, and a jaw of the somewhat angular mould which is supposed to bespeak resolution" (42). Many critics have interpreted this description of Goodwood—his stiffness, fixedness, resolution—as a reflection of his aggressive sexuality, a sexuality that concerns Isabel and that James also found dangerous. While the sexual element is certainly present, Goodwood's hard physique primarily bespeaks a certain political symbolism, what Maxwell Geismar has called a "rude, aggressive symbol of 'New World vitality'" (46). As the narrator reports, "he liked to organise, to contend, to administer; he could make people work his will, believe in him, march before him and justify him. This was the art, as they said, of managing men—which rested, in him, further, on a bold though brooding ambition" (106). Goodwood may remind us, in part, of the founding fathers, of their political zeal and "bold though brooding ambition," but he pushes his leadership role further. He is not a speculative, enlightened thinker; instead, he acts more like a dictator who, rather than work for the people, expects the people to work for him.

While Isabel is attracted to his formidable presence, she is also clearly frightened of him. During his early courtship, she is distinctly put off by his tenacity. She associates him with bellicose imagery—as "naturally plated and steeled, armed essentially for aggression"—and, in her attempt to "escape from him," she wonders what would be her "best weapon" (137). Isabel fears Goodwood's violent aggression primarily because, as she observes, "he seemed to deprive her of the sense of freedom" (104–5). And, while Goodwood insists that he wants to reinforce her individualism—as he says, "it's to make you independent that I want to marry you"—Isabel interprets these lines as a "beautiful sophism" (142). She recognizes that Goodwood stands in stark contrast to her own Emersonian spirit and that, despite his guise as the liberating suitor, he would suffocate her and destroy her search for spiritual independence.

Both Henrietta Stackpole and Caspar Goodwood illustrate the dangers of blind realism. Their project is to replace Isabel's "graceful illusions" with what Henrietta calls "grim reality" (188). These two characters represent a breakdown of the transcendental project: their stubborn insistence on rational thought and objective truth works to extinguish the subjective, transcendent spirit. In a sense, they symbolize progressive American history "following her [Isabel] across the sea," threatening to catch up to and overrun James's heroine (105). Readers are warned of Goodwood's unwavering pursuit when the narrator reveals that "it was a matter of the spirit that sat in his clear-burning eyes like some tireless watcher at a window. She might like it or not, but he insisted, ever, with his whole weight and force: even in one's usual contact with him one had to reckon with that" (105). In Henrietta and Goodwood, Isabel faces her first "reckoning" with the "whole weight and force" of American history itself. They represent a pernicious brand of realism, one that promises to eradicate American romanticism.

Although Isabel successfully contends with these characters, she has a more difficult time evading two other characters, Madame Merle and Gilbert Osmond. Their plotting is far more devious, and therefore far more dangerous. Unlike Henrietta and Goodwood, who represent industry and physical vitality, Merle and Osmond are bourgeois Gilded Age realists concerned primarily with appearance and material possessions. They are not aggressive colonists with a nationalist agenda. Instead, their interest in Isabel is primarily economic, and their goal is to monopolize the heroine. Isabel ultimately falls prey to their plot because they mask their true identity under the cloak of self-reliant individualism. They do not, like Henrietta and Goodwood, wish to subdue her romantic sensibility; rather, they seek to exploit those "graceful illusions" in order to deceive her and literally incorporate her into their scheme.

When Madame Merle is first introduced, she has long since replaced her own romantic dreams, which she describes as "so great—so preposterous," with tangible truths and material gain (174). Thus, she stands in direct opposition to Isabel's Emersonian character; she has renounced the spiritual for the social. Isabel recognizes this quality as Merle's greatest fault: "She was in a word too perfectly the social animal that man and woman are supposed to have intended to be; and she had rid herself of every remnant of that tonic wildness . . . . She existed only in her relations" (167). In an oft-cited conversation between Madame Merle and Isabel, the two characters establish their antithetical natures. Merle tells Isabel: "When you've lived as long as I you'll see that every human being has his shell and that you must take the shell into account. By the shell I mean the whole envelope of circumstances. . . . What shall we call our 'self'? Where does it begin? Where does it end? It overflows into everything that belongs to us—and then it flows back again. I know a large part of myself is in the clothes I choose to wear. I've a great respect for *things*!" (175). Of course, Merle's definition of the self provokes Isabel because it represents the very antithesis of her own Emersonian vision; she challenges

Merle: "I think just the other way. I don't know whether I succeed in express-ing myself, but I know that nothing else expresses me. Nothing that belongs to me is any measure of me . . . . Certainly the clothes which, as you say, I choose to wear, don't express me; and heaven forbid they should!" (175). The contrast is clear. Isabel follows Emerson's proverb that "the world is nothing, the man is all; in yourself is the law of all nature" (70). Merle, on the other hand, is a materialist who is born from and reliant on her relations to the world. To continue her own metaphor, Merle not only has a shell but *is* that shell; she lacks any identity beyond that superficial layer.

The question remains: if Isabel acknowledges their differences, why is she still charmed by the older woman? Isabel is intrigued by Madame Merle pri-marily because what makes Merle bitter also makes her attractive. She embod-ies the knowledge and wisdom that Isabel seeks, and—despite Merle's own contention that "after forty one *can't* really feel" (164)—Isabel is convinced that Merle's suffering makes her feel more deeply: "Life had told upon her; she had felt it strongly, and it was part of the satisfaction to be taken in her society that when the girl talked of what she was pleased to call serious mat-ters this lady understood her so easily and quickly" (164). Isabel embraces her new friend as a mentor who can offer her the experience she lacks. Isabel is particularly vulnerable to Merle at this early stage in the narrative because she still instinctively romanticizes Merle's life experience. As David M. Lubin explains, Isabel's conception of reality is Neoplatonic, in that she sees it as "static, fixed, untouched by history, eternally enduring" (107). It is exactly this warped reading of both history and the individual as inviolable that causes her to misread Merle's unfeeling and spiritually bereft character not only as "charming, sympathetic, intelligent, cultivated," but also as "rare, superior and preëminent" (163).

Perhaps the only characteristic that Isabel actually correctly reads is Madame Merle's intelligence; her shrewdness comes through in her astute ability to ma-nipulate Isabel for her own gain. Unlike Henrietta's plot, which is motivated by nationalism, Merle's plot is, like everything else in her life, materially and socially based. She has no interest in breaking down Isabel's romantic spirit. Instead, she seeks to take advantage of Isabel's "graceful illusions," flattering her with images of resilience: "it will be a great satisfaction to me to see you some years hence. I want to see what life makes of you. One thing's certain—it can't spoil you. It may pull you about horribly, but I defy it to break you up" (164). Isabel's reaction is telling: "Isabel received this assurance as a young sol-dier, still panting from a slight skirmish in which he has come off with hon-our, might receive a pat on the shoulder from his colonel" (164). Merle effec-tively speaks to Isabel's pride and dares her to succeed where she herself has failed. In this way, Merle ensnares Isabel into her plot.

Much like Henrietta, whose plans for Isabel center on Caspar Goodwood, Madame Merle centers her plot around another male suitor, Gilbert Osmond. Osmond is Merle's male counterpart, a social dilettante who embodies superficial materialism. Although Osmond prefers to associate himself with European aristocracy, he is a phony whose identity comes closer to Ralph's conception of him as a "vague, unexplained American" (214). He is described as an effete man, almost feminine in his "light, lean, rather languid-looking figure," who "studied style" (197) and "never . . . tried to earn a penny" (296). Instead of producing, Osmond consumes; he represents both conspicuous leisure and conspicuous consumption. His very identity rests on presentation— or as James calls it, "pose": "Osmond lived exclusively for the world. Far from being its master as he pretended to be, he was its very humble servant, and the degree of its attention was his only measure of success. . . . Everything he did was *pose*—*pose* so subtly considered that if one were not on the lookout one mistook it for impulse. . . . His ambition was not to please the world, but to please himself by exciting the world's curiosity, and then declining to satisfy it" (331). Osmond, whose character ceases to exist without spectators, figures as the antitranscendentalist. Those who know him best repeatedly refer to him in terms of absence. Merle explains that he has "no career, no name, no position, no fortune, no past, no future, no anything" (172), and his sister bluntly says, "there's nothing, nothing, nothing" (233). These characters recognize that, far from lacking social pretensions, Osmond lacks anything outside his pretensions; in Emersonian terms, there is no "me," only the "not me."

It is not surprising, therefore, that Osmond treats people as he does objects, appraising them in terms of their social value. He focuses his efforts primarily on women, whom he seeks to strip of their spiritual identity and render passive representations of his will. For Osmond, women should be "like books—very good and not too long" (198). He has raised his daughter, Pansy, as a work of art, and he expects the same type of service from his wife, whose social successes and failures will become, in his eyes, an extension of himself. For this reason, Lord Warburton's interest in Isabel does not elicit jealousy but rather increases her social capital: "now that he had seen Lord Warburton, whom he thought a very fine example of his race and order, he perceived a new attraction in the idea of taking to himself a young lady who had qualified herself to figure in his collection of choice objects by declining so noble a hand" (258). Here Isabel's association with aristocracy highlights her value as a commodified object. Far from celebrating their self-reliance, Osmond brands women as dependent possessions and personal advertisements.

Osmond's willingness to admit these truths to Isabel—confessing to her, for example, that he is not simply "conventional" but "convention itself"—makes it difficult to fathom why Isabel ultimately succumbs to her suitor and accepts his proposal (265). No matter how many times one reads this novel, the gap between Isabel's Emersonian ideals and her life choices still seems dumbfounding. Even the narrator, second-guessing the reader's confusion, admits: "The working of this young lady's spirit was strange, and I can only give it to you as I see it, not hoping to make it seem altogether natural" (265). The narrator attempts to justify this "strangeness" by adding that "her imagination . . . now hung back: there was a last vague space it couldn't cross—a dusky, uncertain tract which looked ambiguous and even slightly treacherous, like a moorland seen in the winter twilight. But she was to cross it yet" (265). Of course, the "moorland" is history itself, which Isabel is eager to cross because her imagination blinds her, and she believes, like Madame Merle, that the "uncertain tract" of experience will not spoil her.

This blind spot in her imagination makes her the perfect prey for Gilbert Osmond. Osmond caters to Isabel's Emersonian sensibility by attempting to recast his conventional character in ascetic, almost Thoreauvian terms: as a "sweetly provincial" (221) man who practices a "studied, . . . wilful renunciation" (227). He paints a portrait of his life as a sacrificial retreat to Walden Pond, and, as such, Isabel naively celebrates both his "superior enlightenment" (226) and "the success with which he had preserved his independence" (228). Most of all, Isabel falls prey because, as the narrator points out, all the other individuals she knew "belonged to types already present to her mind. Her mind contained no class offering a natural place to Mr. Osmond—he was a specimen apart. . . . He was an original without being an eccentric" (224). Of course, Isabel misses what both Osmond's sister and Merle openly acknowledge: that he has no "type," no "class," no "natural place," because he is "nothing, nothing, nothing." This absence—far from signifying the transcendental spirit—indicates a spiritual vacancy that precludes transcendence.

Isabel's vulnerability is further exacerbated by a critical one-year lapse, a "year she had spent in seeing the world" (270). The reader learns about her movements through flashbacks, through a series of "landscapes" and "figure-pieces" (271). Noticeable first and foremost is an urgency in her travels: "Isabel traveled rapidly and recklessly; she was like a thirsty person draining cup after cup" (274). As much as descriptions of her voyage reveal Isabel's enthusiasm, they also indicate a sense of restlessness, an almost arrogant confidence in her worldly experience: "She flattered herself she had harvested wisdom and learned a great deal more of life than this light-minded creature had even suspected" (270). Isabel mistakes her travels for the "dusty, uncertain tract" of history and believes that in "seeing the world," she has experienced life. Symbolically, Isabel becomes the traveler who has reached the end of the world; she has completed her journey but is still spiritually homeless. After her year traveling, Isabel begins to represent the conflict Georg Lukács describes as "the inadequacy that is due to the soul's being wider and larger than the destinies which life has to offer it" (112). In Osmond, she mistakenly locates a suitable home for her restless soul.

And yet—despite the many reasons why Isabel yields to Osmond—her failure of judgment still feels so monumental, so incomprehensible, that scholars continually mark this failure as James's profound "critique of American 'self-reliance'" (Edel 259) and mockery of "transcendental innocence" (Niemtzow 377). I would argue, instead, that Isabel's faulty imagination, her blind faith in her future, and her ultimate decision to accept Osmond reflect her greatest divergence from Emersonian philosophy. Isabel's absolute confidence in history is, in actuality, thoroughly un-Emersonian. Transcendental philosophy incorporated both a knowledge and distrust of history not found in Isabel's character. Although critics often cite Emerson's "inclination towards ahistoricism," the philosopher clearly had a profound respect for the power of history and experience, and his writings repeatedly tackle the complex relationship between the individual and social experience (Taylor 105). Emerson believed, as Joel Porte notes, that "time will devour us unless we master it" (4); he understood that history was a potentially menacing force that could endanger the individual if not dealt with carefully. Isabel's weakness certainly stems, in part, from her overall romantic sensibility, but her specific ignorance lies in her naive and blind embrace of experience. Isabel's combination of romance and ego allows her to think that she can overcome the forces of history, that she can shape history to accommodate her expansive spirit. The narrator confirms that, in marrying Osmond, Isabel will "cross" that "dusky, uncertain tract," and she will learn the power of history. Importantly, however, Isabel will not easily be defeated, and the text will not easily dismiss Emersonian romance. In the final third of the text, Isabel will attempt to negotiate the difficult binary of romance and realism.

V

When readers next meet Isabel, she has been married to Gilbert Osmond for three years, and while neither the narrator nor Isabel divulges much about her relationship with Osmond, she has clearly both gained the experience she sought and been humbled by it. The reader learns, for example, that Isabel has lost a son in infancy and has become estranged from her husband. The narrator discloses these facts but little else immediately or directly about Isabel's wellbeing, circumstances, or state of mind. Instead, most information comes from the perspective of other characters and Isabel's own subtle, indirect revelations, such as in this scene between Lord Warburton and Isabel:

"You've got an awfully good house."
"Yes, it's very pleasant. But that's not my merit—it's my husband's."

"You mean he has arranged it?"

"Yes, it was nothing when we came."

"He must be very clever."

"He has a genius for upholstery," said Isabel.

"There's a great rage for that sort of thing now. But you must have a taste of your own."

"I enjoy things when they're done, but I've no ideas. I can never propose anything."

"Do you mean you accept what others propose?"

"Very willingly, for the most part." (324)

Isabel now understands that Osmond's "superior enlightenment" is, in fact, nothing more than his "clever" capacity for design and material objects. Furthermore, when Isabel states that she has "no ideas," she hints that Osmond has both crushed and appropriated her spirit. Ralph's perspective of Isabel perpetuates this reading: "The free, keen girl had become quite another person; what he saw was the fine lady who was supposed to represent something. . . . She represented Gilbert Osmond" (331). The apparent breakdown of Isabel's identity would seem to reinforce comments by critics who argue that the text portrays "the weakness of Emersonian idealism" (Millicent Bell 90).

Regardless of her outward appearance, however, there is much to suggest that Isabel is not as easily defeated and disillusioned as critics argue. Instead, Isabel's altered character remains far more ambiguous than most have claimed. What has changed about Isabel is not necessarily her spiritual makeup but rather a new divide between her inner and outer being. Whereas Isabel was once eager to publicly express her every thought and desire, her experience has taught her to shield that inner spirit. In a brief moment of narrative revelation, for example, readers learn that "the years had touched her only to enrich her; the flower of her youth had not faded, it only hung more quietly on its stem. She had lost something of that quick eagerness to which her husband had privately taken exception—she had more the air of being able to wait" (310). There is little question that Isabel's marriage has affected the "graceful illusions" of her youth. Yet, while Isabel has become aware of the force of history, she is still, readers learn, "fertile in [her] resolutions" (340) and continues to "think quite differently" from her husband (303). Most importantly, readers discover that her new life is miserable *precisely* because, contrary to what she tells Lord Warburton, she refuses to relinquish her ideas and become a mere reflection of her husband's ego.

Before her marriage, Isabel lived a life of ideas, of theoretical designs and desires; she had philosophical ideals that she desperately wanted to test, to experience. Most critics assert that, in marrying Osmond, such ideals fail and the "expression of her boundless self" becomes "doomed," but the narrator continually suggests that Isabel's experiment is unfinished (Millicent Bell 90). Even if her ideals are diminished, they are not shattered, and readers sense a recurrent note of possibility: "When Isabel was unhappy she always looked about her . . . for some form of positive exertion. She could never rid herself of the sense that unhappiness was a state of disease—of suffering as opposed to doing. To 'do'—it hardly mattered what—would therefore be an escape, perhaps in some degree a remedy" (348). While Isabel's marriage has clearly tempered her optimism, in her drive to "do" and to "remedy" her suffering, Isabel reveals strong remnants of her earlier determination and expansive spirit. Her premarital illusions have now given way to a new struggle with her growing awareness of realism, which she accepts but still refuses to succumb to passively. Isabel acknowledges an unwritten future and asks: "What was coming—what was before them? That was her constant question. What would he do—what ought *she* to do?" (363). James's altered heroine is a more reticent character, but she is certainly not "doomed." As she later tells Henrietta, "I'm not at all helpless" (417).

This new struggle can be traced through Isabel's growing relationship to Pansy and, more specifically, in her stepdaughter's triangle with Ned Rosier and Lord Warburton. The scenario plays a surprisingly large role in volume 2, particularly as it involves three minor, rather two-dimensional characters. This subplot ultimately reveals more about Isabel than it does about the other characters. Isabel's contradictory duties to her husband, herself, and Pansy mirror her internal conflict between a growing commitment to realism and her lingering ideals of spiritual self-reliance. Her first response to the union between Rosier and Pansy implies passivity. She says simply: "I can do nothing" (344). Yet, she quickly shifts her perspective: "She wished to convince herself that she had done everything possible to content her husband. . . . It would please him greatly to see Pansy married to an English nobleman . . . . It seemed to Isabel that if she could make it her duty to bring about such an event she should play the part of a good wife. She wanted to be that . . . . Then such an undertaking had other recommendations. It would occupy her, and she desired occupation. It would even amuse her, and if she could really amuse herself she perhaps might be saved" (348). In this scene, her thoughts teeter between a desperate need for "occupation" and an almost disturbing, conventional Madame Merle-type sensibility of "assisting her husband to be pleased" (350).

In the end, however, she surprises herself, her readers, and even her husband. In the next scene, she refuses to "play the part of the good wife" : "On the evening I speak of, while Lord Warburton sat there, she had been on the point of taking the great step of going out of the room and leaving her companions alone. I say the great step because it was in this light that Gilbert Osmond would have regarded it, and Isabel was trying as much as possible to take her husband's view. . . . After all she couldn't rise to it; something held

her and made this impossible. . . . There was a vague doubt that interposed—
a sense that she was not quite sure. So she remained in the drawing-room,
and after a while Lord Warburton went on to his party" (350). Despite her
conscious desire to "take her husband's view," Isabel is still guided by a spiritual force more powerful than Osmond's will. In her inability to leave Pansy
and Warburton alone, Isabel temporarily postpones a union she recognizes
as problematic.

Isabel outright defies Osmond when, several days later, she permanently
foils his marriage plans for Lord Warburton and Pansy. In an extended conversation with Warburton, she attempts to discourage his advances. Warburton
questions Isabel: "You told me she would have no wish apart from her father's,
and as I've gathered that he would favor me—!" Isabel responds: "Yes, I told
you she has an immense wish to please her father, and that it would probably
take her very far. . . . But it hardly strikes me as the sort of feeling to which
a man would wish to be indebted for a wife" (372). That her response seems
spontaneous renders it all the more brilliant. Without blatantly insisting that
Warburton end his courtship, she subtly and cleverly speaks to his pride and
noble sensibility to dissuade him. Her interference infuriates Osmond, who
sees it as an act of open defiance, yet Isabel repeatedly makes it clear that she
cares little for petty revenge. Instead, her behavior demonstrates a tenacious
loyalty to her early convictions and a desire to protect Pansy's own freedom.

Isabel's continued loyalty to her Emersonian persona is even more evident
in the growth of her inner consciousness than in her outer deeds. Much of
Isabel's suffering in her marriage comes from her frustrated curiosity, to know
how or why or what "was the work of" her marriage (339). While she tries to
convince herself that there "had been no plot, no snare," that she was a "free
agent" (340), she recognizes some unspoken truth that concerns her: "It was
her deep distrust of her husband—this was what darkened the world. That is a
sentiment easily indicated, but not so easily explained, and so composite in its
character that much time and still more suffering had been needed to bring it
to its actual perfection. Suffering, with Isabel, was an active condition; it was
not a chill, a stupor, a despair; it was a passion of thought, of speculation, of
response to every pressure" (356). Her "deep distrust" has profoundly altered
her perception of reality. Rather than charge recklessly "over roads that one
can't see" (146), she now engages in silent watchfulness and careful judgment:
"Covert observation had become a habit with her; an instinct, of which it is
not an exaggeration to say that it was allied to that of self-defense, had made
it habitual" (350). It is this willful, "covert observation" that defines Isabel's
experience in volume 2.

In chapter 42, the chapter most frequently cited as the focal point of the
text, readers find Isabel sitting in the "silent drawing-room, given up to her

meditation." In this scene, she achieves an "unexpected recognition" (354). Readers may assume that this "unexpected recognition" amounts to Isabel's awakened understanding of Osmond and Merle's true relationship, but in fact what Isabel begins to recognize are those "complications of existence" that James mentions in his preface (5). She begins to acknowledge the importance and value of realism: of witnessing, experiencing, and absorbing history—the "poisoned drink"—despite the potential consequences of such consciousness (134). Novick ties the scene directly back to American realism: "The long passage . . . was the perfect expression of his [James's] theory and his practice of realism. Here he portrayed one of the true pivots of history, an event in the consciousness of a person deeply engaged in living. Isabel was his reader . . . , trying to understand the reality that lay behind the scattered clues of the fiction" (*Young Master* 421). In this critical moment, James emphasizes both to Isabel and to his reader the palpable force of plot.

While the scene in Isabel's drawing room reinforces the importance of realism—of the search for objective truth—it does not serve to minimize an earlier romantic vision. Isabel's growing consciousness may temper the "graceful illusions" of her youth, but they will also help her foster spiritual transcendence: "For herself, she lingered in the soundless saloon long after the fire had gone out. There was no danger of her feeling the cold; she was in a fever. She heard the small hours strike, and then the great ones, but her vigil took no heed of time. Her mind, assailed by vision, was in a state of extraordinary activity, and her visions might as well come to her there, where she sat up to meet them, as on her pillow, to make a mockery of rest" (364). James denies his reader an overt epiphany, and Isabel's "fever" does not easily alleviate her suffering. By the same token, this scene should not be read as James's denunciation of romance. Isabel's enlightenment may not offer her immediate relief, but it presents her with a clear sense of spiritual empowerment and acts as a form of "self-defense" (350). After her marriage, Isabel seems reserved and almost sedated, wearing what Ralph reads as a "fixed and mechanical" expression (330); with her "unexpected recognition," Isabel recaptures an earlier spiritual fervor (or "fever") and begins "to wake from a long pernicious dream" (428).

A passage in chapter 49—a poignant and pivotal moment often overlooked by critics—symbolizes the delicate balance between Isabel's growing awareness of history and her renewed loyalty to transcendental ideals. James's heroine, searching for quiet contemplation, visits Roman ruins. The description of her experience is extensive and telling:

> Isabel took a drive alone that afternoon; she wished to be far away, under the sky, where she could descend from her carriage and tread upon the daisies. She had long before this taken old Rome into her confidence,

for in a world of ruins the ruin of her happiness seemed a less unnatural catastrophe. She rested her weariness upon things that had crumbled for centuries and yet still were upright; she dropped her secret sadness into the silence of lonely places, where its very modern quality detached itself and grew objective, so that as she sat in a sun-warmed angle on a winter's day, or stood in a mouldy church to which no one came, she could almost smile at it and think of its smallness. Small it was, in the large Roman record, and her haunting sense of the continuity of the human lot easily carried her from the less to the greater. . . . There was no gentler nor less consistent heretic than Isabel; the firmest of worshippers, gazing at dark altar-pictures or clustered candles, could not have felt more intimately the suggestiveness of these objects nor have been more liable at such moments to a spiritual visitation. . . . The carriage, leaving the walls of Rome behind, rolled through narrow lanes where the wild honeysuckle had begun to tangle itself in the hedges, or waited for her in quiet places where the fields lay near, while she strolled further and further over the flower-freckled turf, or sat on a stone that had once had a use and gazed through the veil of her personal sadness at the splendid sadness of the scene—at the dense, warm light, the far gradations and soft confusions of colour, the motionless shepherds in lonely attitudes, the hills where the cloud-shadows had the lightness of a blush. (430–31)

The scene is presented almost in its entirety not only because it is one of James's most beautiful passages but also because it highlights Isabel's altered consciousness. It offers a stark contrast to that earlier scene in which Isabel describes her idea of happiness as a "swift carriage, of a dark night, rattling with four horses over roads that one can't see" (146). In both a literal and figurative sense, Isabel now "descend[s] from her carriage" not only to "see" but to "tread upon the daisies."

One could argue that this moment represents Isabel's most marked association with realism: she rejects her earlier naive, Emersonian nature and awakens to the breadth and power of history. A close reading of the scene, however, indicates that as much as Isabel acknowledges the "continuity of the human lot," she also merges this vision of history with a profound, new spiritual awareness: "the firmest of worshippers, gazing at dark altar-pictures or clustered candles, could not have felt more intimately the suggestiveness of these objects nor have been more liable at such moments to a spiritual visitation." She achieves a type of "negative capability," where one accepts within nature the "uncertainties, Mysteries, doubts, without any irritable reaching after fact & reason" (Keats 41–42). More importantly, her romantic connection to nature is situated within the historic ruins of old Rome; it is here that James connects the binary voices of spirituality and material history, which exist concurrently as simultaneous layers in Isabel's consciousness. Thus, Rome is "crumbled" and yet still "upright"; the ancient city is old and lonely and yet still maintains a "modern quality"; the "mouldy church" is small and yet still part of the large Roman record. All of these opposing elements are meant to reflect Isabel's own dialogic imagination. Through the Roman ruins, Isabel both loses herself in history—allowing her "silent sadness" to become part of a larger past—and simultaneously achieves her most intense spiritual visitation. Although Isabel embraces the objective truth of history, readers find her—particularly in the passage's final emphasis on light—engaged in a type of Emersonian awakening where man "learn[s] to detect and watch that gleam of light which flashes across his mind from within" (Emerson, "Self-Reliance" 259). Her experience echoes a memorable and oft-cited line from *Nature*: "Standing on the bare ground,—my head bathed by the blithe air, and uplifted into infinite space,— all mean egotism vanishes" (10). Much like Emerson's man in nature, Isabel now becomes "part or particle" of something much greater than herself (10). The difference is that James reconfigures the binary of romance and realism by *merging* Emerson's idea of nature not only with the eternal present but also with the past. In James's rendering, with the pastoral images of the "motionless shepherds in lonely attitudes," history itself becomes part of nature.

While the text might end here, in this quieting pastoral moment, Isabel's plot continues. Despite her awakening, Isabel's vision is still somewhat skewed by the "soft confusions of colour" (431). As readers learn, she still "had no personal acquaintance with wickedness. She had desired a large acquaintance with human life, and in spite of her having flattered herself that she cultivated it with some success this elementary privilege had been denied her" (431); her "prayer to be enlightened" has yet to be fulfilled (430). Her prayer is eventually answered by perhaps the most superficial character in the text, the Countess Gemini, who professes to be her "aid to innocent ignorance" and uncovers the truth of Pansy's real parentage (451). Isabel is "troubled and puzzled" (451) by the revelation, but even this new "personal acquaintance with wickedness" does not destroy her romantic sensibility (431). The Countess is, therefore, shocked and even somewhat dismayed to discover that Isabel's reaction is not one of passionate revenge but quiet sympathy and compassion. Isabel uses the term "poor woman" several times, not only in reference to Osmond's first wife but also in reference to Pansy's mother, the "vile" Madame Merle herself (452). She is less concerned with regaining her social pride and more interested in reclaiming her personal liberty. The revelation, while painful, triggers that "gleam of light . . . from within" (Emerson 259). Rather than a "critique of Emersonian individualism," her growing consciousness represents James's symbolic struggle to relocate Emersonian individualism in the post-bellum American subject (Eakin 169).

The question becomes: how does one maintain spiritual individualism in the face of history? How does one merge the dual truths of romance and realism? Although James does not offer easy answers to these questions, he presents readers with a newly matured heroine who, while maybe lacking the answers herself, certainly begins a quest to locate some possible synthesis. Isabel's new insight, for example, prompts her to reconsider her personal moral obligations. Once concerned with playing "the part of the good wife" and doing "everything possible to content her husband," she now makes a series of choices that illustrate her renewed insistence on self-reliance (348). Isabel's first choice is to openly disobey Osmond by returning to Gardencourt to see Ralph. While Isabel had been undecided regarding her voyage, after meeting with the Countess she appears resolved; chapter 52 begins: "There was a train for Turin and Paris that evening" (456). Before she leaves, she visits Pansy at the convent. In the past, Isabel has only quietly and hesitantly supported Pansy, but she now proposes to liberate Pansy from the convent and take her away to England; although Pansy proves incapable of acting against her father, Isabel promises to come back, indicating a firm sense of purpose as well as the ability to think independently and, more importantly, to translate that thought into action. Finally, Isabel announces her spiritual independence when she once again meets Caspar Goodwood, with whom she "she wished to set herself right." With a clearer sense of both self and society, Isabel now locates the courage to act for herself and "put her spiritual affairs in order" (405).

Many critics regard Isabel's final meeting with Goodwood, and the novel's ending in general, as evidence of her failure and, by extension, the ultimate failure of transcendentalism. There are those, for example, who read Goodwood as a symbol of liberty, which Isabel turns down in favor of a constricted, conventional life. Oscar Cargill is one critic who recognizes Goodwood's renewed proposal as "an offer of complete freedom and a restoration of independence to Isabel" (282); likewise, Carren Kaston claims that Goodwood offers Isabel the "Emersonian freedom of a self-designed life" (55); Judith H. Montgomery is more forthright, stating that in returning to Rome Isabel "returns herself to a lifetime of servitude" and chooses "fulfillment of the image" over "fulfillment of the self" (896). These critics view Goodwood as "the most Emersonian of her wooers" and suggest that, in rejecting him and returning to Rome, Isabel submits both physically and spiritually to the text's least Emersonian wooer, Osmond (Millicent Bell 105). In such a reading, the novel ends with the final defeat of spiritual individualism.

It is easy to understand why so many readers interpret Isabel's rejection of Goodwood as a failure. After all, Goodwood is a highly attractive figure who appears to present Isabel with an easy solution to her oppressive marriage. The reader wants to believe Goodwood when he tells Isabel: "You must save what you can of your life; you mustn't lose it all simply because you've lost a part. . . . We can do absolutely as we please; to whom under the sun do we owe anything? What is it that holds us, what is it that has the smallest right to interfere in such a question as this?" (488–89). Goodwood delivers a powerful, poetic speech, one that has been linked to the final words of Milton's *Paradise Lost*:

> The world was all before them, where to choose
> Their place of rest, and Providence their guide:
> They hand in hand with wandering steps and slow,
> Through Eden took their solitary way. (12: 646–69)[15]

This literary connection highlights Goodwood's purpose: to proclaim himself an innocent Adamic figure who offers his Eve a life renewed.

Caspar Goodwood's words, however, also recall an earlier promise to Isabel: "It's to make you independent that I want to marry you." Just as Isabel has earlier read these words as nothing more than a "beautiful sophism," so readers too must now detect a note of pretense in Goodwood's rhetoric (142). Rather than spiritual resolve, in this scene Goodwood displays a type of desperation associated with physical aggression. He literally frightens Isabel with his forcefulness: "She had a new sensation; he had never produced it before; it was a feeling of danger. There was indeed something really formidable in his resolution" (486). Far from liberating her, Goodwood wants to possess her, and, in a moment of sheer passion, he exposes his true intentions: "His kiss was like white lightning, a flash that spread, and spread again, and stayed; and it was extraordinarily as if, while she took it, she felt each thing in his hard manhood that had least pleased her, each aggressive fact of his face, his figure, his presence, justified of its intense identity and made one with this act of possession. So had she heard of those wrecked and under water following a train of images before they sink. But when darkness returned she was free. She never looked about her; she only darted from the spot" (489). Goodwood's passion is intoxicating and powerful in a way that Osmond can never be; for this reason the reader wants Isabel to submit to Goodwood's desires. Yet, Isabel runs away from him precisely because she realizes that his physical power also amounts to "an act of possession." Submitting to Goodwood would result in the destruction of her expanded consciousness.

What disturbs Isabel, in addition to Goodwood's overall "intense identity," is her recognition that "this act of possession" is just another attempt to plot her future. Goodwood explains that it was Ralph who convinced him to approach her again: "'He told me how the case stands for you. He explained everything; he guessed my sentiments. . . . He left you—so long as you should be in England—to my care,' said Goodwood as if he were making a great point. 'Do you know what he said to me the last time I saw him—as he lay there where he died? He said: "Do everything you can do for her; do everything she'll let you."'" Isabel's subsequent reaction reveals her distaste for such paternalism: "You had no business to talk about me!" (487). Her shock and frustration clearly stem from the fact that she has, yet again, been plotted against. Despite Ralph's best intentions, his dying wish violates the very element of her spiritual being that he had hoped to preserve: her independence. In volume 2, Isabel has come first and foremost to realize that her narrative has been the product of external plotting rather than a product of her personal will. Through her expanded consciousness (both of herself and the world around her), Isabel has not only begun to recognize the power of plot but has also worked to maintain her spiritual integrity in the face of such recognition. Now Goodwood insults her spiritual and psychological growth by offering her a proposal based on yet another deception. Her decision to go back to Rome, therefore, may disturb many readers, but, as Poirier contends, it is "absolutely within the logic of her Emersonian idealism" (*Comic Sense* 246). In fact, Isabel's decision to return to Rome becomes a physical manifestation of her renewed ability to act independently.

It is difficult to view Isabel's return to Rome as an easy or great victory; as Stone aptly notes, "by the end of the novel, Isabel manages a curious sort of success" (208). Readers can only speculate what will happen to Isabel, and the book ends with same question that Isabel has asked earlier: "What was coming—what was before them?" (363). Many critics attempt to complete Isabel's plot. Poirier, for example, ends his discussion of the text by stating that "returning to Rome will, as Caspar admonishes, cost her her life" (*Comic Sense* 246). Richard Chase similarly claims that, at the end of the text, Isabel "seems veritably to belong to the sisterhood of Hester Prynne" (128). By contrast, Anthony J. Mazzella argues that Isabel's return to Rome will allow her to "counter his [Osmond's] intransigence and relieve Pansy's plight" (611). In fact, James denies readers both of these clear, alternative endings. Isabel's decision amounts to a rejection of both extremes, a refusal to either romanticize reality or renounce romance. In returning to Rome, Isabel does not attempt to escape reality; instead, she faces what James believes nineteenth-century transcendentalists such as Emerson and Thoreau tried to avoid. The text clearly warns against the postbellum American who attempts to create alternative, socially removed transcendental spaces, who becomes isolated and immersed in a Walden Pond or Brook Farm. One must concede the truth of and engage with history. As Jill M. Kress stresses, Isabel "cannot bolt the door against the public world; even the innermost sanctuary of personal thought expands to include social relations" (85–86). Although the novel does not allow Isabel to "bolt the door against the public world," it also strongly affirms Emerson's emphasis on the power and "integrity of . . . [one's] own mind." Rome is the site where Isabel attempts to synthesize both visions, to locate history within nature; furthermore, it is Rome that is simultaneously "crumbled" and "upright," old and new. As such, Rome symbolizes Isabel's own uncertain and yet conceivably hopeful future, a future that will attempt to incorporate both the "complications of existence" and, via consciousness, the possibility for spiritual integrity.

VI

While James leaves Isabel with an uncertain future, he constructs more definitive futures for the other characters in the novel. The text's finale offers a review of the players, all of whose endings call into question both ends of the romance/realism binary. As discussed, Ralph is the character who has dedicated the remainder of his life to watching Isabel renew the hope of Emersonian romance. He embodies the romantic side of James that wonders if spiritual individualism may still survive, unimpeded by history. Isabel's narrative, of course, proves him wrong. Most critics agree with Poirier when he contends that "with Ralph's death, Isabel ceases to live in the imagination of freedom, and he dies because her life no longer allows him to imagine the possibility that freedom and the life of the world are compatible" (*Comic Sense* 241). In one sense, Ralph dies when his narrative project collapses, when he realizes that plot cannot easily contain Isabel's Emersonian character. His death is the death of pure Emersonian romance.

If James offers a bleak picture of unadulterated romance, his vision of stark realism is even harsher. The text's realist characters—Merle, Osmond, Goodwood, and Henrietta—are all either punished or, by the end, reformed. Madame Merle and Gilbert Osmond, the material realists, are certainly not destroyed, but their plot has in essence proved unsuccessful. Merle quite blatantly admits her failure with her concluding (and rather satisfying) lines in chapter 49: "'Have I been so vile all for nothing?' she vaguely wailed" (437). Her plot uncovered, her past revealed, Merle is left defeated; as she tells Isabel: "You're very unhappy, I know. But I'm more so. . . . I shall go to America" (464). In *The Prison of Womanhood*, Elizabeth Jean Sabiston astutely links Merle's return to America with her need for "a refresher course in innocence" (137). If Isabel has had to learn the power of history, Merle must revisit the possibility for spiritual renewal. Merle's faith in material realism proves entirely flawed.

Gilbert Osmond, the reader must feel, does not suffer nearly enough for his part in Isabel's unhappiness; yet, there are several facets of his own plot that satisfy the reader's desire for redress. First, Isabel defies Osmond, particularly by thwarting his marriage plot for Pansy. While it is difficult to argue that Isabel leaves Gardencourt solely to save Pansy, it seems clear that her return serves, in part, to protect Pansy from her father. There is also the implication that even Isabel's money has provided Osmond with little beyond his trinkets and weekly salon. When the Countess instructs Isabel not to "give [Pansy] a *dot*" of her money, she intimates that Isabel's inheritance is still her own to do with as she wishes (455). Even more than Isabel's money, however, Osmond has always sought to appropriate Isabel's spiritual identity, to obliterate her independence and her ideas. He ultimately fails. Rather than renounce her independence, in volume 2 Isabel actually reclaims her individual identity. Osmond hates Isabel precisely because he cannot change her. Stone argues that Osmond's defeat lies even deeper: "After she marries him, she does worse than defy him; she sees through him" (221). While readers never actually witness Osmond admit his failure as Merle does, it is evident that his plot to obliterate Isabel's identity has been largely ineffective.

Neither Caspar Goodwood's character nor his circumstances appear to change at all during the course of the narrative. At the beginning of the text, he is the aggressive postbellum American industrialist, a militaristic suitor who tirelessly pursues Isabel. At the end of the text, he is still an aggressive, dominant force whose pursuit of Isabel remains hopeless. His final attempt to woo Isabel demonstrates his continued frustration: "She had had time only to rise when, with a motion that looked like violence, but felt like—she knew not what, he grasped her by the wrist and made her sink again into the seat." (486). Despite his resolution, his strength, and his Miltonic speeches, he is turned down yet again. At the end of the novel, readers are left with one final, pathetic image of him: Henrietta tells Goodwood that Isabel has left England and returned to Rome, and he leaves dejected, with little hope beyond "the key to patience" (490). Goodwood's future promises to be an endless series of rejections, a wasted life.

Henrietta offers the most humorous finale. She is the only one of the four realists who proves a round character capable of change. The novel's staunch champion of American democracy and objective, often superficial notions of truth learns to reject her own stubborn sensibility. While she seems the perfect wife for Goodwood—both are domineering, highly rational, and ultranationalist—Henrietta ends up with Bob Bantling, a simple, somewhat sensitive British subject. Her description of Bantling produces, as Isabel observes, her first disparaging statement "against . . . [her] native land": "He is not intellectual, but he appreciates intellect. On the other hand, he doesn't exaggerate its claims. I sometimes think we do in the United States" (470). Henrietta's uncharacteristically unpatriotic comment speaks specifically to the rigidity of American subjects, a fault she herself has been guilty of. By the end of the novel, she becomes a better reader—both of herself and her nation—and learns to see through the interpretive lens of others.

The text makes clear that Henrietta's growing friendship with Ralph Touchett is at least partially responsible for her softened persona. Henrietta once had little more interest in Ralph than "to show him up," but now the journalist has become both his caretaker and friend (83). Their connection is the key to Henrietta's development: Ralph's romantic nature acts as a counter to Henrietta's rigid character. Their burgeoning friendship and its positive effect on Henrietta demonstrate the problem with unilateral thinking, embodied by the other main figures in the novel. Ralph, Merle, Osmond, Goodwood, and Henrietta all stand in contrast to Isabel, who alone struggles to negotiate the conflict between romance and realism within a single character.

There remains one final figure in the novel who helps reinforce the romance/realism binary in this text. Daniel Touchett's early exit tends to remove him from critical interest, but he proves an important character who mirrors a central shift in nineteenth-century thought, a shift the younger characters must contend with. Ralph's father is representative of Emerson's generation, the last remnant of true transcendentalism. The very first image of him emphasizes his distinct individualism: "The old man had his cup in his hand; it was an unusually large cup, *of a different pattern from the rest of the set* and painted in brilliant colours" (17; emphasis added). His cup signifies his cultural and historical distance from the other characters; much like the cup, he too is "of a different pattern from the rest of the set." His difference manifests itself most visibly in his world outlook. Daniel Touchett is the only character in the text who not only understands the power of history but also recognizes its dangers. He embodies that element of transcendentalism that Isabel initially overlooks: like Emerson, he reads history as sinister, as an "impertinence and injury" (Emerson, "Self-Reliance" 270). Thus, he warns his son and Lord Warburton that "there will be great changes; and not all for the better" (22).

Despite his recognition of impending "social and political changes," he alone manages to live independent of such historical shifts (23). He is a native Vermonter who fully acknowledges his identity as an American despite his residence in England; he uses his native tongue to emphasize this distance: "I ain't a lord," he says (72). Yet, he lives comfortably in England, in his Gardencourt, an Eden separate from nationhood and history. He manages a type of totality of self discussed by Lukács, where the subject is at ease in the objective world. For this reason, he is not only the lone American who seems at home in England, but he is also the only character who does not plot against

Isabel. He experiences a type of unification of self and world that the other characters do not. Of course, Daniel Touchett is quite literally a dying breed. He exhibits the shift in "the history of the American mind" that James describes in *Hawthorne*; he becomes part of the generation of older romantics who, after the Civil War, had nothing left but "to hang their heads and close their eyes" (114).

Even more than Ralph, it is Isabel who becomes Daniel Touchett's transcendental child, the inheritor of his Emersonian values and the character who contends with those "social and political changes" that he warns against. She is almost forcibly removed from her isolated, ahistorical home of books and transcendental teachings and brought out into the world, and she alone attempts to locate a synthesis of Emersonian romance and the "complications of existence." Carrying with her an Emersonian spirit, but one devoid of the essential caution of history, she charges into experience "over roads that one can't see" (146). After her marriage to Osmond, if Isabel becomes disillusioned at all, then it is not, as critics contend, with Emersonian romance. Isabel eats "of the tree of knowledge" and awakens to the reality of history itself (*Hawthorne* 114). Through consciousness, she works to reclaim self-reliance in a new, postbellum world, one that James understands as "a more complicated place than it had hitherto seemed, the future more treacherous, success more difficult" (*Hawthorne* 114).[16] Isabel's ending is left open simply because success is, as James contends, now more difficult, and Isabel's consciousness becomes a burgeoning idea not yet fulfilled. As she tells Henrietta: "There are many things I mean to do" (417). *The Portrait of a Lady* becomes James's own experiment, an attempt to investigate a complex binary: the dynamic relationship between two cultural moments—romanticism and realism—that are found in both *Hawthorne* and James's own life. Through Isabel, James attempts to synthesize a residual romantic trend with the dominant culture of realism. Consciousness, he suggests, will become this new battleground, but an easy, definitive solution is only imagined, not easily enacted.

3
Edith Wharton's

The House of Mirth

> Every spirit makes its house; but afterwards the house confines the spirit.
> —Ralph Waldo Emerson, "Fate," *Essays*

I

Edith Wharton begins her memoir, *A Backward Glance*, with her "earliest definite memory" (3): "It was on a bright day of midwinter, in New York. The little girl who eventually became me, but as yet was neither me nor anybody else in particular, but merely a soft anonymous morsel of humanity— this little girl, who bore my name, was going for a walk with her father. The episode is literally the first thing I can remember about her, and therefore I date the birth of her identity from that day. . . . It was always an event in the little girl's life to take a walk with her father, and more particularly so today, because she had on her new winter bonnet, which was so beautiful (and so becoming) that for the first time she woke to the importance of dress, and of herself as a subject for adornment—so that I may date from that hour the birth of the conscious and feminine *me* in the little girl's vague soul" (1–2). Through her description of this "little girl," Wharton reveals her deep-seated interest in questions of individual identity, a subject that resonates in each of her novels. By using the third person, she casts herself as a literary character, a heroine attempting to develop a sense of self amidst the presence of material culture. Her romantic rhetoric, her focused meditation on individual identity, and her concern with the social body all speak directly to those primary concerns of Ralph Waldo Emerson, whom she thought one of the three "best" American poets and whose writing she described as "some beautiful bit of pink crystal" (qtd. in Lewis, *Edith Wharton* 236).[1]

In "Undine Spragg and the Transcendental I," Julie Olin-Ammentorp and

Ann Ryan compare and contrast the role that Emerson played in Wharton's life and literature with the figure of Emerson adopted by late-nineteenth-century American popular culture. They explain that "at the close of the nineteenth century, reading Emerson was a nostalgic gesture in a culture obsessively concerned not only with its own changing identity, but also with the consequent worth of American individualism and the possibility of American idealism" (1). Olin-Ammentorp and Ryan specifically identify this "nostalgic gesture" with a lowbrow, commodified adaptation of Emerson, one in which his writings were translated into aphorisms and "sewn into samplers and hung on parlor walls, copied into primers, and recited at any and every type of rhetorical event" (1). Emerson was, in this way, a celebrity in Wharton's Gilded Age America, but his pop-cultural presence had become largely detached from his philosophy; in fact, his philosophy of spiritual self-reliance had ironically (and unfortunately) been transformed into a material product to be bought, traded, and sold.

Olin-Ammentorp and Ryan emphasize Wharton's appreciation of Emerson by juxtaposing her own view of the philosopher with this pop culture, material rendering of Emerson: "Wharton clearly admired what she perceived as the 'real' Emerson, but was critical of popular, cheapening readings of his works" (3). Support for such an argument can be found in Wharton's own library of books at her historic home in the Berkshires ("The Mount"), which contains multiple volumes of Emerson's work—his essays, poetry, and journals—and unveils her personal and intellectual interest in his writing. In her copies of Emerson's published texts, Wharton carefully highlighted and annotated his language, singling out quotes in his essay "Character," for example, where Emerson writes that "society is frivolous, and shreds its day into scraps, its conversation into ceremonies and escapes" (Wharton, Marginalia 98).[2] Far from accepting Emerson as a cultural fad, Wharton respected his writing—that "beautiful bit of pink crystal"—precisely for its opposition to such popular convention. Rather than a mere sampler or displaced quotation, Emerson's prose and poetry offered Wharton—like so many other intellectuals of the period—a language and vision with which to structure her deepest concerns of spiritual transcendence. In her troubled relationship with her mother, in her sterile marriage, in her fulfilling career as a writer, in her friendships with Henry James and Walter Berry, and in her passionate love affair with Morton Fullerton, Wharton continually struggled to protect her "vague soul" from the social world around her.[3]

The impact of Emerson's legacy on Wharton's life and literature is most evident in her 1905 novel about a "society of irresponsible pleasure-seekers," *The House of Mirth* (Wharton *Backward* 207). Emerson's central tenets—reconfigured as what Lawrence Selden calls a "republic of the spirit"—form the central philosophical framework for the novel (*Mirth* 55). *The House of Mirth* addresses several core concerns of transcendentalism: man's relationship to society, his aptitude for self-reliance, and his ability to sustain those "voices which we hear in solitude . . . as we enter into the world" (Emerson, "Self-Reliance" 261). The novel acts as Wharton's profound conversation not only with the "irresponsible" New York society of her youth but also with larger questions of its transcendental alternative.

While *The House of Mirth* engages with Emerson's mid-nineteenth-century ideology, it revisits these doctrines during a very different moment in American history. When Emerson published "Self-Reliance" in 1841, his ideas resonated with previously conceived democratic ideals; transcendentalism was harmonious with American tropes of man in nature and the divine self. Emerson brilliantly articulated a core value of the national ethos: the desire to maintain a sense of the democratic individual above the trappings of society and government. By the beginning of the twentieth century that national ethos had changed. The metaphor of "the spirit and the house"—a metaphor that appears in both Emerson's and Wharton's literature and serves as an epigraph for this chapter—helps articulate this change.[4] Before the Civil War, the American spirit had been busy constructing its house, specifically defining what it meant to be "American." After the Civil War, the house—an emblem of America's national identity—now seemed to confine the spirit.

Evidence of such a shift can be found early in *The House of Mirth*, when Lily and Selden discuss the popular fad of collecting Americana. Lily asks Selden whether the owners of Americana are historians, and Selden responds: "No; very few of the historians can afford to buy them" (11). In early-twentieth-century America, national artifacts had become a collectable commodity (much like Emerson himself). Instead of forging a new identity, Americanness was now something to be purchased and amassed. In postbellum America, while man-made institutions of business and technology began to explode, the land's untapped natural resources were being mined, developed, and settled. The progression from agrarian to industrial became symptomatic: the social machine had replaced the individual. Americans had constructed a web of social and material structures that now appeared ubiquitous and impenetrable.

By 1905, when *The House of Mirth* was published, even Walden Pond—a transcendental symbol of nature and self-reliance—had become a crowded tourist trap, beset by thousands in the summer, intruded upon by automobiles, and sought after by filmmakers (Maynard 218–19). In *Walden Pond: A History*, W. Barksdale Maynard carefully details early-twentieth-century accounts of Walden's transformation: of the garbage, for example, that was left at Walden by the mass of picnicking families and, in 1902, of Concord's thwarted plans to construct a beef-packing plant on the site of the old hut (217–19). Much like Emerson's writing, which was now "identified with an emerging market-place economy," the American landscape itself had become a social and commercial pecking ground (Olin-Ammentorp and Ryan 1).

In *The House of Mirth*, Emerson's philosophy is reenacted in this new historical moment. Like Mark Twain's *Adventures of Huckleberry Finn* and Henry James's *The Portrait of a Lady*, Edith Wharton's *The House of Mirth* becomes a cultural litmus test, an investigation into the complex relationship between American philosophy and history.[5] What happens to the Emersonian "spirit" when "its house" has transformed that spirit into a commodity? This critical question becomes the focus of Wharton's novel. In *The House of Mirth*, Wharton explores, tests, and ultimately proves Emerson's adage: "Every spirit makes its house; but afterwards the house confines the spirit."

Wharton fills her "house of mirth" with an array of characters, each of whom plays a distinct role in the architecture of her argument with postbellum America. Her exploration of nineteenth-century romantic philosophy begins with Lawrence Selden, who becomes Wharton's initial spokesperson for spiritual self-reliance. Although Wharton applauds Selden's basic message of spiritual fortitude, she also makes clear the hidden fractures in his philosophy. Selden plainly misreads transcendentalism and comes to represent the false Emersonian figure, a Gilded Age mutation of Emersonianism. In place of Selden, Lily Bart becomes the true Emersonian heroine, the character who ultimately escapes the psychological trappings of the Gilded Age. Her plot becomes a quest to navigate what Lukács terms "the separation of man and world" (32), to rectify the breach between the romantic and real. Her quest reads like a journey through Dante's *Inferno*, where one encounters a rift between "man and world" in every sinful circle of society—from the old money Trenors, to the nouveau-riche Jewish real estate mogul Simon Rosedale, all the way down to the bribing charwoman Mrs. Haffen. In one sense, by the end of the novel, Lily fails; her plot illustrates the danger of asserting one's individual will in postbellum America. On the other hand, her spiritual experiment acts as the central, heroic act of the novel. She alone has the courage to place character before plot and seek Emersonian individualism in the postbellum world.

II

Lawrence Selden—a charming, somewhat aloof bachelor who stands on the edge of New York's upper-class society—provides readers a preliminary blueprint of the novel's philosophical framework. He posits his abstract and idealistic philosophy to Lily Bart early in the text, when they are "ascending the long slopes beyond the high-road" to the heights of Bellomont, Gus and Judy

Trenor's fashionable country estate (51): "My idea of success . . . is personal freedom. . . . From everything—from money, from poverty, from ease and anxiety, from all the material accidents. To keep a kind of republic of the spirit—that's what I call success" (55). Selden's "idea of success" exposes two crucial components of his philosophy. First, he belittles popular, bourgeois assumptions of material happiness, or what he calls "material accidents"; in their place, he promotes a less conventional view, one that privileges spiritual fulfillment. Second, his philosophy speaks to the preeminence of self; his ideas of "personal freedom" and the "republic of the spirit" focus on the individual rather than the group.

On the surface, Selden's republic of the spirit faithfully follows Emerson's nineteenth-century transcendental philosophy of spiritual self-reliance. His rhetoric parallels Emerson's critique of material culture and his conviction that "to stand for the private verdict against popular clamor is the office of the noble" (227). Like Emerson, Selden laments that "so much human nature is used up" in social production (*Mirth* 56). Furthermore, Selden notably sounds his philosophic yawp on a hilltop, in the text's only pastoral scene: "The afternoon was perfect. . . . In the woody hollows of the park there was already a faint chill; but as the ground rose the air grew lighter, and ascending the long slopes beyond the high-road, Lily and her companion reached a zone of lingering summer. The path wound across a meadow with scattered trees; then it dipped into a lane plumed with asters and purpling sprays of bramble, whence, through the light quiver of ash-leaves, the country unrolled itself in pastoral distances" (51). This scene—with its "woody hollows," "purpling sprays of bramble," and "ash-leaves"—is the closest the novel comes to pastoral harmony between man and nature; as such, it reinforces the connection between Selden's own spiritual leanings and the transcendental philosopher. The other obvious reference here is to the Sermon on the Mount: "And seeing the multitudes, he went up into a mountain: and when he was set, his disciples came unto him: And he opened his mouth, and taught them" (Matthew 5:1–2). Not only does Lily describe the scene as an ascent up "the long slopes beyond the high-road," but the location of Selden's own sermon is called "Bellomont," the beautiful mount. In his Biblical reenactment, Selden becomes the Jesus figure ministering to Lily, his eager disciple, showing her the correct path toward righteousness and virtue. He preaches on the depraved evils of society—the "house of mirth"—and promotes an alternate divine path: a form of Emersonian romanticism that points toward Wharton's own vision of spirituality.

Selden's sermon ends, however, with a "remote sound, like the hum of a giant insect"; the car, a reminder of industrial modernity, interrupts their pastoral moment, and—"their flight over"—they descend both literally and figuratively (59). What readers quickly learn, having returned from this ephemeral moment, is that they too must "beware of false prophets" (Matthew 7:15). Even as Selden introduces the theme of Emersonian romanticism, a closer look at his sermon exposes major problems, both with his theories and his character. First and foremost, Selden proves reliant on the society he critiques. As Lily reminds him: "It seems to me . . . that you spend a good deal of your time in the element you disapprove of" (56). Her comment is certainly apt: he delivers his sermon on "material accidents" while vacationing at the pastoral estate of his wealthy New York friends. Selden himself admits that he is an "amphibious" creature who moves in and out of the social fray, but he self-righteously maintains that, as a spectator rather than a participant, he can become one of "the critics on the fence" (56). In truth, he remains just remote enough to judge society and yet still enjoy all of its privileges.

Even as spectator, Selden unknowingly becomes an irreplaceable part of the social wheel. Lily, for example, attributes Selden's charm to his "social detachment, a happy air of viewing the show objectively, of having points of contact outside the great gilt cage in which they were all huddled for the mob to gape at" (45). The irony is that, in his attempt to step out of "the great gilt cage" and maintain "social detachment," he becomes part of the same gaping mob. In *The Social Construction of American Realism*, Amy Kaplan highlights the interdependent roles of actor and audience in Gilded Age American society. In postbellum New York, she explains, the competition for class status played itself out in the form of "extravagant public spectacles" (92), during which the spectator reifies the power of the spectacle and "serves as a mirror" for the patron's class status (95). In this way, Selden's pretense of social detachment affirms both his arrogance and ignorance: while he views his role as a powerful voyeur, he actually provides a critical social function, serving to legitimate Gilded Age culture.

Although Selden himself relies on society, he maintains a selfish indifference to social responsibility and manipulates Emerson's philosophy to justify his own moral limitations. He openly patronizes Lily, belittling her values and lecturing her on the correct path to "personal freedom," but he fails to offer her the necessary support and community to translate those ideals into realities. When Lily complains that she never had anyone to tell her "about the republic of the spirit," for instance, Selden responds that the republic is "a country one has to find the way to one's self" (55). And when Lily explains to Selden that she is a "*jeune fille à marier*," he retorts: "Ah, then I'm afraid we can't let you into the republic. . . . There are not many married people in it" (56).

Lily immediately recognizes and attempts to point out the fallacies in Selden's logic. As Dale M. Bauer observes, Lily tries to "draw him out of his monologically closed world" (111). She questions, for example, his seemingly undemocratic and exclusionary ideas: "Ah, you are as bad as the other sectarians, . . .

why do you call your republic a republic? It is a close corporation, and you create arbitrary objections in order to keep people out." Selden blithely replies: "It is not *my* republic; if it were, I should have a *coup d'état* and seat you on the throne" (*Mirth* 57). Here Selden lays bare the contradictions in his philosophy: what should be a communal republic amounts to a monarchy. When Selden comments that the republic is a "country one has to find the way to one's self," Lily insists: "But I should never have found my way there if you hadn't told me. . . . Whenever I see you, I find myself spelling out a letter of the sign—and yesterday—and last evening at dinner—I suddenly saw a little way into your republic" (55). The difference between the two characters is clear: where Selden sees his abstract spirituality as completely self-contained, Lily embraces a notion of spirituality that can be shared.

Selden's warped vision of self-reliance comes, in part, from his inability to acknowledge the difficulties of those who are disempowered, specifically financially dependent women and the lower classes. While not rich, Selden is, unlike Lily, a financially independent male bachelor who fails to grasp basic issues of economic survival. His ignorance becomes particularly evident when he includes Ned Silverton as an example of society's frivolous waste of "good material." Although Selden's complaint—that "so much of human nature is used up" in "the decorative side of life"—is well founded, his idea is made manifest not by Ned Silverton but by the woman before him (56). As has been repeatedly noted by critics, Lily is the character in the novel whose struggle as a beautiful object becomes a prime example of social waste.[6] Rather than acknowledge Lily's own challenges, however, Selden empathizes with another man, an idle male bachelor whose selfish relationship with Bertha Dorset will ultimately result in Lily's social downfall. Selden's privileged social position allows him to speak glibly about what he calls "material accidents," and it blinds him to Lily's recognition that, for an economically dependent single woman, financial stability is more than merely an accident.

Critics regularly charge Emerson with similar faults, pointing out in particular that the Boston Brahmin was removed from the lives of average nineteenth-century Americans.[7] The novel is often read, therefore, as a critique of Emersonian philosophy, particularly its distance from historical, social, and economic reality. While Selden and Emerson may share certain social privileges, they nonetheless differ greatly in their visions of community. Emerson focused on the importance of individualism, but he did not disavow notions of community. Emerson's own republic of the spirit included dedication to family, an emphasis on friendship, and the emotional support of Henry David Thoreau and other transcendentalists. While he espoused similar ideas of personal freedom, his own philosophy allowed for a community of individuals dictated not by society but instead governed by higher laws than those created by mortal men. The binaries of community and self-reliance were not as clear-cut for Emerson as they are for Selden. Emerson's own circle in Concord as well as his published writings attest to his focus on community. In his essay "Friendship," for example, he argues that "our intellectual and active powers increase with our affection" (341); in his essay "Love," he defines love as the "enchantment of human life," which "seizes on man at one period, and works a revolution in his mind and body; unites him to his race, . . . and gives permanence to human society" (327). Most importantly, in his essay "The Over-Soul," Emerson complains that "we live in succession, in division, in parts, in particles. Meantime within man is the soul of the whole; the wise silence; the universal beauty, to which every part and particle is equally related; the eternal ONE" (386).

Emerson's philosophy incorporates an ecumenical vision of humanity that Selden's lacks. Lily highlights Selden's incapacity for community when she poses the following rhetorical question: "Why do you make the things I have chosen seem hateful to me, if you have nothing to give me instead?" (*Mirth* 58). While Emerson emphasized the dangers of society and traditional notions of success, unlike Selden he was not simply a glib "critic . . . on the fence" (56). Selden's republic is flawed because he rewrites ideas of transcendentalism to justify his own moral indifference; he neglects Emerson's ideas of the "over-soul," "the universal beauty," "the eternal ONE." His appropriation of Emerson allows him the false presumption of spiritual authority, but he adapts Emerson's philosophy to Gilded Age culture: ideas of personal freedom now work to validate self-interest and emotional detachment. He represents the "fervent mystic" whom Emerson warns about in "The Over-Soul," the false prophet who speaks "from without, as spectators merely" (395).

III

The inconsistencies and contradictions in Selden's republic of the spirit philosophy are evident not only during his sermon at Bellomont but throughout the narrative, particularly in his relationship with three women in the novel: Lily Bart, Bertha Dorset, and Gerty Farish. Selden's problematic perspective on women is evident even in the novel's opening paragraph: "Selden paused in surprise. In the afternoon rush of the Grand Central station his eyes had been refreshed by the sight of Miss Lily Bart" (5). The first glimpse of Lily comes quite unexpectedly, not from the objective perspective of the third-person narrator but instead through the highly subjective viewpoint of Lawrence Selden. In this introductory scene, Selden becomes the subject, Lily the object, and it can be assumed that Selden will be the primary focalizer and hero. Yet readers quickly realize that, rather than identify with him, they are meant to criticize his overtly shallow and materialistic description of Lily. He enjoys, for example, her physical features: "the modelling of her little ear, the crisp upward wave of her hair . . . and the thick planting of her straight black lashes" (7). His discussion of her beauty, however, moves beyond appreciation and toward misogyny: "He led her through the throng of returning holiday-makers, past swallow-faced girls in preposterous hats, and flat-chested women struggling with paper bundles and palm-leaf fans. Was it possible that she belonged to the same race? The dinginess, the crudity of this average section of womanhood made him feel how highly specialized she was. . . . He had a confused sense that she must have cost a great deal to make, that a great many dull and ugly people must, in some mysterious way, have been sacrificed to produce her. He was aware that the qualities distinguishing her from the herd of her sex were chiefly external: as though a fine glaze of beauty and fastidiousness had been applied to vulgar clay" (6–7). This scene exposes far more about Selden, particularly his attitude toward women, than it does about Lily. Selden's description of Lily may initially seem flattering, but only in so far as he dislikes women in general. In admiring her, Selden reads Lily as an exception to the "average section of womanhood." He frames Lily's superiority as "chiefly external" rather than spiritual; he recognizes, underneath her "glaze of beauty," the normal "vulgar clay" of the female "herd." His elevated vision of Lily is thereby cast in opposition to his insulting and debasing view of women as "vulgar" and, in his use of the term "herd," even animalistic. Finally, his description of Lily confirms his symbolic association with the Gilded Age. In his "confused sense that she must have cost a great deal to make," he highlights his allegiance to a dominant culture of materialism, greed, and Wall Street speculation. Selden's thoughts in the opening scene reflect his split vision of the novel's heroine: a deep-seated attraction to her partnered with a self-righteous attitude of disapproval and repulsion.

Selden maintains his conflicted view of Lily throughout the text. Despite his apparent love for her, Selden never proposes. Contemporary responses to *The House of Mirth* expressed widespread dissatisfaction with the fact that Selden never marries Lily, but such criticism fails to account for the important symbolism inherent in Selden and Lily's failed relationship (Lewis, *Edith Wharton* 152). According to his own admission, Selden remains a bachelor because his spiritual leanings preclude emotional commitment; as he tells Lily, "there are not many married people" in his republic (56). In fact, while Selden would have readers believe that his detachment stems from his own spiritual transcendence, his actions prove otherwise. During their early walk at Bellomont, Lily asks Selden quite plainly: "Do you want to marry me?" His retort is childish: "No, I don't want to—but perhaps I should if you did!" (58). As they return to the house, his defensive response lays bare his fragile ego: "He drew his cigarette-case from his pocket and slowly lit a cigarette. It seemed to him necessary, at that moment, to proclaim, by some habitual gesture of this sort, his recovered hold on the actual: he had an almost puerile wish to let his companion see that, their flight over, he had landed on his feet" (59). His commitment to bachelorhood clearly stems more from ego than spiritual individualism. He uses his philosophy to compensate for his own material shortcomings; as he himself says: "I . . . belittle all the things I can't offer you" (58). His spiritual convictions act as a front for his pride.

Selden's distortion of Emersonian romance becomes most blatant at the Wellington Brys' tableaux vivants party, where Selden comes closest to satisfying Wharton's readers and declaring his love for Lily. When he sees Lily in her own tableaux vivant—as a mute and motionless statue of Joshua Reynolds's painting *Mrs. Lloyd*—he experiences a false awakening in which he tragically mistakes Lily's acting for spiritual transcendence: "The noble buoyancy of her attitude, its suggestion of soaring grace, revealed the touch of poetry in her beauty that Selden always felt in her presence, yet lost the sense of when he was not with her. Its expression was now so vivid that for the first time he seemed to see before him the real Lily Bart, divested of the trivialities of her little world" (106). In this scene Lily is certainly not "divested of the trivialities of her little world." Instead, she becomes a commodity, a work of art, which she performs for that "little world." Selden misreads Lily's role as a living statue, an image produced by and for upper-class society. He inverts Emerson's notions of the "me" and "not me"; he takes the most base, objectifying, and dehumanizing version of Lily—the ideal, social Lily—and rereads it as her "real," spiritual self. The tragedy, and the reason why most readers of the novel do not get their sentimental wish, is that Selden falls in love with a false social facade, the very antithesis of all that Emerson celebrated.

Selden's hypocrisy becomes evident not only in his relationship with Lily but with two other women in the novel: Bertha Dorset and Gerty Farish. Bertha is portrayed, and even acknowledged by her friends, as a "nasty woman" (37). She is a keen materialist who exemplifies the empty, idle world of upper-class leisure that Selden criticizes. She lacks spiritual virtues, is not self-reliant, and, in fact, depends upon the destruction of others to satisfy her selfish whims and desires. As Linda Wagner-Martin notes: "Bertha has power because Bertha represents the system, and whatever she does, her behavior is sanctioned by that system" ("Novel of Admonition" 119). Bertha violates the most basic principles of Selden's republic.

And yet, early in the novel the reader discovers that Selden has had an affair with this "nasty woman." Ironically, the affair is revealed only pages before Selden's smug spiritual sermon, in which he hypocritically mocks Lily's own interaction with the Dorset social scene. His rhetoric belies his own actions. Bertha is one of the least spiritual characters in the novel, and Selden's attraction to her obviously stems from her superficial charm and beauty. Far from Lily's natural beauty, Bertha's good looks are artificial, acquired through financial means and leisure time. The narrator observes that "Mrs. Dorset never came down till luncheon: her doctors, she averred, had forbidden her to expose herself to the crude air of the morning" (48). Selden, who criticizes materialism, is incapable of seeing beneath the physical appearance that Bertha's wealth affords her. He becomes intimately involved with a woman who stands in stark contrast to his abstract idealism. His secret affair with Bertha is, in short, an affair with the system; he uses society when it suits him and condemns those elements of society that are, for him, untenable. The love letters between Bertha and Selden, which Lily later acquires and keeps throughout the novel, act as a keen reminder of Selden's hypocrisy, a reminder that Selden enjoys all that he professes to disdain.

While Bertha Dorset's attraction to Selden is primarily sexual and generated by upper-class ennui, Gerty Farish's love for him is heartfelt and genuine. As a single, relatively poor social worker, a woman who is socially impotent but financially and emotionally self-reliant, she is Bertha Dorset's opposite. In many ways, she represents the New Woman of early-twentieth-century America, the confident woman who breaks away from the subservient, dependent female mold and works to help other women gain their independence. In this sense, Gerty's ardent attraction to Selden seems logical: socially, financially, and spiritually, they seem well suited. That Selden often uses her as an example to Lily of an alternative route—as a way to transcend her own materialist trappings—underscores the association of Gerty with his own republic.

Selden respects Gerty Farish and celebrates her spiritual accomplishments, but he does not return her affections. Hard work, financial woes, and years spent in a "cramped flat" have all taken their toll on Gerty's looks (23); the narrator explains, quite bluntly, that she "typified the mediocre and the ineffectual" (70). It is, in fact, only when Selden is giddy with love for Lily that he even tepidly concedes Gerty's worth: "He had never before noticed that she had 'points'—really, some good fellow might do worse" (122). This patent and patronizing acknowledgment reflects Selden's typical reaction to women. Just as he courts Bertha, the charming yet spiritually empty woman, so he finds Gerty, the spiritually wealthy yet unattractive woman, average and dull. At the beginning of the novel, when Lily asks Selden about his book collection—"You collect, don't you—you know about first editions and things?"—Selden responds: "As much as a man may who has no money to spend. Now and then I pick up something in the rubbish heap; and I go and look on at the big sales" (11). Selden treats women much as he treats his book collection. He might "now and then . . . pick up something in the rubbish heap," but Selden goes after the "big sales," the beautiful, rich, and charming women of upper-class society. The tragic paradox of Selden's philosophy is that the women who most closely approximate the values of his republic will ultimately be thrown into the rubbish heap of undesirable women.

Furthermore, Selden's reading of Gerty's life is tragically inaccurate. Though she is one of the most spiritual and morally responsible characters in the novel, she is also unhappy and lonely. Because of his personal philosophy—his Gilded Age mutation of Emersonianism—Selden mistakenly assumes that Gerty's spiritual strength obviates the need for companionship or community, but her character, in fact, symbolizes the emotional cost of spiritual detachment. Without companionship or community, Gerty sees her "future stretched out interminably, with her lonely figure toiling down it, a mere speck on the solitude" (123). Her only respite from loneliness comes in those rare moments when she is invited to social functions, where she acts as a voyeur, living vicariously through others: "Miss Farish . . . was accustomed, in the way of happiness, to such scant light as shone through the cracks of other people's lives" (118). Like Selden, she plays the role of spectator, but unlike Selden—who as an attractive bachelor is a genuinely desirable addition to social gatherings—Gerty's invitations stem entirely from familial charity. Rather than an emblem of spiritual transcendence, Gerty represents a woman who, cast out on the margins of genteel society, has become self-reliant only by necessity. Selden's ignorance of Gerty's social and romantic desires as well as his inability to reciprocate her feelings remind the reader what is missing in Selden's republic.

Narrative descriptions of Selden's mother help account for his skewed perception of women. While not wealthy, his mother manages to maintain her primary function as an upper-class woman in Gilded Age America—to display leisure, or what Thorstein Veblen refers to as the "non-productive consumption of time" (46): "Now it had been Selden's fate to have a charming mother: her graceful portrait, all smiles and Cashmere, still emitted a faded scent of the undefinable quality" (Wharton, *Mirth* 120). The mention of cashmere associates his mother's grace and charm with her material wealth, but she downplays this connection between money and beauty and gives Selden the impression that such grace and charm are inherent in all women: "his views of womankind in especial were tinged by the remembrance of the one woman who had given him his sense of 'values.' It was from her [his mother] that he inherited his detachment from the sumptuary side of life: the stoic's carelessness of material things, combined with the Epicurean's pleasure in them. Life shorn of either feeling appeared to him a diminished thing; and nowhere was the blending of the two ingredients so essential as in the character of a pretty woman" (120–21). Selden's own misguided image of women seems firmly rooted in his relationship with his mother, specifically in her simultaneous "carelessness of material things" and "Epicurean's pleasure in them." She gives him the false sense that a woman's material beauty signifies her spiritual worth. It is precisely for this reason that, in Lily's tableau vivant, Selden is incapable of distinguishing the true woman from her physical ideal. He enjoys his romantic vision but, in the process, loses sight of the real.

Selden's republic of the spirit, therefore, acts as a conflicted and even arrogant revision of Emersonian transcendentalism. It is not simply that Selden lacks Emersonian underpinnings. He is one of the few characters who acknowledges and even acts as a spokesperson for the spiritual values of self-reliance. As Lily notes, despite his enjoyment of the "great gilt cage," Selden "had never forgotten the way out" (45). Selden's problem amounts to fear. His gender and financial security allow him to sit comfortably, too comfortably, "on the fence" (56). He hides behind his romantic rhetoric, espousing spiritual values and judging others, yet he proves incapable of relinquishing his own social privileges. His misogynistic image of women as material creatures justifies his moral self-righteousness, keeps him safely distanced from Lily, and allows him to rewrite Emersonian romance as spiritual detachment. His ego and pride, along with his dread of what lies outside the gilt cage, mislead him and prevent him from transcending the "joint-stock company" and fully immersing himself in any real republic (Emerson, "Self-Reliance" 261).

IV

While Selden masquerades as an Emersonian hero, Lily Bart ultimately comes to embody the core philosophies of Emerson. She translates Selden's misguided romance into a more literal rendering of Emerson, reinvesting his romantic ideas with an emotional awareness of community. More importantly, rather than simply theorize, Lily enacts this republic in real terms; she puts Selden's abstract theory to the test. Far from simply declaiming a sermon on the mount, Lily becomes a full-fledged romantic figure attempting to forge an individual identity in a society that privileges materialism and conformity. In short, she infuses into his monologic romantic world a dialogic blend of both Emersonian romance and realism. As Lily attempts to locate Emersonian possibility in Gilded Age America, readers discover the paradox of her quest for individualism: although she achieves spiritual self-reliance, her moral strength leaves her particularly vulnerable. Survival outside of society, outside "the midst of the crowd," no longer seems physically possible (Emerson 263).

Reading Lily as the victim of a debased society is certainly not a new interpretation of *The House of Mirth*. Critics generally agree that the novel reflects Wharton's own contention that "a frivolous society can acquire dramatic significance only through what its frivolity destroys" (*Backward* 207). This quote, and the novel in general, has overwhelmingly been interpreted in feminist terms: Lily is the victim of a patriarchal society that privileges women for being ornamental objects rather than individual beings. Judith Fetterley claims, for example, that Wharton's "symbol of social waste is specifically a beautiful woman" and, as such, the novel serves as a "powerful denunciation of patriarchal culture" ("The Temptation" 200). Cynthia Griffin Wolff similarly contends that "in Wharton's estimation the deformities of a debased society will always be shown most clearly in the plight of those who are disempowered" ("Lily Bart and the Drama of Femininity" 213).

I do not wish to underestimate the importance of gender in Wharton's novel. Misogyny, stereotypes, and double standards all undoubtedly play a critical role in Lily's struggles. As readers have seen, Selden's relationships with Lily, Bertha, and Gerty attest to the significance of gender in the novel. I do, however, want to emphasize that Wharton's analysis is as much a commentary on history and nation as it is on gender. Her focus is on the stifling effects of American society at the turn of the century, and her scope is far-reaching. Reading the text only in terms of its "powerful denunciation of patriarchal culture" misses the scale of Wharton's critique. In her own life, Wharton tended to shy away from burgeoning feminist ideas. Hermione Lee claims that "the politics of sexual injustice and inequality are very strongly felt [in Wharton's literature], though she would have been appalled to be called a feminist" (*Edith* 187–88). Elizabeth Ammons further acknowledges that Wharton was "not among the activists" for women's rights: "she held herself aloof on the question of the vote; and she certainly joined no women's club" (2). While biography should not limit one's reading of Wharton's fiction, her life indicates concerns that include but also extend beyond gender.

In the novel, Wharton examines issues of gender and class, but in doing so she negotiates a larger historical and national concern: the search for Emersonian idealism in postbellum America. In *A Backward Glance*, Wharton attempts to make sense of her own oppressive youth by considering the historical conflict between the national spirit and material history: "Looking back at that little world, and remembering the 'hoard of petty maxims' with which its elders preached down every sort of initiative, I have often wondered at such lassitude in the descendants of the men who cleared a place for themselves in a new world, and then fought for the right to be masters there. What had become of the spirit of the pioneers and the revolutionaries? Perhaps the very violence of their effort had caused it to exhaust itself in the next generation, or the too great prosperity succeeding on almost unexampled hardships had produced, if not inertia, at least indifference in all matters except business or family affairs" (55–56). In this passage, Wharton contemplates the ideal of clearing a place—literally and figuratively—for one's self. In *The House of*

Mirth, she questions how to live appropriately in the space one has cleared: can one transcend "business and family affairs" and rediscover the "spirit of the pioneers and the revolutionaries," or has history rendered those ideals inaccessible? Wharton's biographical meditations communicate her interest not simply in society and gender but also in society and nation.

The House of Mirth does not discriminate in its depiction of Gilded Age social ills; rather than exclusively female, social waste is ubiquitous. Although they may not necessarily share the same plots or suffer the same consequences, both men and women in the novel prove equally miserable. And while Wharton sympathizes with the plight of the lower classes, tragedy strikes every class level of society. She exposes a system where depravity is purely democratic: spread across all ranks, from working to middle class, from old to new money. From Gus Trenor, the depressed Wall Street banker, to Mrs. Haffen, the beaten-down charwoman, Wharton evokes an image of America where man and nature have become equally trapped by the same artificial, material confines. In the novel, business and family matters have, in fact, largely squashed the "spirit of the pioneers and the revolutionaries."

Importantly, in the midst of this national and spiritual crisis, Wharton casts the role of the self-reliant pioneer—the Huck Finn figure who lights out for "the Territory"—with a woman, a heroine rather than a hero. In "Melodramas of Beset Manhood," Nina Baym argues that in traditional American literature "the matter of American experience is inherently male" (130): women play the role of the domesticator and men play the role of the "individual against society" (132).[8] In *The House of Mirth*, however, it is Lily Bart who becomes the fully realized quest figure, the character who comes to signify the mythic American experience. Rather than simply relegated to the domestic sphere, in this novel the heroine plays the archetypal role of the individual caught between transcendental desire and historical necessity. Lily is, therefore, more than a female victim carried on by the weight of her gender. She is representative of a specific historical moment, of the realist struggle to locate Emersonian romanticism in Gilded Age America.

V

At the beginning of the novel Lily, far from a self-reliant maverick, is largely concerned with the material world around her. She is, much like Lawrence Selden, a "victim of the civilization which had produced her" (8). The narrator describes some of Lily's earliest memories: "Ruling the turbulent element called home was the vigorous and determined figure of a mother still young enough to dance her ball-dresses to rags, while the hazy outline of a neutral-tinted father filled an intermediate space between the butler and the man who came to wind the clocks. Even to the eyes of infancy, Mrs. Hudson Bart had appeared young; but Lily could not recall the time when her father had not been bald and slightly stooping, with streaks of grey in his hair, and a tired walk. It was a shock to her to learn afterward that he was but two years older than her mother" (25–26). In this upper-class environment, her mother is in charge of conspicuous consumption and her father is run ragged by the "perpetual need—the need of more money" (26).[9] Elaine Showalter astutely pegs Lily's father as an automaton, a wealthy version of Herman Melville's Bartleby (366). When her father loses all of his money, presumably in the stock market, he becomes valueless ("he had become extinct when he ceased to fulfil his purpose") and, shorn of any identity or purpose, dies shortly thereafter (Wharton, *Mirth* 28). For Lily, her future is determined. Her mother has raised her as an ornament and a commodity: "Lily's beauty . . . was the last asset in their fortunes, the nucleus around which their life was to be rebuilt. . . . She watched it jealously, as though it were her own property and Lily its mere custodian" (29). When faced with an unsure economic future, her mother tells her "with a kind of fierce vindictiveness: 'But you'll get it all back—you'll get it all back, with your face'" (25). Because of her upbringing, Lily becomes a decided pragmatist who understands the reality of women's lot; as she tells Selden: "We are expected to be pretty and well-dressed till we drop—and if we can't keep it up alone, we have to go into partnership" (12).

At times, Lily's sense of stark realism becomes rather dark, as when she envisions a "future of servitude to the whims of others, never the possibility of asserting her own eager individuality" (80). Inherent in her negativity is the desire for something more, for the chance to assert that "eager individuality." Despite her keen social awareness, Lily displays a romantic yearning to escape the confines of her gilt cage. During her country walk with Selden, she demonstrates early signs of revolt: "There were in her at the moment two beings, one drawing deep breaths of freedom and exhilaration, the other gasping for air in a little black prison-house of fears. But gradually the captive's gasps grew fainter, or the other paid less heed to them: the horizon expanded, the air grew stronger, and the free spirit quivered for flight" (52). At her core, Lily is an unconventional being, one who—despite her pragmatic approach to life—struggles between conflicting ideas of realism and romance.

Selden's sermon on the mount moves Lily toward social rebellion. As Annette L. Benert observes, "Lily knows the speciousness, even the hypocrisy, of Selden's republic. Yet she cherishes this ideal as her only moral reference point" (33). Lily's dilemma is that, as a financially dependent woman, she lacks Selden's "joyous irresponsibility of a free man" and cannot simply fly in and out of that gilt cage as he can (44). Every choice she makes becomes significant in deciding both her financial and spiritual future. Book 1 marks Lily's slow and wavering search for a transcendental alternative to her social bondage. Lily makes critical choices that solidify her increasingly socially liberated spirit but, at the same time, place her in increasing danger of excommunication and homelessness.

Lily's moral and spiritual evolution becomes visible shortly after her trip to Bellomont. Her first act of rebellion occurs when, after being blackmailed by Mrs. Haffen, she purchases Lawrence Selden and Bertha Dorset's private love letters. Although Lily is desperate for money and has a chance to profit by selling the letters back to Bertha, she rejects these material rewards: "she was aware only of feeling that Selden would wish the letters rescued, and that therefore she must obtain possession of them. Beyond that her mind did not travel" (83). Shortly thereafter, Lily reinforces her new spiritual commitment by donating money to Gerty's charity, the Girls' Club: "The satisfaction derived from this act was all that the most ardent moralist could have desired. Lily felt a new interest in herself as a person of charitable instincts: she had never before thought of doing good with the wealth she had so often dreamed of possessing, but now her horizon was enlarged by the vision of a prodigal philanthropy" (88). A sarcastic undercurrent runs through these lines, as Lily aggrandizes a seemingly moderate contribution. Regardless, Lily—who had earlier "found herself scanning her little world through his retina"—now attempts to enact Selden's philosophic vision (45).

Ironically, of course, each moral gesture results from the money she has borrowed from Gus Trenor. It is unclear how much Lily knows when Gus offers to "make a handsome sum of money for her" (67). The narrator suggests that Lily remains willingly naive about its source: "the haziness enveloping the transaction served as a veil for her embarrassment, and through the general blur her hopes dilated like lamps in a fog. She understood only that her modest investments were to be mysteriously multiplied without risk to herself" (68). Lily's moral hesitancy is in keeping with her wavering spiritual ethos. She unknowingly takes money from a married man and reinvests it in the morally righteous acts of buying Selden's letters and donating to charity. In doing so, she tries to rectify her conflicting spiritual and financial needs.

It is only in the climactic scene of book 1, when Gus Trenor lures Lily to his house under false pretenses, that Lily finally confronts the truth: her earnings have actually been payments from Gus for "services" not yet rendered. This moment becomes a turning point for Lily, who must now choose between economic necessity and spiritual ascendency. In a "society of irresponsible pleasure seekers," the most socially viable act would also be the most morally reprehensible: for Lily to play the game, become Gus's mistress, satisfy him, and gain both sexual and social leverage. Lily's first real moral awakening comes at this critical moment when she not only refuses Gus's advances but simultaneously experiences a growing self-awareness: "She seemed a stranger to herself, or rather there were two selves in her, the one she had always known, and a new abhorrent being to which it found itself chained" (117). Until now, Lily has "liked to think of her beauty as a power for good," but here she realizes the full meaning of her mother's persistent message—that her beauty is purely an economic asset and sexual prize (30). It is therefore fitting that, in this scene, Lily observes "her helpless useless hands" (117). Lily's growing awareness reveals a central paradox in the novel: her economic survival is itself "chained" to this "new abhorrent being." She must choose between character or plot, spirit or life, romance or realism.

Lily's subsequent reliance on Gerty Farish highlights her moral and spiritual epiphany. As discussed, Gerty Farish is the female character who most closely approximates the text's idealized republic. The problem is that Gerty (much like Selden) is incapable of forging a supportive, spiritual community. When Lily seeks shelter with Gerty immediately after her tragic interaction with Gus Trenor, for example, readers learn that Gerty "hated Lily Bart": "It closed with her in the darkness like some formless evil to be blindly grappled with. Reason, judgment, renunciation, all the sane daylight forces, were beaten back in the sharp struggle for self-preservation. She wanted happiness—wanted it as fiercely and unscrupulously as Lily did, but without Lily's power of obtaining it. And in her conscious impotence she lay shivering, and hated her friend" (128–29). By now, Gerty has become consumed with jealousy over Lily's relationship with Selden. Her own desperate desire for social acceptance precludes any sustained spiritual connection with Lily; as a result, Lily's asylum with Gerty proves futile.

In a parallel scene, Selden illustrates his own spiritual limitations. While Lily struggles to regain her pride at Gus Trenor's house, Selden searches for her at Mrs. Fisher's dinner party. Ever since seeing Lily in her tableau, Selden has been sailing on romantic thoughts of their bright future together. He pictures himself as Lily's rescuer: "he would lift her out of it, take her beyond!" (125). Although he declares his determination to take her "beyond" and transcend material society, his actions prove otherwise. Returning home from Mrs. Fisher's house, he and Van Alstyne see Lily emerging from the residence of Gus Trenor. The scene is a short one: "Van Alstyne dropped his eye-glass with a low whistle. 'A—hem—nothing of this, eh, Selden? As one of the family, I know I may count on you—appearances are deceptive—and Fifth Avenue is so imperfectly lighted—.' 'Goodnight,' said Selden, turning sharply down the side street without seeing the other's extended hand" (127). This brief encounter becomes a pivotal moment in the novel. Despite his own contention, Selden proves incapable of distinguishing "the woman he knew from the vulgar estimate of her" (121). Even as Van Alstyne warns him that "appearances are deceptive," he judges Lily precisely on such superficial markers. Instead of taking her "beyond," he runs away to Monte Carlo. At the exact moment when Lily most desperately needs Selden's faith, he fails to see the "real" Lily behind the "vulgar" social image; he sacrifices Lily to his own myopic vision and leaves her alone to face the "Furies" (117).

VI

If book 1 portrays Lily's spiritual awakening, book 2 represents the tragic unraveling of Lily's plot as she confronts her "displaced relationship between life and essence" (Lukács 44). Critics often treat book 2 as evidence that the novel is primarily a work of naturalism rather than realism. Larry Rubin, for example, argues that in book 2, "having been made what she is by forces beyond her control, she [Lily] eventually falls victim to those same forces. Dogged by poverty and hounded by scandal, she is 'tossed as helplessly as a cork in the whirls and eddies of the social stream—tossed and buffeted and finally dragged under with her eyes wide open to her own helplessness'" (182). Such readings center around one critical tenet of American naturalism: "environment becomes the force which crushes the protagonist" (Rubin 184). There is no doubt that book 2 condemns social convention and proves Wharton's contention that the twentieth-century American had spun an elaborate "web of customs, manners, [and] culture" around himself (qtd. in Nevius 64). Labeling the text naturalistic, however, is problematic. Naturalism focuses on the idea that forces of nature, in particular fate and chance, are stronger than human will; the movement specifically takes aim at Emerson's adage: "Trust thyself: every heart vibrates to that iron string" (260).

While it is certainly true that social forces seem to control Lily in book 1, "like manacles chaining her to her fate," book 2 is defined by Lily's spiritual rebellion against that fate (*Mirth* 8). Unlike Wharton's infamous heroine Undine Spragg in *The Custom of the Country*, Lily makes critical moral choices that defy cultural determinants and spare her from both Gus Trenor's sexual demands and an undesirable marriage plot. Amy Kaplan maintains that Wharton's rejection of "marriage as the narrative teleology of the domestic novel . . . implicitly calls attention to her own narrative as realistic" (94). In this reading, Lily's ability to avoid the marriage plot serves to reinforce the narrative's connection to realism. I would argue that Lily's rejection of marriage simultaneously connects her to a romantic ideology of individualism. Like Huck Finn and Isabel Archer, the choices Lily makes are motivated by her romantic desire, specifically her quest for self-reliance. As an Emersonian figure negotiating the historical confines of postbellum America, she embodies this dominant dialogic voice inherent in American realism. Lily's eventual death confirms her transcendental homelessness and proves that for "noncomformity the world whips you with its displeasure" (Emerson, "Self-Reliance" 264). It is Lily's personal determination, in fact, that causes her physical demise; her death becomes her sacrifice of the material body for the transcendental spirit. Her death, however, does not necessarily detract from her quest; instead, it reflects the power of the system she disobeys. If critics are correct that *The House of Mirth* is indeed a naturalist novel, then Lily Bart is its one clear representative of realism, the only individual aware of and eager to transcend her fate.

In book 2, Lily's narrative struggles highlight the particular hardships of women, who must contend with obstacles to spiritual self-worth and financial stability. Lily's plot exposes the reality of the Gilded Age: society has no place for a woman who chooses spiritual self-reliance over the comforts of material culture. While Lily's quest reveals much about the difficulties women faced in Gilded Age America, Wharton's critical scope nevertheless extends beyond gender. Lily's fall down the social ladder acts as a barometer of society's general malaise. Her plot includes a bevy of characters—across class and gender lines—who are all either morally reproachable, spiritually defunct, or deeply unhappy. Wharton refuses to portray a society in which men and the financially privileged enjoy unadulterated bliss, leaving the disenfranchised the sole inheritors of miserable misfortune. Rather, Wharton's text depicts a train of social ills that has spread all across America. The "house of mirth" does not discriminate based on race, class, or gender: from the wealthiest to the most impoverished, the "house confines the spirit."

Lily's social demise begins with the most fashionable upper-class set: the Trenors. Judy Trenor, like most of the upper-class women in the novel, seems devoid of an identity outside her social facade: "she seemed to exist only as a hostess, not so much from any exaggerated instinct of hospitality as because she could not sustain life except in a crowd" (34). Her husband, Gus Trenor, is far more emotive than his wife but most frequently communicates these emotions in the form of violence, expressing his anger at the "hard work" it takes "to keep the machinery running" (65). His repeated, often aggressive passes at Lily expose his sexual frustration, moral vacancy, and unhappy marriage. In addition, while Gus and Judy Trenor have children, they are primarily absent from view and are clearly both physically and spiritually detached from their parents: "It was Mrs. Trenor's theory that her daughters actually did go to church every Sunday; but their French governess's convictions calling her to the rival fane, and the fatigues of the week keeping their mother in her room till luncheon, there was seldom any one present to verify the fact" (42). They live in a spiritual and moral vacuum that characterizes the misery and malaise at the very pinnacle of New York society.

When Lily turns down Gus Trenor's advances, she assures her rejection from the Trenors' society; her fall from their high social peak brings her to the level of the Dorsets, who, as Irving Howe humorously observes, "no longer pretend to care about traditional styles and values. Bertha Dorset is a ferocious bitch, her husband a limp dyspeptic" (123). The Dorsets' relationship clearly calls into question Judith Fetterley's claim that in this novel "social waste is female" ("The Temptation" 200). George Dorset is, perhaps, the most miserable character in the text; he symbolizes the universal presence of despair in this society. The first time George is introduced, the narrator communicates that his "long sallow face and distrustful eyes seemed always barricaded against the expansive emotions" (94). Later, when the barricades come down, readers witness a man so wrecked by his marriage that he literally begs Lily to help him: "You do see, don't you? You understand? I'm desperate—I'm at the end of my tether. I want to be free, and you can free me. I know you can. You don't want to keep me bound fast in hell, do you?" (191). Here it is not the woman who garners the reader's sympathies. Rather, Wharton reverses the traditional gender roles, placing the man in the position of helpless victim begging to be rescued by his female savior.

If Lily plays the role of the white knight, Bertha Dorset plays the role of the evil villain, the master who keeps her prisoner hostage. She is indeed a "nasty woman" whose main source of pleasure is the perpetuation of others' misery (37). She is portrayed—in anachronistic terms—as a Dementor ripped from the pages of a Harry Potter novel: "She was smaller and thinner than Lily Bart, with a restless pliability of pose, as if she could have been crumpled up and run through a ring, like the sinuous draperies she affected. . . . She was like a disembodied spirit who took up a great deal of room" (Wharton, *Mirth* 21–22). It would be impossible to assess Bertha's happiness because happiness requires a soul, and Bertha's "disembodied spirit" clearly marks its absence. She is a spiritual wasteland, a hollow creature with an aggressive drive to acquire more and more material to compensate for her derisory existence. Bertha represents American capitalism at its worst.

Given the unadulterated sterility of Bertha's character, Lily's decision to escape her "crushing difficulties" by joining the Dorsets on their European cruise seems particularly foolish. Lily's new spiritual awakening, however, lowers her guard against the vicissitudes of social reality and thus blinds her to Bertha's serpentine behavior. When Bertha has her disastrous affair with Ned Silverton, all the other characters involved understand that Bertha will try to scapegoat Lily; yet Lily, because of her vulnerability, fails to even recognize that the affair has taken place. When George tells her of Bertha's "dénouement"—of her failure to return to the boat the previous night—Lily appears woefully ingenuous: "*Dénouement*—isn't that too big a word for such a small incident? The worst of it, after all, is the fatigue which Bertha has probably slept off by this time" (158). Although Lily has always maintained a keen sense of figurative irony and blistering social awareness, here she fails to see beyond the surface narrative.

Lily's shift from social awareness to moral consciousness accounts for her naivety. Her newfound compassion dulls her earlier cynicism. Thus, rather than attempt to defeat Bertha, she now works "undividedly in her friend's interest": "all the disadvantages of such a situation were for the woman; and it was to Bertha that Lily's sympathies now went out" (160). While Lily sympathizes with Bertha, Selden blames Lily for her social failure. He asks: "What had brought her to this pass? What weakness had placed her so abominably at her enemy's mercy?" (170). His reaction illustrates the problem with a naturalist reading of the novel, specifically one that sees Lily's plot as a consequence of fate or chance. What Selden labels "weakness" is not the product of some external force. Instead, it can be linked directly back to Selden's earlier sermon at Bellomont: Lily is now "so abominably at her enemy's mercy" precisely because of her newfound dedication to conscience rather than custom.

Lily's moral fortitude is, of course, repaid with social exile. Carry Fisher—a social-climbing divorcee who ironically displays a level of effectiveness, resilience, and even kindness not found elsewhere in society—helps to find Lily refuge with the Gormers, a family on the "social out-skirt" (182). In one sense, these nominal social figurines parody their more high-ranking social counterparts: they are "caricature[s] approximating the real thing" (182). Fisher describes the Gormers' gatherings as "a sort of continuous performance of their own, a kind of social Coney Island, where everybody is welcome who can make noise enough and doesn't put on airs" (181). Their set attempts to outdo their social superiors in every regard—"Everything was pitched in a higher key, and there was more of each thing: more noise, more colour, more champagne, more familiarity" (182). While such descriptions paint the Gormers as a relatively innocuous group, a specific New York phenomenon, Lily's trip to Alaska with the family illustrates how far the ills of this society extend. She is invited as Mattie Gormer's plaything, as "an expensive toy in the hands of a spoiled child" (189). Far from a pastoral alternative to urban society, Alaska appears not much different from Monte Carlo. The trip is "the Gormers' tumultuous progress across their native continent" and is representative of an important shift in the history of America's frontier (185). Their trip mocks American ideals of man in nature and illustrates how the Gilded Age has become a gilded cage. Nature—once embodied in those "essences unchanged by man; space, the air, the river, the leaf"—is now the last stomping ground of the rich and spoiled (Emerson, *Nature* 8). As Jennie A. Kassanoff maintains, *The House of Mirth* explores a world where "distinctions between the genuine and the imitative, the natural and the cultural, have all but collapsed" (315).

Lily's expulsion from the Gormer set may be seen as the cruel result of

Bertha's final attempt to poison Lily's reputation in society. Lily is not, however, "tossed as helplessly as a cork in the whirls and eddies of the social stream" (Rubin 182). Rather, she plays a critical role in deciding her own future. Carry presents Lily with a possible alternative to social exile: "the only thing to save you from Bertha is to marry somebody else" (197). Two potential marriage plots immediately present themselves: Carry advises Lily to marry George Dorset as a "particular form of retaliation," and Simon Rosedale offers to marry Lily, provided she use her incriminating letters to blackmail Bertha and reclaim her social position (197). Lily, importantly, opposes both of these marriage plots. She foregoes her social welfare in favor of self-reliance. Despite the narrator's admission—"there had been nothing in her training to develop any continuity of moral strength"—she still manages to reject "Rosedale's effort without conscious effort; her whole being had risen against it" (204). In her rejection of Rosedale, Lily dodges social pressure and follows Emerson's counsel in "Self-Reliance": "No law can be sacred to me but that of my nature. Good and bad are but names very readily transferable to that or this; the only right is what is after my constitution, the only wrong is what is against it" (Emerson 262).

By contrast, Selden continually proves incapable of making any "independent, genuine verdict" (Emerson, "Self-Reliance" 261). During Lily's fall down the social scale, he purposefully avoids her. She notices his absence and feels it "as one of the chief bitternesses" of her social exile (216). Selden justifies his emotional and physical distance based on her ill-advised friendship with the Gormers, but the narrator suggests that Selden's reason is far more selfish: "It was much simpler for him to judge Miss Bart by her habitual conduct than by the rare deviations from it which had thrown her so disturbingly in his way; and every act of hers which made the recurrence of such deviations more unlikely, confirmed the sense of relief with which he returned to the conventional view of her" (212). His "conventional view" of Lily sanctions his role as indifferent spectator and reinforces the reader's vision of him as the false Emersonian prophet. His so-called philosophy of self-reliance and emotional separation amounts to a philosophy of self-concern.

Lily, meanwhile, remains the true Emersonian hero, sacrificing her financial and social security by rejecting George Dorset's and Simon Rosedale's marriage propositions. She does this in spite of the fact that these choices propel her one step further down the social ladder and into the position of social secretary for Norma Hatch, "the wealthy divorcee who lives in a chaos of indolence, forever a prey to sharpers and schemers" (Howe 123). It is here that Selden finally visits Lily, but only in order to castigate her for taking a job with the social climber. While Selden's intentions may seem honorable, his approach and execution are problematic. In this scene, he acts in an emotionally reserved manner, alert "to the fear of her attaching a personal significance to his visit" (216). He is so anxious to appear emotionally indifferent that he is incapable of acknowledging her very real, very pressing financial concerns. Instead, he manufactures his own romantic narrative; he self-righteously claims that "starvation is not . . . [her] only alternative" and recommends that she "contrive a life together" with Gerty (218). Clearly blind to Gerty's own unhappiness and social ambitions, Selden offers Lily a solution that amounts to a prison sentence, a life for Lily that deviates far from any republic of the spirit.

Lily sees through Selden's presumptuous behavior and, in fact, points him toward his hypocrisy: "My relation to Mrs. Hatch is one I have no reason to be ashamed of. She has helped me to earn a living when my old friends were quite resigned to seeing me starve" (218). The next chapter, however, ironically begins: "Look at those spangles, Miss Bart—every one of 'em sewed on crooked" (219). In an exceptional narrative juxtaposition, Wharton takes her readers directly from Selden and Lily's meeting to the millinery factory where Lily is now employed, sewing spangles on hats. Once again, Lily accepts Selden's advice even though she knows it is flawed. Selden becomes a reminder of her own transcendental desires. He feeds her independent spirit and prods it forward.

Many critics sentimentalize Lily's role as a hat trimmer, reading these women as spiritually superior to their upper-class counterparts. Elaine Showalter, for example, envisions Lily's new position as a "genuinely awakened woman, who fully recognizes her own position in the community of women workers" (370), and Wai-Chee Dimock argues that Wharton grafts "her ideal on a lower social order, the working class" (389). In fact, these women in the lowest social caste are as enmeshed in the social structure as their upper-class sisters. Physically, they are described as "dull and colourless," and they prove painfully envious of the more colorful upper class. As a result, they find their joy and comfort in living vicariously through the lives of the women whose hats they trim:

> It was the strangest part of Lily's strange experience, the hearing of these names [the Trenors and the Dorsets], the seeing the fragmentary and distorted image of the world she had lived in reflected in the mirror of the working-girls' minds. She had never before suspected the mixture of insatiable curiosity and contemptuous freedom with which she and her kind were discussed in this underworld of toilers who lived on their vanity and self-indulgence. Every girl in Mme. Regina's work-room knew to whom the headgear in her hands was destined, and had her opinion of its future wearer, and a definite knowledge of the latter's place in the social system. That Lily was a star fallen from that sky did not, after the

first stir of curiosity had subsided, materially add to their interest in her. She had fallen, she had "gone under," and true to the ideal of the race, they were awed only by success—by the gross tangible image of material achievement. (223)

Far from "genuinely awakened," these "toilers" are thoroughly mired in the corrupt society they serve. As Bauer notes, the "hat-trimmers have internalized the ideals of the authoritative cultural discourse" (120). In addition, as hat trimmers for the rich, they become important cogs in the social wheel: their survival depends on the Wall Street earnings of men who need suitable ornaments for their rich wives. They idealize "the gross tangible image of material achievement" and help promote conspicuous consumption. The argument that these working women act as Wharton's model, that they offer a communal alternative to competitive female society or act as an escape from Gilded Age culture, discounts Wharton's searing critique of the trimmers, of their social envy and material aspirations.

Even more than the factory workers, critics often sentimentalize another working-class woman: Nettie Struther. Nettie appears late in the novel, when Lily—who has by now lost her job as a milliner and become virtually homeless—rests in Bryant Park. Nettie sees her sitting on a bench and approaches her. In this scene, readers learn that Lily's earlier financial contributions to the Girls' Club helped rescue this "thin shabby figure" from tuberculosis and that Nettie has since closely followed Lily's social career (243). Nettie is frequently read as Wharton's preferred social alternative because, despite her lack of money and beauty, she is one of the only characters (male or female) who seems relatively content: "Nettie Struther's frail envelope was now alive with hope and energy" (243). She has gained her "hope and energy" from the love, support, and faith of her husband, George. Critics tend to interpret this supportive marriage, along with Nettie's maternal nature, as evidence of her ideal, spiritual status. Carol J. Singley, for example, argues: "Wharton offers her heroine a singular form of domestic shelter in Nettie Struther's kitchen. . . . The scene is reminiscent of those found in sentimental novels by nineteenth-century writers such as Harriet Beecher Stowe, Susan Warner, and Louisa May Alcott, and the encounter between the two women is suggestive of the strength of female bonds and the restorative properties of home and hearth—qualities hailed in nineteenth-century domestic fiction as antidotes to a callous, materialistic world" (12). Showalter also locates female community as the novel's solution to social ills: "*The House of Mirth* ends not only with a death but with the vision of a new world of female solidarity, a world in which women like Gerty Farish and Nettie Struther will struggle hopefully and courageously" (370).[10]

The problem with these readings is that they assume an ideal that Wharton simply refuses to offer. Nettie Struther is as dependent on upper-class society as her milliner peers. The stock market, as David Stineback reasons, is "the one institution that is responsible for virtually everyone's fate in *The House of Mirth*" (91). Nettie is no exception. Her recovery from tuberculosis depends almost entirely on Lily's own social fortunes: "The episode of Nettie Crane's timely rescue from disease had been one of the most satisfying incidents of her connection with Gerty's charitable work. She had furnished the girl with the means to go to a sanatorium in the mountains: it struck her now with a peculiar irony that the money she had used had been Gus Trenor's" (*Mirth* 243). In a symbolic sense, Nettie's very existence depends upon the most demoralizing social incident in Lily's life. Lower-class survival relies on the commerce and charity of upper-class materialism; in return, the lower classes worship and envy upper-class culture. Nettie, for example, idealizes Lily. When Lily tells Nettie that she has been "unhappy—in great trouble," Nettie responds: "*You* in trouble? I've always thought of you as being so high up, where everything was just grand. Sometimes, when I felt real mean, and got to wondering why things were so queerly fixed in the world, I used to remember that you were having a lovely time, anyhow, and that seemed to show there was a kind of justice somewhere" (243). Nettie's naivety becomes almost parodic when readers discover that she has named her baby "Marry Anto'nette": Nettie chooses the name because the actress portraying "the French queen in that play at the Garden" reminds her of Lily (244). The baby's name symbolically reflects Nettie's own envy, an emotion that promises to be reproduced in her lower-class daughter. In effect, Nettie becomes part of the "gaping mob" that—as Amy Kaplan has shown—functions to legitimate the upper-class order of early-twentieth-century America (102).

Beneath her subtle parody of Nettie, Wharton certainly applauds the intimacy and spiritual companionship reflected in George and Nettie's marriage. Lily herself praises Nettie's marriage: "All the men and women she knew were like atoms whirling away from each other in some wild centrifugal dance: her first glimpse of the continuity of life had come to her that evening in Nettie Struther's kitchen. The poor little working-girl . . . seemed to Lily to have reached the central truth of existence. It was a meagre enough life, on the grim edge of poverty, with scant margin for possibilities of sickness or mischance, but it had the frail audacious permanence of a bird's nest built on the edge of a cliff—a mere wisp of leaves and straw, yet so put together that the lives entrusted to it may hang safely over the abyss" (248). There is no doubt that Lily envisions Nettie's life as a spiritual alternative—"the central truth of existence"—to the "wild centrifugal dance" of New York's social scene. Wharton may very well share Lily's vision; here she clearly indicates the importance of love and community in forging a spiritual life.

Although Nettie achieves a type of community the other characters lack, she should not be read as Wharton's idealized portrayal of a woman who escapes the strictures of society. Nettie's poverty remains a constant threat to her existence. As Gavin Jones has argued, "the very point of Wharton's nest image is its vulnerability not its permanence, its precarious position above an 'abyss' of dependence" (101). Furthermore, any attempt to sentimentalize Nettie's role in the novel falls flat upon examination of another, older working-class woman, one who does in fact succumb to "sickness and mischance." Nettie can be seen as a younger, more fortunate version of Mrs. Haffen, the charwoman who blackmails Lily with Selden and Bertha's love letters. Early in the novel, readers learn that an illness and operation have left Mrs. Haffen and her family without money or food for survival. Like Nettie, she too exhibits maternal tendencies, worrying about the safety of her husband and children, but she also illustrates the vulnerability of the poor and the lengths to which one must go in order to protect family. This older woman, whose "sickness and mischance" have forced her to sacrifice her scruples for subsistence, plainly does not represent an ideal spiritual alternative. As she admits when she blackmails Lily: "I ain't got no other way of raising money, and if we don't pay our rent tomorrow night we'll be put out. I never done anythin' of the kind before" (83). The gender, class, and social connections between Nettie and Mrs. Haffen—both live "on the grim edge of poverty," on the "edge of a cliff"— signify Wharton's refusal to locate any simple panacea for Gilded Age corruption. Rather than the ultimate New Woman ideal, Nettie acts as a final rung on the social ladder, the last measure of society's general malaise.[11]

VII

In *The House of Mirth*, Wharton endorses Emerson's assertion: "Society everywhere is in conspiracy against the manhood of every one of its members. Society is a joint-stock company, in which the members agree, for the better securing of his bread to each shareholder, to surrender the liberty and culture of the eater" (261). In this novel, Wharton extends Emerson's assault on society. She depicts an image of America where, by 1905, there is no alternative, nowhere to avoid the "joint-stock company." Lily becomes the spiritual alternative, the only genuinely self-reliant individual, and yet her plot keenly portrays her own transcendental homelessness. She ultimately locates the spirit but lacks the republic, the country to which she can escape. "Beyond"—the symbolic insignia on her stationary—simply does not exist.

Lily's struggle is best summed up in two contiguous scenes at the end of the novel. By this point, Lily is unemployed, has no job prospects, and spends much of her time walking the streets of New York City. There she runs into

Simon Rosedale, who, because he is Jewish, is presented as an outsider.[12] Because of his religious identity and status as nouveau riche, Rosedale lacks the social privilege of Lawrence Selden. Unlike Selden, he is a social realist who quite consciously and matter-of-factly understands that, just as money determines his value, so ornamentality governs an upper-class woman's worth. Rosedale thereby acts as Selden's antithesis. While they are the only two characters who seem to truly love Lily, they are physical and cultural opposites. Where Selden represents the blind idealist, so caught up in his romantic vision that he overlooks Lily's very real struggles, Rosedale is the pure realist, the character who, as Gloria C. Erlich notes, is an "almost omniscient observer" (72). Rosedale's unadulterated realism allows him to distinguish between objective truth and social fiction; despite his purely materialist values and his business-like marriage proposition to Lily, he ironically proves a more sensitive and understanding man than the intellectual philosopher.

Lily reveals the true story of her debts to Rosedale because she understands that he "was the fitting person to receive and transmit her version of the facts" (Wharton, *Mirth* 228). Rosedale is free from Selden's blind idealism and therefore has a greater capacity for empathy. When Lily tells Rosedale that she is out of work, for example, he responds: "'Out of work—out of work! What a way for you to talk! The idea of your having to work—it's preposterous.' He brought out his sentences in short violent jerks, as though they were forced up from a deep inner crater of indignation. 'It's a farce—a crazy farce,' he repeated" (233). Rosedale's response reflects a genuine concern for Lily, "a rather helpless fidelity of sentiment, which seemed to be struggling through the hard surface of his material ambitions" (234). He asks Lily to reconsider their "business arrangement," to use her proof of Bertha and Selden's affair to reclaim her social position and to marry him (233). His offer is crude and unfeeling, but, compared to Selden's ignorance, his honest realism and ability to see the truth is refreshing. The problem is that, while Rosedale reinforces the importance of realism, he lacks any romantic imagination. Lily's story emits sympathy from Rosedale, but his social ambitions never falter. He is as incapable of taking Lily "beyond" as Selden is.

With Rosedale's proposal, Lily faces her final moral crisis: whether to embrace her romantic spirit or accept material reality. Unlike the more nuanced plot James constructs for Isabel Archer in *The Portrait of a Lady*, Wharton seems to provide her heroine with a more direct either/or alternative. Lily ultimately decides to accept Rosedale's offer when she realizes that spiritual transcendence will not realistically afford her material stability; the two are incompatible in Wharton's fictional world. On her way to the Dorset house to bribe Bertha, she passes by Selden's apartment and feels, yet again, drawn in by his spiritual influence: "It was strange to find herself passing his house on such an errand. She seemed suddenly to see her action as he would see it—and the fact of his own connection with it, the fact that, to attain her end, she must trade on his name, and profit by a secret of his past, chilled her blood with shame" (237). She decides to visit him and, as her desire to live up to Selden's ideals mounts, she burns the letters, her only remaining asset, the symbolic embodiment of "her old self" (241). Rather than suffer a naturalistic fall from grace, here Lily employs individual will in order to free herself from her fate as a material ornament. She chooses romance in the face of realism.

This scene reveals Lily's spiritual fortitude at the same time that it under-scores Selden's spiritual limitations. With the destruction of Selden's letters, Lily sacrifices her final chance to save herself from poverty. While she exhib-its her greatest moment of moral courage, Selden proves utterly incapable of spiritual communion. As Lily throws the letters in the fire, Selden does not see her all-important act; instead, he notices how thin her hands look against the rising light of the flames: "He saw too, under the loose lines of her dress, how the curves of her figure had shrunk to angularity; he remembered long after-ward how the red play of the flame sharpened the depression of her nostrils, and intensified the blackness of the shadows which struck up from her cheek-bones to her eyes" (241). Selden is too busy focusing on her loss of beauty, on the physical effects of her growing poverty, to notice her selfless act. Selden's vision of Lily is even more disturbing when one remembers his earlier blithe comment that "starvation is not the only alternative" (218). Starvation has, by now, become a critical concern for Lily.

At two earlier points in the novel, Selden seemingly revels in Lily's weak-ness. During their walk at Bellomont, he observes that her "emotional weak-ness . . . had become the most interesting thing about her" (55). Again, at the Van Osburgh wedding: "The appeal of her helplessness touched in him, as it always did, a latent chord of inclination" (75). Selden has had an almost perverse interest in his ability to affect Lily's composure. Yet now, when the physical effects of her weakness and growing frailty are real and severe, he is not amused, but feels instead "a rising tinge of embarrassment" (238). That Lily has actually followed his advice and sacrificed her material worth—her beauty and charm—to follow his spiritual republic proves unpleasant for him. His romantic philosophy has never accounted for these social truths. The re-ality of her situation makes him self-conscious. Rather than support her moral and spiritual development, he represses the truth and fails her. His ahistorical romantic vision blinds him to the reality of her historical moment.

As with the earlier scene between Lily and George Dorset, Wharton once again reverses stereotypical gender roles. Selden has always envisioned himself as Lily's rescuer, taking her "beyond the ugliness, the pettiness, the attrition and corrosion of the soul," but it is Lily who actually plays the heroic figure

(122). She sacrifices her own social position and financial survival in order to shield Selden from the hard truth that he, the false prophet, is too weak to bear. Lily replaces Selden as Wharton's spiritual spokesperson and stoically accepts the consequences. Unlike Rosedale, who represents pure realism, and Selden, who represents pure romance, Lily is the character who fuses her romantic vision with the courage to accept and address history. She offers a dialogic alternative to those two monologic male characters.

And yet, despite her heroic efforts, at the end of the novel Lily dies. Critics continually argue over whether Lily's death, induced by an overdose of chloral, is intentional or accidental. In their need to find a tidy ending, readers tend to emphasize Lily's last thoughts—either of the fading word that she wants to tell Selden or of "Nettie Strether's child . . . lying on her arm"—in order to settle on Wharton's final message (251). Her death, however, is not tidy—"slowly the thought of the word faded"—and suggests that Lily can have no "real" end (251). After her death, the text, like reality, continues: "The next morning rose mild and bright, with a promise of summer in the air" (251). Lily's quest has resembled Christian's in *The Pilgrim's Progress*, and her narrative— her search for spiritual righteousness as well as her social and physical decline toward death—feels largely allegorical. In *The House of Mirth*, however, there is no Celestial City, no easy word or neat maternal message. In order to locate Emersonian romance, Lily has to transcend material reality.

In *A Backward Glance*, Wharton writes: "My last page is always latent in my first" (208). It is therefore appropriate that *The House of Mirth* ends with Selden alone in Lily's room, imagining her much as he did in the first pages. In attempting to make sense of her death, he constructs his own sentimental ending to absolve himself and secure his complacency. He comforts himself with the thought that their separation was caused by a mixture of social conditions and fate: "He saw that all the conditions of life had conspired to keep them apart; since his very detachment from the external influences which swayed her had increased his spiritual fastidiousness, and made it more difficult for him to live and love uncritically. But at least he *had* loved her—had been willing to stake his future on his faith in her—and if the moment had been fated to pass from them before they could seize it, he saw now that, for both, it had been saved out of the ruin of their lives" (255). Selden's reading is problematic on several levels. First, his mention of "faith" and "love" is highly ironic. His faith in and love for Lily reach their pinnacle when she is a mute tableau and fade when she most desperately needs him. Contrary to his musings, it is precisely his lack of faith that has proved his greatest weakness. More importantly, Selden refuses to take any credit for their ruined lives. Instead, as Frances L. Restuccia notes, in this scene "Selden interprets Lily's story as a romantic tragedy" (410). Like the critics who undermine Lily's fortitude by reading Wharton's text as naturalistic, Selden mitigates his own failure by blaming her death on deterministic forces; he uses naturalism as a false romantic narrative. As discussed, Lily's downward spiral is far from deterministic; it results from her own strong will and Selden's corresponding weakness. In a letter to her friend Sara Norton, Edith Wharton labeled Selden "a negative hero" (qtd. in Lewis, *Edith Wharton* 155). This appears the proper category. Selden is an intellectual man who means well and truly believes in the value of his spiritual philosophy, but his philosophy still mistakes self-reliance for self-concern and social criticism for complacency. In Selden, Wharton illustrates the most dangerous elements of unguarded romanticism and reminds readers of the need to temper Emersonian romance with realism.[13]

Thus, while Lawrence Selden represents the "negative" or ineffectual hero who substitutes a misguided philosophy for the courage to act, Lily Bart comes to symbolize Wharton's central theme in *The House of Mirth*: that realism is neither a disavowal of romantic Emersonian philosophy nor a facile rejection of history. Realism, instead, becomes the struggle to negotiate the binaries of Emersonian desire and historical truth in postbellum America. Lily's plot embodies this struggle. It is therefore misguided to read Lily solely as a victim of her gender, to label Lily's plot naturalistic, or even to envision her death as symbolic of her spiritual failure. The text repudiates each of these claims. Lily is not a failure; rather, she is the only character with the determination to place character before plot and heroically seek Emersonian individualism in the postbellum world. She alone points readers back to the lost "spirit of the pioneers and the revolutionaries," to those "who cleared a place for themselves in a new world, and then fought for the right to be masters there" (*Backward* 55).

4
Willa Cather's

My Ántonia

The world exists for the education of each man. . . . He should see that
he can live all history in his own person. He must sit solidly at home,
and not suffer himself to be bullied by kings or empires, but know that
he is greater than all the geography and all the government of the world;
he must transfer the point of view from which history is commonly
read, from Rome and Athens and London to himself, and not deny his
conviction that he is the court, and if England or Egypt have any thing
to say to him, he will try the case; if not, let them for ever be silent. . . .
"What is History," said Napoleon, "but a fable agreed upon?"
                            —Ralph Waldo Emerson, "History," *Essays*

I

In 1924, Willa Cather denounced "this passion for Americanizing everything
and everybody," calling it a "deadly disease" (qtd. in Reynolds, *Willa Cather
in Context* 73). Although Cather was specifically referring to the nationalis-
tic impulse to transform ethnic immigrants into "Americans," her protest is
certainly relevant to the more general question of her role in American literary history. As Susan J. Rosowski notes, "a writer is important not because
she represents transcendent values or universal truths, but because she is inscribed into a culture" ("Prospects" 147). In attempting to understand how
My Ántonia "fits" into American literary culture, it would seem I am participating in exactly this type of "diseased" activity.

And yet, in order to integrate Cather's *My Ántonia* into a discussion of
American realism—in order to consider her text in conversation with *Adventures of Huckleberry Finn*, *The Portrait of a Lady*, and *The House of Mirth*—
I must first address her place in the American literary tradition. Historically,
critics have disagreed over Cather's literary allegiances and have alternately
situated her within the traditions of romance, realism, naturalism, impressionism, and modernism. James Woodress, for example, claims that Cather was
a "devoted Romantic" (386); John J. Murphy "credits Cather with combin-
ing both realistic and naturalistic traditions" (Introduction 16); David Stouck

asserts that Cather's literature "had its roots in those large movements in the arts in the late nineteenth-century—impressionism and symbolism" (52); and Linda Wagner-Martin specifically marks *My Ántonia* as a "classic modernist text" (*The Modern American Novel* 16). Janis P. Stout highlights the contradictory nature of such readings when she states: "Long regarded as a romantic realist, Willa Cather has in recent years also been read as a modernist, or more precisely a minimalist modernist" (168).[1] Scholars are left, finally, with the conclusion drawn up by Elsa Nettles: "There is no critical consensus that Cather belongs in any one literary tradition." (7).

What makes Cather a slippery literary figure? Why do critics have such difficulty linking her to a specific literary movement? Critical disagreement in Cather studies is, in part, a product of her historical breadth; she published her first short story ("Peter") in 1892, at the height of American realism, and her last complete novel (*Sapphira and the Slave Girl*) in 1940, when modernism was already giving way to postmodernism. Guy Reynolds argues that space, as well as time, helps explain her contested literary identity: "The range of her works, especially the geographical variety of their settings, would make Cather's identity problematic" (Introduction x). Critical disagreement also seems to stem from what scholars generally recognize as the overall elusive quality of Cather's life and literature. Hermione Lee poignantly writes that "like the image of the rock which she places at the centre of many of her books, she is a resistant subject, even an obstructive one. When you set out to write about her, you feel she would not have liked what you are doing, and would not have liked you either" (*Willa* 3). Susan J. Rosowski adds that *My Ántonia*, in particular, "defies analysis, a quality critics often note when beginning a discussion of it" (*The Voyage Perilous* 75).

I begin my own discussion of *My Ántonia* by acknowledging the elusive quality of Cather's life and literature, not to imply that her work defies analysis but, on the contrary, to situate the novel within a very specific moment in American literary history. I recognize that, in attempting to pin her down, Cather would very likely "not have liked what . . . [I am] doing, and would not have liked . . . [me] either." At the risk of offending Cather, I nevertheless want to reclaim the text as a work of late American realism and argue that history, despite critical contentions, plays a central role in the novel. When one reads through the critical history of *My Ántonia*, one is struck by the overwhelming insistence on the text's ahistorical, mythical qualities. Critics tend to reconfigure the elusive nature of the novel as evidence of a romantic parable: *My Ántonia* is most frequently read as a timeless portrayal of the American pastoral—as a reflection of what Robert E. Scholes labels "the myth of Adam in America" (19) and Harold Bloom calls "our intense vision of a lost America" (Introduction 1).

Claims of Cather's ahistoricism begin as early as the 1920s and 1930s, when Marxist critic Granville Hicks made his much-publicized objection to Cather's artistic distance from contemporary life: "Miss Cather has never once tried to see contemporary life as it is; she sees only that it lacks what the past, at least in her idealization of it, had. Thus she has been barred from the task that has occupied most of the world's great artists, the expression of what is central and fundamental in her own age" (708). Hicks reads what he terms her "supine romanticism" as the greatest "case against Willa Cather" (710). Although the Cold War myth and symbol school of criticism reaffirmed Cather's importance, these scholars did so not by contradicting Hicks's most basic claims but rather by celebrating the text's ahistoricism and its relationship to predominant romantic tropes. James E. Miller Jr. remarks, for example: "In some dark sense, Jim's experience is the American experience, his melancholy sense of loss also his country's, his longing for something missed in the past a national longing. The lost promise, the misplaced vision, is America's loss—our loss—and it haunts us all, still" (123).

In the past several decades, Cather critics have taken aim at certain assumptions inherent in these earlier arguments. Feminist and queer readings, in particular, tend to disagree with critics such as Marcus Cunliffe—who asserts that "Willa Cather did not stake out a claim for herself as a woman writer"—and instead stress the importance of gender and sexuality in *My Ántonia* (24–25).[2] Many of these analyses, however, remain primarily ahistorical. In "Creative Fertility and the National Romance in Willa Cather's *O Pioneers!* and *My Ántonia*," for example, Mary Paniccia Carden preserves a similar mythological perspective but argues that the text "recasts the starring role in the national romance with pioneering women" (295); and in *Sons and Daughters of Self-Made Men*, Carden focuses, alternately, on the "impossibility of mythic American masculinity" (117). Here the critical lens shifts, but the emphasis on myth in the novel prevails.

Even where new historicist readings have worked to reinscribe Cather into a historical framework, there seems to remain a stubborn allegiance to *My Ántonia*'s mythic qualities. In *Willa Cather in Context*, for example, Guy Reynolds ties Cather's novels to the Progressive Era of 1890–1920 but grafts his reading back onto ideas of archetypes and myths, as when he states that Cather "writes myth into her novels, self-consciously foregrounding a symbolic parable-like form of story-telling" (20). Since the 1996 publication of *Willa Cather in Context*, there has been a renewed and dedicated attempt to rehistoricize Cather. Among these groundbreaking new studies, *Cather Studies, Volume 6: History, Memory, and War* (2006) focuses on "themes central to the so-called American century and to our own historical moment" (Trout xii) and includes a chapter on *My Ántonia*, which convincingly argues that the novel "is a highly charged exercise of political memory" (Gorman 29). Likewise, *Cather Studies, Volume 9: Willa Cather and Modern Cultures* (2011) "demonstrates how far Cather criticism has come" (Homestead and Reynolds xi) and describes "Cather as a writer of transition: she straddled the late-Victorian and modernist eras and saw many aspects of the contemporary world emerge over time" (xix). These more recent contextualized interpretations still spend little time discussing *My Ántonia* and concentrate, instead, on her other titles that are seemingly more appropriate to historical analysis. Since its publication, critical interpretations of *My Ántonia*—whether symbolic, feminist, queer, or even new historicist—overwhelmingly assume the centrality of the two fundamental American myths in the text: the myth of romantic possibility, which R. W. B. Lewis outlines in *The American Adam*, and the myth of loss, described by Leo Marx as the metaphor of the "machine in the garden" in his book with that title.

In grounding *My Ántonia* largely in national, archetypal, and timeless myths, critics often mystify rather than clarify the novel's specific place in American literary history. Such confusion circulates particularly in critical assumptions about the text's historical setting. Critics who read the novel as "an intense vision of a lost America," for example, tend to locate the text at the cusp of modernity (Bloom, Introduction 1). According to these assumptions, the story begins with Jim's childhood promises of pastoral possibility, before technology has reared its reaping hook, and ends with his disillusionment, after the machine has raped the garden; in this reading, the novel becomes an elegy of America's former innocence and lost potential. One might argue that a novel such as Mark Twain's *Adventures of Huckleberry Finn*—which is set in the 1840s—retreats to a similar preindustrial period of pastoral purity. Jim Burden's story, however, begins in 1885 and takes readers to 1916 (Giannone 84). By 1885—the start of Burden's narrative and the year *Adventures of Huckleberry Finn* was published—the machine had not only been introduced but had fully invaded the garden. As Alfred Kazin explains, the 1880s and 1890s were defined by "impending change [that] became almost oppressive in its vividness" (xxii). By the start of *My Ántonia*, Americans had already begun to acknowledge this irreversible sense of loss; the promise of an agrarian wilderness and the possibilities of a new world had disintegrated in the American consciousness.

One might conclude that Cather sacrificed historical accuracy—that, having herself been born in 1873, she was not fully aware of the historical complexities of her childhood America. But such an assumption is challenged by the figure of Jim, who in the opening pages of his narrative arrives in Nebraska as a young boy traveling on the transcontinental railroad. Perhaps the most potent symbol of the "machine in the garden," the transcontinental railroad would not be an apt image for a novel set in the heart of a supposed golden era. Rather than in a period of ahistorical romantic idealism, Cather locates her story after the Civil War, after the influx of modern technology, after the Homestead Act, after the completion of the railroad, and thus at the end of the pioneering period. She sets her plot during the heyday of American realism, when Americans were, indeed, facing facts rather than escaping from them. To assume that Cather was idealizing 1885 America would be to assume a certain historical naivety on her part.

In truth, Cather was not historically naive. *My Ántonia*, and Cather's literature in general, reveals a profound awareness of history and the American individual's increasingly unstable relationship to his environment. While the novel incorporates mythology and encompasses, as I will argue, salient principles of Ralph Waldo Emerson's philosophy, the text is not a timeless "commentary on the American experience" but rather a commentary on a specific moment in American history (Miller 112). *My Ántonia* should be read in terms of its engagement with this historical moment. By accepting Cather as "a resistant subject, even an obstructive one," critics miss the significant contextual element of the novel and overlook its relationship to American literary history (Lee, *Willa* 3). In fact, this novel, both in terms of its style and its theme, reproduces many of the tenets that realist critics such as William Dean Howells and Henry James had earlier outlined.[3] Including *My Ántonia* in a discussion of American realism not only illuminates meaning in the text but ultimately sheds light on the movement itself.

II

Biographers do not hesitate to point out Willa Cather's aversion to realism, noting her distaste in particular for the literary philosophies of Howells: she "blamed William Dean Howells for being too tame" (Murphy, *The Road Home* 2), "thought him something of a pompous ass," and complained of his literary style that "he might as well write a detailed account of how he had the measles and the whooping cough" (Woodress 107). Despite her less than flattering descriptions of Howells, Cather nevertheless admired Mark Twain and Henry James.[4] In one of her early columns as a journalist, for example, she labels James "that mighty master of language and keen student of human actions and motives," and reports that he is the only "English-speaking author who is really keeping his self-respect and sticking for perfection" (qtd. in Woodress 108). Furthermore, she read Twain's *Adventures of Huckleberry Finn* at least twenty times and listed the novel as one of "three American books which have the possibility of a long, long life" (qtd. in Orvell 31). While Cather may have disliked what Frank Norris referred to as Howells's novels about the "drama of a broken teacup" (Norris 278), she often deferred to the work of other literary realists and was highly engaged with the cultural period.[5]

Scholars tend to emphasize Cather's *critique* of realism, but few analyze how she wrote *within* the literary movement.[6] Cather's own literary criticism, in fact, marks her as a spokesperson for realism. Cather wrote essays in support of realism and, not unlike Howells in *Criticism and Fiction*, attempted to map out its stylistic and thematic properties. In her essay "The Novel Démeublé," for example, she discusses common misreadings of realism and delineates how the literary style should be defined: "There is a popular superstition that 'realism' asserts itself in the cataloguing of a great number of material processes, the methods of operating manufactories and trades, and in minutely and unsparingly describing physical sensations. But is not realism, more than it is anything else, an attitude of mind on the part of the writer toward his material, a vague indication of the sympathy and candour with which he accepts, rather than chooses, his theme?" (37). Cather was more interested in describing character than cataloguing "material processes," in "break[ing] away from mere verisimilitude," and in presenting "scene by suggestion rather than by enumeration" (Cather, "The Novel" 40). In this sense, she confirms her literary allegiance to James's style of realism over Howells's "minute and unsparing" "enumeration," for example, of a grasshopper.[7] Her comments, specifically regarding the organic relationship between author and theme, echo James's own critical discussions of literature. Her vision of the realist writer who "accepts, rather than chooses, his theme," in particular, recalls James, who writes in his preface to *The Portrait of a Lady* that theme grows from the "soil" of the "artist's prime sensibility" (6). In "The Novel Démeublé," Cather locates herself within the realist tradition and simultaneously becomes an important link in its development.

My Ántonia incorporates aesthetic elements associated with this tradition. Cather's use of the framing device, most notably, reflects the type of verisimilitude that American realists privileged. In her introduction, she establishes Jim's story as the product of an agreement between two friends to "set down on paper" all that they remember of their old friend, Ántonia (713). The internal story that follows becomes Jim's impressionistic account of the young Bohemian girl and displays a similar "fidelity to experience and probability of motive" that Howells earlier argued for in *Criticism and Fiction* (15). Miles Orvell specifically connects Cather's narrative style in *My Ántonia* back to Twain's in *Adventures of Huckleberry Finn*: "Cather, like Twain, is making a virtue out of the seeming naiveté of her narrator, exploiting the resources of the vernacular, opposing her narrator's artlessness and the presumed artificiality of the 'editor'" (35). *My Ántonia* employs these "vernacular resources" as early as chapter 1, when the farm hand Jake Marpole tries to reproduce Ántonia's limited English skills: "They can't any of them speak English, except one little girl and all she can say is 'We go Black Hawk, Nebraska'" (715–16). Again, in chapter 2, Jim recognizes his grandmother's seemingly foreign regional dialect:

"'Down to the kitchen' struck me as curious; it was always 'out in the kitchen' at home" (719). These two representations—of both immigrant and Midwestern dialects—demonstrate Cather's attention to the plurality of regional and ethnic cultures. Through her use of the authentic vernacular, Cather contrasts Jim's own educated voice of the East with both the uneducated American farmers and the Bohemian immigrants of the prairie.

Cather's allegiance to realism emanates not only from her style but, more importantly, from her use of theme; like other realist texts discussed in this book, *My Ántonia* reflects the thematic struggle between the Emersonian hero/ine and her plot. Biographers continually note Cather's knowledge and appreciation of Emerson's work as well as her literary debt to him. James Woodress, for example, maintains that Cather's "worldview derives . . . from Emerson" (242). Readers can specifically trace this Emersonian worldview in *My Ántonia*. Through setting, symbolism, character, and plot, *My Ántonia* reflects core Emersonian ideals: of spiritual individualism, freedom from social constraints, and an organic relationship with nature. Even as the novel applauds the Emersonian individual, however, it also sets American transcendentalism against the backdrop of postbellum history. The text struggles with the same question found in Twain's *Adventures of Huckleberry Finn*, James's *The Portrait of a Lady*, and Wharton's *The House of Mirth*: can the modern world accommodate the romantic Emersonian spirit? As much as Jim purports to tell Ántonia's story, he also tells his own; and Jim's story in many ways mirrors the stories of Huck Finn, Isabel Archer, and Lily Bart. Like those earlier hero/ines, as Jim grows up he experiences a sense of "transcendental homelessness," where the individual "enters into competition with the outside world" (Lukács 112). Jim's narrative progression represents his perennial search for a home, and the central theme of Jim's story becomes this conflict between the individual and history. The text belongs in a discussion of American realism, therefore, in part because the narrative confronts the same dialogic extremes that I argue are inherent in American realism. *My Ántonia* endorses Emersonian transcendentalism but also recognizes its philosophic ideals as fictions.

In *The Sense of an Ending*, Frank Kermode specifically distinguishes between myth and fiction: "Fictions can degenerate into myths whenever they are not consciously held to be fictive. . . . Myth operates within the diagrams of ritual, which presupposes total and adequate explanations of things as they are and were; it is a sequence of radically unchangeable gestures. Fictions are for finding things out, and they change as the needs of sense-making change. Myths are the agents of stability, fictions the agents of change. Myths call for absolute, fictions for conditional assent" (39). Kermode's distinction between myth and fiction is useful when discussing American realism because, in much the same way, that movement offered a "conditional" rather than "absolute" embrace of Emersonian romanticism. While American realists acknowledged their literary debt to Emerson, they criticized the philosopher's tendency to "presuppose . . . total and adequate explanations of things as they are and were." History, they argued, simply would not allow for such a "sequence of radically unchangeable gestures"; the individual would have to own up to the power of plot. In a sense, Jim acts as the realist author: in his rendering of Ántonia, he celebrates the Emersonian ideal but, in doing so, acknowledges that myth as fiction.[8]

My Ántonia is particularly instructive, however, because it not only is inscribed within the realist tradition but also begins to move beyond it. While the text disapproves of the transcendentalist's tendency to *bypass* history, the novel simultaneously examines and questions the realist's strict *confidence* in history. Against Jim's realist narrative, Cather offers readers another story, one that honors Jim's vision but also qualifies it. Specifically, this alternative story identifies Jim as an unreliable narrator and questions his reading of history. Jim, it is revealed, puts too much emphasis on the power of plot; his version of history is *too* "absolute." He blindly blames the "machine in the garden" for the loss of his childhood Emersonian spirit and naturalizes his seeming loss of innocence onto the inevitable passage of time. In staging Jim's narrative shortcomings, the text rereads the American struggling to preserve his individualism not as the passive victim of history but rather as the enabler of his own destruction. Much like *Adventures of Huckleberry Finn*, *The Portrait of a Lady*, and *The House of Mirth*, *My Ántonia* acknowledges the power of history and recognizes that man may not be "greater than all the geography and all the government of the world." Yet, unlike these previous realist novels, *My Ántonia* simultaneously suggests that history, indeed, may also be "a fable agreed upon" (Emerson, "History" 240); the novel implies that both binaries—romantic philosophy and material realism—may, in fact, be guilty of "presuppos[ing] . . . total and adequate explanations of things as they are and were" (Kermode 39). While realism tends to fictionalize the myth of the Emersonian individual unbound by history or society, Cather now begins to call for the "conditional assent" of history itself. In this way, *My Ántonia* embodies the dominant cultural movement of its time—American realism—and yet also begins to locate a new emerging literary culture.

III

In the introductory narrative that frames Jim Burden's story, the unnamed first-person narrator depicts the older Jim as a realist character who lives a sterile, unromantic life.[9] Even though he continues to love the "never-ending miles of ripe wheat," he has moved from the "freemasonry" of the West to the urban metropolis of New York in order to work as "legal counsel for one of the great Western railways" (*My Ántonia* 711). As a lawyer for the railways, he presumably now works to defend and support those who develop the land he loves. Furthermore, his wife is a cold and detached woman, whom Jim has married, the narrator hints, only to foster his career. The narrator very clearly does "not like his wife" (711) and notes that she "seems unimpressionable and temperamentally incapable of enthusiasm" (712). Their marriage appears loveless, a union based solely on social convenience and material gain.

According to the narrator, despite Jim's lackluster adult life, his disposition has remained "naturally romantic and ardent" (712). Time, however, seems to have rendered Jim's romantic desires inaccessible, and his romantic sensibility has, instead, become largely destructive. Readers learn, for example, that his ardent spirit has been "one of the strongest elements in his [business] success": "He loves with a personal passion the great country through which his railway runs and branches. His faith in it and his knowledge of it have played an important part in its development. He is always able to raise capital for new enterprises in Wyoming or Montana, and has helped young men out there to do remarkable things in mines and timber and oil. . . . Jim is still able to lose himself in those big Western dreams" (712). The great irony of Jim's "big Western dreams" is that, while his "faith in" and "knowledge of" the land "have played an important part in its development," they have also helped to ensure its ruin. As a lawyer in the East, his only avenue to romance is through money and development; that development, of course, works to transform nature into Gilded Age capital. Jim's "romantic and ardent disposition" now paradoxically serves to corrode romance.

Memory acts as Jim's alternative outlet for his "naturally romantic and ardent disposition." His entire narrative of Ántonia Shimerda emerges from his nostalgic longing. In the introduction, readers find the frame narrator and Jim Burden both traveling away from New York City, through the plains of Iowa. The narrator's description of the land captures this yearning for the pastoral delights of their childhood: "We were talking about what it is like to spend one's childhood in little towns like these, buried in wheat and corn, under stimulating extremes of climate: burning summers when the world lies green and billowy beneath a brilliant sky, when one is fairly stifled in vegetation, in the color and smell of strong weeds and heavy harvests" (711). This vision elicits the memory of the Bohemian girl Ántonia Shimerda, who seems to embody the innocence of the landscape; each agrees to write down and share a narrative of Ántonia, "in this way to get a picture of her" (713). Jim completes his manuscript first and decides to name it not "Ántonia" but, rather, "*My Ántonia*." Many critics have commented on the importance of this title, in particular Jim's all-important use of the first-person possessive; as Jim himself acknowledges, his narrative will not be an objective portrait of the Bohemian girl but a remembrance of things past, a personal, unorganized impression of what "Ántonia's name recalls to me" (714). Although the story will be about Ántonia, readers sense that it will also be about Jim, about his childhood and subsequent loss. Jim's narrative will honor his romantic childhood but will also explain how plot has led him so far from that "little prairie town" toward New York City, the epicenter of Gilded Age materialism (711).[10]

In book 1, readers are immersed in Jim's Emersonian childhood and thrust into the paradise of the Nebraska prairies. Jim, at age ten, moves from Virginia to Nebraska to live with his grandparents. Like Huck Finn, Isabel Archer, and Lily Bart, Jim Burden is an orphan and preserves a similar "original relation to the universe" (Emerson, *Nature* 7). He reads this potential for new experience as Emerson does in the opening pages of *Nature*, in the form of "new lands, new men, new thoughts" (7). As such, his first impression of the prairie is not as "a country at all, but the material out of which countries are made" (*My Ántonia* 718). Jim, like Emerson, chooses not to be retrospective, not to "grope among the dry bones of the past," but to search for a "poetry and philosophy of insight," a "religion by revelation" (Emerson, *Nature* 7).

Jim immediately locates that "poetry and philosophy of insight," that "religion by revelation," in nature. His first encounters with the land seem to come right out of the pages of Emerson, his descriptions "enumerating the values of nature and casting up their sum" (Emerson, *Nature* 8). Emerson's concept of the "transparent eye-ball" is notoriously difficult to express or conceive of within the realm of experience, but Jim's descriptions of Nebraska embody just this concept. Bumping along the road to his grandparents' farm, Jim notes the empty landscape: "There was nothing but land: not a country at all, but the material out of which countries are made. . . . The wagon jolted on, carrying me I knew not whither. I don't think I was homesick. If we never arrived anywhere, it did not matter. Between that earth and that sky I felt erased, blotted out" (*My Ántonia* 718). When Jim reports that "between that earth and that sky [he] . . . felt erased, blotted out," he approximates Emerson's metaphor of the "transparent eye-ball": "I am nothing; I see all; the currents of the Universal Being circulate through me; I am part or particle of God" (Emerson, *Nature* 10). Much like Emerson, who instructs his readers that in nature "all mean egotism vanishes," Jim's identity gets lost in the landscape around him (Emerson, *Nature* 10). As Jim explains: "I did not say my prayers that night: here, I felt what would be would be" (*My Ántonia* 718). On the western prairies, Jim accepts nature as his new religion.

Jim's spiritual surrender to nature is reinforced shortly thereafter when— alone in his grandmother's garden—he feels "motion in the landscape; in the fresh, easy-blowing morning wind, and in the earth itself, as if the shaggy grass were a sort of loose hide, and underneath it herds of wild buffalo were galloping, galloping" (723). He leans against a "warm yellow pumpkin" and, feeling as if he is at the edge of the world, merges his spirit with the landscape around him: "I was something that lay under the sun and felt it, like the pumpkins, and I did not want to be anything more. I was entirely happy. Perhaps we feel like that when we die and become a part of something entire . . . . At any rate, that is happiness; to be dissolved into something complete and great" (724).[11] These lines beg comparison to Emerson's words in *Nature*: "I have no hostility to nature, but a child's love to it. I expand and live in the warm day like corn and melons" (Emerson 38). In both of these passages, particularly through the use of simile, the distinction between man and nature disappears, and—rather than the personification of the landscape—it is now man who assumes the characteristics of the harvest. The striking similarity between these two passages could be entirely coincidental; whether intentional or not, the echoes of Emerson resonate, as Jim's childhood becomes a living embodiment of transcendental philosophy. As Hermione Lee asserts, "Jim could be another Thoreau or Emerson ('I am nothing, I see all') . . . as the narrator contemplates his 'intimations of immortality' in the language of American transcendentalism" (*Willa* 141).

These early romantic encounters with nature continue throughout book 1, as Jim explores each of his first four seasons on the prairie with his new Bohemian friend and neighbor, Ántonia. Because readers do not have access to Ántonia's consciousness, it is more difficult to gauge her own relationship to nature. On the one hand, her experience with her environment is quite different from Jim's. As an immigrant without the comforts of a house or the assurance of food, Ántonia must view the pumpkins not simply as a resting place but as a vital source of sustenance. Her responsibilities contrast with Jim's sustained sense of ease. While Jim delights in the "dazzling light" of his first winter, for example, Ántonia suffers from cold and hunger (*My Ántonia* 753).

In spite of their cultural and class differences, in childhood these two characters nevertheless share a similar Emersonian vision. In particular, they both maintain the same freshness, vitality, and spiritual awareness of landscape. Jim notes that, while Ántonia struggles with poverty, she is also "light-hearted and never complained" (733). She is amazed by the beauty of the sky and enjoys "scaring rabbits or starting up flocks of quail" (733); when she is cold, she builds a nest for herself "in the long red grass" (729). Her communion with nature is portrayed most visibly on a cold autumn day when she revitalizes a suffering grasshopper: "While we were lying there against the warm bank, a little insect of the palest, frailest green hopped painfully out of the buffalo grass and tried to leap into a bunch of bluestem. He missed it, fell back, and sat with his head sunk between his long legs, his antennae quivering, as if he were waiting for something to come and finish him. Tony made a warm nest for him in her hands; talked to him gaily and indulgently in Bohemian. Presently he began to sing for us—a thin, rusty little chirp" (736). On the way home, as a chill sets in, she nurtures the "frail little creature": "Tony . . . carefully put the green insect in her hair, tying her big handkerchief down loosely over her curls" (737). Emerson writes that "in the presence of nature, a wild delight runs through the man, in spite of real sorrows" (Emerson, *Nature* 10). For Ántonia, nature's presence functions precisely as this reprieve from "real sorrows"; it allows her, like Jim, to "be dissolved into something complete and great." Edwin T. Bowden observes that "on the prairie farm she expands to the limit of her being, and her inner horizon stretches toward the outer until the two join in one complete circle" (15). Book 1 comes to embody each of the central tenets outlined in Emerson's *Nature*: nature becomes commodity, beauty, language, discipline, idealism, spirit, and prospects. The story of Jim's and Ántonia's childhoods is based on these classic American ideals; Emersonian possibility comes to life through their "unaffected, unbiased, unbribable, unaffrighted innocence" (Emerson, "Self-Reliance" 261).

IV

If book 1 offers the promise of uncorrupted nature and spiritual integrity, then books 2 through 5 test the characters' resilience against the forces of history. Readers find that life continually pulls Jim further away from Emersonian possibility and toward what he reads as the inevitable progression of time. In book 2, his grandparents retire to the town of Black Hawk and send Jim to a local school. An older and more restless Jim expresses the town's sterility: "People's speech, their voices, their very glances, became furtive and repressed. Every individual taste, every natural appetite, was bridled by caution. . . . The growing piles of ashes and cinders in the back yards were the only evidence that the wasteful, consuming process of life went on at all" (*My Ántonia* 851). Jim reads the introduction of bourgeois civilization—the "wasteful, consuming process of life"—as corrupt. The townspeople's stifled and "guarded mode of existence" contrasts with earlier scenes of Jim's and Ántonia's uninhibited lives on the prairie (851). C. Hugh Holman maintains that Jim "is the medium for expressing this recognition of the nostalgic sense that, as the obligations of civilization and history increasingly impress their weight upon the individual, they carry him further and further away from the good, simple, and pastoral life" (34). Jim thus communicates the vision of the American realist, who acknowledges the individual's battle against the "obligations of civilization and history."

As early as book 2, however, Jim's narrow reading of history begins to prove problematic. Where Jim has idealized each of the four seasons on the farm in book 1, even noting the delight of winter, he now rereads nature in terms of his own spiritual loss. Jim writes, for example, that "on the farm the weather was the great fact, and men's affairs went on underneath it, as the streams creep under the ice. But in Black Hawk the scene of human life was spread out shrunken and pinched, frozen down to the bare stalk" (828). In fact, he now recasts nature as a "bitter song" (823): "The pale, cold light of the winter sunset did not beautify—it was like the light of truth itself. . . . The wind sprang up afresh, with a kind of bitter song, as if it said: 'This is *reality*, whether you like it or not. All those frivolities of summer, the light and shadow, the living mask of green that trembled over everything, they were lies, and this is what was underneath. This is the *truth*'" (823; emphasis added). This short passage exposes Jim's shifting perception of "reality," of what he reads as "truth." He passes off his reading of "reality" as objective, as a force that can only temporarily be mitigated through illusion. In a sense, he naturalizes his personal deprivation and, rather than take responsibility for his spiritual conflict, deflects his own failure of will back onto the landscape. It is not that Jim loses all sense of his childhood idealism. He still maintains a pastoral vision of America, where country life is viewed as fruitful and town life as "wasteful" and "consuming," but he begins to justify a life removed from that vision by rewriting it as an impossible dream (851). He suggests—much like the American realist himself—that sooner or later the individual must "face facts" and accept the truth of history.

At the end of book 2, Jim moves further from the country, this time to the city of Lincoln to continue his education. Again, rather than attribute his move to personal choice, Jim interprets the shift as the unavoidable process of growing up. Soon before Jim leaves Black Hawk, he spends a day in the country with the three "hired girls"—Tiny, Ántonia, and Lena. In this scene, Jim's famous description of a plough joins man and nature in one stunning image: "Presently we saw a curious thing: There were no clouds, the sun was going down in a limpid, gold-washed sky. Just as the lower edge of the red disc rested on the high fields against the horizon, a great black figure suddenly appeared on the face of the sun. . . . On some upland farm, a plough had been left standing in the field. The sun was sinking just behind it. Magnified across the distance by the horizontal light, it stood out against the sun, was exactly contained within the circle of the disc; the handles, the tongue, the share—black against the molten red. There it was, heroic in size, a picture writing on the sun" (865–66). This passage presents the reader with one of the most spectacular images in American literature. It translates into words the sublimity of nature and recalls Emerson's own perspective in *Nature*: "To the body and mind which have been cramped by noxious work or company, nature is medicinal and restores their tone. . . . The tradesman, the attorney comes out of the din and craft of the street, and sees the sky and the woods, and is man again. . . . The health of the eye seems to demand a horizon. We are never tired, so long as we can see far enough" (Emerson 14–15). Cather's image reinforces this restorative, "medicinal" element of nature. Here the plough—the symbolic representation of "noxious work"—is contained by the setting sun, and, through this image of the horizon, through the "sky and the woods," the farmers and the "hired girls" become "[hu]man again." Equally important is how Jim specifically emphasizes the *ephemeral* nature of the plough figure: "Even while we whispered about it, our vision disappeared" (*My Ántonia* 866). Thus, while the image is restorative, it is also—like Jim's own Emersonian youth—fleeting. As natural as the sun setting, he must grow up, and his romantic vision must give way to reality. He laments: "When boys and girls are growing up, life can't stand still, not even in the quietest of country towns; and they *have* to grow up, whether they will or no" (835; emphasis added). Jim mourns the "obligations of civilization and history," which seem to direct human lives toward their inevitable ends.

In book 2, Jim's personal narrative is cast against the background of Ántonia's own plot. Like Jim, Ántonia moves to town, not for school but rather out of financial necessity. Unlike Jim, however, Ántonia does not mourn the loss of her childhood but adapts well to changing circumstances. Despite her new surroundings, she is able to maintain her same youthful vitality, individual integrity, and Emersonian self-reliance. Jim notes that town life seemed to make his neighbors "furtive and repressed," incapable of expressing "individual taste" or "natural appetite" (851), but he observes by contrast that "everything she [Ántonia] said seemed to come right out of her heart" (825). Even as the limitations of the townspeople are dictated by their reliance on environment, property, and social approval for happiness, Ántonia still seems to live by Emerson's adage that "nothing can bring you peace but yourself" (282).

Ántonia's spiritual individualism now becomes associated with a larger group of immigrant women, all of whom live outside the strict conventions of American society and exhibit a similar "vigor," a "positive carriage and freedom of movement" that stands in contrast to their American neighbors (838). As a result of their vitality, they are "considered a menace to the social order": "Their beauty shone out too boldly against a conventional background" (840). In fact, Ántonia loses her job with the Harlings when she chooses to attend the forbidden Vannis' dances despite their wishes. While Ántonia's actions potentially threaten her financial and physical security, her choice is an important one, as it signifies her continued spiritual energy and her ability to overcome external pressures and resist conformity.

Lena Lingard is another immigrant, Norwegian rather than Bohemian, who stands out against the "furtive and repressed" town of Black Hawk. It is interesting that critics have marked this other central female figure in the novel as Ántonia's "literary foil" (Bowden 16).[12] Although Ántonia and Lena do not ultimately share similar plots, they do share core values. Like Ántonia, Lena exhibits "a positive carriage and freedom of movement." Jim explains his earliest memories of Lena as "out among her cattle, bareheaded and barefooted, scantily dressed in tattered clothing, always knitting as she watched her herd." He describes her as "something wild," quite unabashed about her "ragged clothes," with an "easy" and "gentle" disposition matched equally against her ruggedness (*My Ántonia* 817). Unlike those "furtive and repressed" townspeople, Lena is comfortable with her body and her environment.

Despite the fact that Lena comes to represent an urban contrast to the earthy Ántonia, both women share the same heroic individualism, the same fierce sense of self-reliance that privileges personal integrity and independence above conformity and social convention. Jim considers, for example, how Lena manages to succeed in Lincoln's business environment without giving in to the capitalist American model: "Lena's success puzzled me. She was so easygoing; had none of the push and self-assertiveness that get people ahead in business" (885). As a dressmaker, Lena is consistently more dedicated to the product than the capital. Unlike Jim, her interest is not in prospecting and making money but on clothing the human figure to look as "fresh as the spring morning" (885–86). Even as Jim's movement away from nature contributes to his spiritual decline, Lena maintains her "blissful expression of countenance" despite her move to the big city of Lincoln, Nebraska (885). Jim admits that, even in Lincoln, Lena remains "almost as candid as Nature" (886). Rather than a foil, Lena Lingard is more like Ántonia's doppelganger; their paths may diverge, sending one out into the world and the other back to the earth, but their similar spiritual drive and self-possession render them complementary Emersonian heroines.[13]

This idea is highlighted by the fact that Jim comes to idealize and love both Ántonia and Lena. In spite of his feelings, however, he pursues neither of them and instead distances himself from both. As discussed, he resigns himself to a vision of reality that reads the loss of romance as an inevitable part of growing up. In books 3 and 4, Jim denies himself the opportunity to create a deeper spiritual connection with either of these Emersonian heroines. In book 3, he becomes physically and spiritually close to Lena.[14] Yet, at a critical moment Jim chooses to detach. He has the choice to remain in the West or to move to the East and study at Harvard. He appears to make this decision during a conversation with Lena, who teases Jim: "What's on your mind, Jim? Are you afraid I'll want you to marry me some day?" (893). Jim's response is telling: "Then I told her I was going away." Although Lena has made it clear that she has no intention of getting married, the juxtaposition of the two lines exposes Jim's fear, not simply the fear of marriage but of all that Lena symbolizes. In turning away from Lena, he rejects an Emersonian vision of self-determination and rugged individualism that he has already written off as lost.

In book 4, Jim—having removed himself from Lena—now avoids another spiritual connection, this time with Ántonia. Having gone away and finished his studies at Harvard, he returns to Black Hawk for the summer and learns that Ántonia has been deserted by her American lover and is now unmarried with a baby girl. Jim observes Ántonia's continued spiritual strength and calm, despite her hardship: "She was thinner than I had ever seen her, and looked as Mrs. Steavens said, 'worked down,' but there was a new kind of strength in the gravity of her face, and her color still gave that look of deep-seated health and ardor" (909). Recognizing the beauty and vitality intrinsic in her character, Jim confesses: "Do you know, Ántonia, since I've been away, I think of you more often than of any one else in this part of the world. I'd have liked to have you for a sweetheart, or a wife, or my mother or my sister—anything that a woman can be to a man. The *idea* of you is a part of my mind; you influence my likes and dislikes, all my tastes, hundreds of times when I don't realize it. You really are a part of me" (910; emphasis added). The obvious question becomes: why does he not, then, choose to "have . . . [Ántonia] for a sweetheart, or a wife"? He even admits that he feels the "old pull of the earth," and yet despite this desire he still decides to return back East, away from the country, toward the center of sterile materialism (910). The key word in this passage is "idea," which renders Ántonia an unattainable ideal rather than a palpable reality.

Jim does not recognize the faultiness of his own logic. Instead, he once again deflects his loss onto the natural landscape. He describes the setting sun and rising moon that he and Ántonia witness as they walk home: "As we walked homeward across the fields, the sun dropped and lay like a great golden globe in the low west. While it hung there, the moon rose in the east, as big as a cart-wheel, pale silver and streaked with rose color, thin as a bubble or a ghost-moon. For five, perhaps ten minutes, the two luminaries confronted each other across the level land, resting on opposite edges of the world" (910). Jim borrows the image of the sun and moon in order to symbolize the grown man and woman who walk "homeward across the fields" and "rest . . . on opposite edges of the world." His metaphor serves to naturalize, and thus rationalize, the position in which he and Ántonia now find themselves. Just as Ántonia will remain the figure of the sun setting in the West (Nebraska), so Jim must become the figure of the moon rising in the East (New York). The "idea" of Ántonia is offset by an alternate, naturalist reading, one that justifies his search for material rewards over spiritual communion.

Jim relieves himself of the "burden" to act by relegating both Lena and Ántonia to the world of ideas and assigning them the status of muses. In Lincoln, Jim writes the two women into the poetry of Virgil. He actually sees the image of Lena within the pages of Virgil's *Georgics*: "It floated before me on the page like a picture" (880). Blanche H. Gelfant ties this scene to Jim's fear of sexuality, which she argues acts as "a determining force in his story" (62). Gelfant makes the important point that Jim, "by relegating Lena to the ideal but unreachable world of art . . . assures their separation" (69). Jim clearly attempts to create distance between himself and Lena, but he seems motivated by more than just his fear of sexuality. Jim is driven as well by his stubborn allegiance to history, by his firm belief that the Emersonian values of his youth—as magnificent and heroic as they were—must ultimately give way to the narrative of the industrial, urban machine invading the pastoral garden.

In mythologizing the two women, Jim not only ensures his separation from them but also transfigures his own narrative into myth. He describes the symbolic connection between the "hired girls" and Virgil's poetry: "It came over me, as it had never done before, the relation between girls like those and the poetry of Virgil. If there were no girls like them in the world, there would be no poetry. I understood that clearly, for the first time" (*My Ántonia* 880). In many ways, Jim's connection to these women mirrors America's historical connection to the land. Jim first responded to the Nebraska prairie as "the material out of which countries are made" (718). Here the women become the material out of which poetry is made. Just as America's myth of manifest destiny emerged out of the need to rewrite expansion and appropriation as ennobling, Jim similarly inscribes the women into the poetry of Virgil as a way to ennoble his own problematic narrative. Ántonia's and Lena's ability to maintain their vitality and independence threatens Jim's inability to maintain such ideals. By writing them into myth, and thus making them inherently impalpable and intangible, he relegates them to the world of romance, maintains his position as the realist, and justifies his own failure to locate the ideal within the real. Furthermore, by recasting them into the role of muses and himself into the role of epic poet, Jim effectively rewrites Virgil into his own epic American narrative. He transforms his failure into heroism.

Jim also manages to preserve his illusion through the act of writing his narrative, his "My Ántonia." In *Reading for the Plot*, Peter Brooks argues that "narrative demarcates, encloses, establishes limits, orders" (4). The reader's impulse for narrative derives from the need for mastery and control. One significant incident in the text supports Brooks's narrative theory and exposes Jim's own authorial need to contain and control meaning. In book 2, Jim offers to housesit at the Cutters' in place of Ántonia, who fears Wick Cutter's sexual advances. Cutter returns that night and attacks Jim, mistaking him for Ántonia.

Readers expect Jim to be proud of having saved Ántonia and concomitantly angry at Cutter's misconduct. It is therefore noteworthy that, rather than sympathize with Ántonia, Jim blames her: "I heard Ántonia sobbing outside my door, but I asked grandmother to send her away. I felt that I never wanted to see her again. I hated her almost as much as I hated Cutter. She had let me in for all this disgustingness" (*My Ántonia* 869). Critics often read this scene in terms of Jim's problematic relationship to women or, again, in terms of his fear of sexuality.[15] While his reaction clearly illustrates his selfish disregard for women's sexual struggles, the word "disgustingness," in particular, suggests an alternative reading. The scene represents one of the few narrative moments in the text that Jim, as author, cannot seem to contain. Ántonia's reality—the "disgustingness" of her economic and physical vulnerability—stains Jim's reading of her as his fresh, angelic muse, as the material out of which poetry is made; it removes her from the cordoned-off space of illusory romance. He later tells readers that "the idea is one that no circumstances can frustrate" (884). But in this scene, the circumstances corrupt the idea. Jim's heroic revision of reality—his reading of Virgil and his writing of "My Ántonia"—works to counter the potential frustration and "shape the recovery of meaning within time" (Brooks 36).

Nowhere is this tendency more obvious than in the last paragraph of book 5. While Jim's role up until now has been riddled with inconsistencies, it is here that his unreliability as narrator is solidified and the essence of his story can be understood. In one of the most beautiful passages in the book, Jim explains the circle of man's experience: "For Ántonia and for me, this had been the road of Destiny; had taken us to those early accidents of fortune which predetermined for us all that we can ever be. Now I understood that the same road was to bring us together again. Whatever we had missed, we possessed together the precious, the incommunicable past" (*My Ántonia* 937). Despite the poetic brilliance of the language, there are certain troubling contradictions in Jim's seeming "epiphany" (Helmick 113).[16] In particular, the words "Destiny" and "predetermined" are completely out of sync with Jim's story. In the passage, Jim projects his personal failure—his empty marriage, his destructive job, and his overall parasitic relationship to both nature and society—onto some larger force that lies beyond individual choice. Jim understands the larger force, those "accidents of fortune," as history.

Jim's narrative, of course, undermines such a strict and deterministic reading of history. Far from being controlled by history, Jim has determined his own plot through conscious choices, each of which has worked to replace the Emersonian ideals of his youth with urban material culture. As Demaree C. Peck observes, Jim has not traveled the "road of Destiny" but "has traveled the road of desire" (157). After book 1, each book begins with a decision that transports Jim farther and farther away from the land he loves. In book 2, Jim's grandparents *choose* to move to town, in part to send Jim to school and help him integrate into American society. Book 3 opens with Jim's move to Lincoln, where he *chooses* the realm of ideas over experience. At the end of book 3, Jim *chooses* to leave Lena and follow his teacher East to the center of urban life. At the end of book 4, Jim *chooses* to return to New York, to go to law school rather than stay in the country with Ántonia. And now, Jim blames history in order to make sense of his empty life. His use of the words "Destiny" and "predetermined" belie the facts of his own narrative.

V

Jim's final lines urge the reader to go back and reconsider his entire narrative. In book 1, Jim establishes his role as the Emersonian romantic by reflecting on and deeply honoring his childhood vision. Yet, even as he honors the transcendental project, he reads this mythic philosophy as a fiction. He becomes the realist author who accepts that Emerson's ideas, while expressing a crucial and vital element of spiritual desire, conflict with experience and do not, alone, represent truth. Cather supports Jim's reading of Emersonian romance and writes within this same tradition of realism. In books 2 through 5, however, Cather illustrates what happens when Jim's vision is taken to its extreme: history becomes a scapegoat for personal failure, and spiritual loss becomes as natural as the image of the setting sun and rising moon. Jim thereby mythologizes history in much the same way that Emerson mythologized the individual, by presupposing within this larger force "total and adequate explanations of things as they are and were" (Kermode 39). Such is the teleological narrative, the myth, which Cather ultimately questions.

By reviewing Ántonia's and Lena's narratives through this larger critical lens, readers recognize within them the voice of Cather. The women do not suffer from Jim's experience of transcendental homelessness because they temper their reading of both binaries, Emersonian idealism and historical reality; they understand romance as less than ideal and history as less than real. The novel, therefore, celebrates Lena and Ántonia as Emersonian figures and applauds their persistence, despite all odds, to preserve their individualism. There is no doubt that *My Ántonia* favors the integrity of Ántonia and Lena over Jim. Still, far from idealizing their plots, the novel makes clear that, in attempting to maintain their transcendental values, they have had to battle historical forces in ways that Jim has not.

Book 1 stresses the difficult lives of Ántonia and her family. Ántonia grows up "in the crowded clutter of their cave," working the land instead of going to school (768). Out of pride, she hides her jealousy of Jim, but at one point she reveals her envy of Jim's privileged childhood: "Sometime you will tell me all those nice things you learn at the school, won't you, Jimmy?" (792). By contrast, Jim grows up not having to worry about his difficult future. Instead, much like Tom Sawyer, he spends his leisure time writing himself into romantic adventures, such as those of Jesse James and Coronado. One snowy winter day, he finds himself busy with constant chores and calls this "a strange, unnatural sort of day" (774); he fails to recognize that this is Ántonia's typical day. Before he moves to Black Hawk, she tells Jim: "If I live here, like you, that is different. Things will be easy for you. But they will be hard for us" (802). Ántonia enjoys a pastoral childhood but does not blindly romanticize it. She experiences tremendous hardship and, in the face of such adversity, struggles courageously to preserve her spiritual values.

In book 5, when Jim finally returns from the East and visits Ántonia, readers are introduced to a grown woman with a husband and "ten or eleven" children (913). Ántonia explains to Jim that her children help her to tend the farm: "Oh, we don't have to work so hard now! We've got plenty to help us, papa and me" (916). Despite her optimism, it is also evident that multiple childbirths and hard farm labor have affected Ántonia's external beauty. Although critics often cite her at the end of the text as an Earth Mother, Jim's description of her suggests a less idealistic picture. He presents her as "a stalwart, brown woman, flat-chested, her curly brown hair a little grizzled" (914).[17] Her divergent life—one reliant on nature and manual labor—has proven physically damaging.

At the same time, Jim recognizes within his old friend a continued organic relationship, both to self and nature. He remarks that "whatever else was gone, Ántonia had not lost the fire of life" (917): "She was a battered woman now, not a lovely girl; but she still had that something which fires the imagination, could still stop one's breath for a moment by a look or gesture that somehow revealed the meaning in common things. She had only to stand in the orchard, to put her hand on a little crab tree and look up at the apples, to make you feel the goodness of planting and tending and harvesting at last" (926). Ántonia never seems to lose her commitment to Emersonian philosophy. In her natural vitality, her connection to the land, and her spiritual integrity, she manages to preserve the transcendental essence of her character. As John J. Murphy acknowledges: "She has successfully accomplished a version of the Emersonian ideal he [Jim] so fervently craved when he first came to Nebraska, 'happiness; to be dissolved into something complete and great'" (*The Road Home* 93). Even though she continues her commitment to these romantic ideas, however, she simultaneously remains a realist. She accepts the physical and emotional sacrifices one must make in order to renounce Jim's more modern, material existence and remain on the prairie.

Eudora Welty observes that Willa Cather "saw the landscape had mystery as well as reality. She was undaunted by both" (6). Welty's observation also applies to Ántonia, who, like Cather, accepts both the romantic "mystery" and the brutal "reality" in the landscape.

Lena also maintains her Emersonian values, specifically her self-reliance and freedom from social convention, but she too qualifies these ideals in order to preserve them. If Lena and Ántonia act as complementary heroines, they also lack what the other incorporates. While Ántonia's commitment to nature and family results in physical degeneration, for example, Lena holds onto her youthful energy; as Tiny observes, she is "the only person . . . who never gets any older" (*My Ántonia* 896). By contrast, she sacrifices what Ántonia does not: community and family. Each woman retains her spiritual independence, regardless of external hardships, but neither lives a bucolic life. In both cases, any sense of pure idealism is mitigated by stark reality. Hence Lena and Ántonia actually succeed in finding homes for their transcendental spirits. Although Ántonia finds her home on the Nebraska prairies and Lena in the opposite world of San Francisco, they both manage to merge their Emersonian spirits with the external world. That said, their narratives are fraught, and neither is offered an easy, happy ending.[18]

More importantly, even this tempered vision of Emersonianism is figuratively relocated outside America. Neither Lena nor Ántonia is American born, and Ántonia ultimately reintegrates into Bohemian culture.[19] Even Ántonia's American-born children—who exhibit her same Emersonian relationship to nature, who enjoy playing in the fields and sleeping in the barn—all speak Bohemian and do not learn English until they go to school. These "new Americans" give up the American myth of unadulterated idealism because they are willing to transform the ideal into the real. That Cather locates a new spiritual/ social synthesis in the figure of the immigrant indicates her subtle distrust of American culture, specifically of Americans' ability to live outside of myth.[20] In order to locate Emersonianism in modern America, she argues, one must demythologize romance and accept historical struggle and material sacrifice.

In questioning the myth of the ahistorical Emersonian figure, Cather channels a primary concern of American realism. She acknowledges, as have the realists before her, the intrusion of modern industrial America and its threat to earlier romantic ideas of individual transcendence. Through the characters of Jim, Ántonia, and Lena, she examines how the Emersonian hero attempts to negotiate a changing world. While she envisions a home for the text's two transcendental characters, Lena and Ántonia, she complicates the reductive trope of the "individual standing alone, self-reliant and self-propelling, ready to confront whatever awaited him" (Lewis, *American Adam* 5). She exposes the myth of the American Adam and alters that overly simplistic reading of the Emersonian hero.

Her text, however, also provides an early modernist response to American realism and, in particular, to the questionable faith that realist writers had in their scientific trust of objective truth. Through Jim's narrative, she asks: do we, indeed, fear the "inadequacy that is due to the soul's being wider and larger than the destinies which life has to offer it"? (Lukács 112). Does the spiritual individual struggle against a greater force called "history," a force that—despite our desires—threatens Emersonian possibility? Or is it we who create our own history? Do we purposefully construct a narrow universe and limit our spiritual potential because we actually fear a world that is too large? Jim's story—what John J. Murphy has labeled his "journey through the stages of civilization"—becomes the story of an American Everyman who involves himself in increasingly confining social environments in an attempt to "determine" his role as an individual (*The Road Home* 2). In *The American Adam*, R. W. B. Lewis expresses the same myth that Jim embraces as truth: "Instead of looking forward to new possibilities, we direct our tired attention to the burden of history, observing repeatedly that it is later than you think" (196). Jim Burden buys into this myth and writes himself into the novel as a symbol of the great "burden of history," as the character who must accept the power of plot. Unlike Jim, Cather reads the myth as fiction, and Jim becomes the "burden" of all Americans who blame external forces on their own spiritual failures.

Jim's real dilemma is, therefore, not that he has limited choices but rather that he has *too many* choices. As Catherine D. Holmes argues, "Jim's true burden in the new world is unrestricted freedom of movement and choice" (340). In his essay "From the World to the Wilderness: Renewal in Thoreau and Cather," John Jacobs makes a critical point about wilderness as metaphor: "Most elementally, wilderness exists when a solitary individual confronts nature without easy access to the material and psychological securities of the civilized world. Since wilderness, ultimately, is a metaphor, what is essentially confronted in the wilderness is the self and/or the ineluctable power that transcends the wilderness condition" (12). Jacobs adds that, for those who are "prepared by predisposition and discipline to wrest meaning from the wilderness, the wilderness experience yields great creative power," but, for those ill prepared, the wilderness can result in dislocation and despair (12). Jim does not openly express feelings of dislocation and despair; as an unreliable narrator, he tends to rewrite such emotions into romantic tropes of memory and desire. Jim's journey nevertheless illustrates a fear of the wilderness, in particular a certain fear of "unrestricted freedom of movement and choice" (Holmes 340).

Jim's early experiences on the prairie reveal this hidden fear. In the novel's early scenes, particularly in the wagon on the way to his grandmother's house and shortly thereafter as he lies in her garden, he speaks in the language of American transcendentalism. He presents readers with an image of the child immersing himself in his environment and joining his spirit with nature. Despite his overt Emersonian discourse, however, there still remains a troubling undertone in Jim's language. In both scenes, he admits feeling as if "the world was left behind, that we had got over the edge of it" (*My Ántonia* 718). In the garden scene, he elaborates: "the light air about me told me that the world ended here: only the ground and sun and sky were left, and if one went a little farther there would be only sun and sky, and one would float off into them" (723). There is a clear note of transcendental poetry in these lines, but one senses in them an additional level of uncertainty. While Jim admires and honors this type of infinite union, he also fears it; he fears that he may walk over the edge, that he may be forever "erased, blotted out" (718). His narrative lays bare his simultaneous attraction to and pervading anxiety over such an expansive philosophy. After his childhood, Jim therefore retreats further and further from the edge toward the machine, toward "the material and psychological securities of the civilized world" (Jacobs 12).

Jim's own fears are mirrored by those of two other minor but important characters. Early on in the novel, two men commit suicide: Mr. Shimerda and the tramp at Ole Iverson's. Both of these men experience an intense weariness as a result of transcendental homelessness: Mr. Shimerda travels from Bohemia until he reaches the Nebraskan "edge of the world," and the tramp shows up at Ole Iverson's farm claiming that he's "tired of trampin'" and "won't go no farther" (*My Ántonia* 826). They both find themselves far from the "material and psychological securities of the civilized world" and struggle to manage the infinite space and dislocation of their travels (Jacobs 12). As a final choice, they embrace the machine, the great symbol of man over nature, as a way to regain control and end their lives. While Mr. Shimerda shoots himself in the head with his hunting gun, the tramp literally throws himself into the thresher. In a metaphorical sense, their actions illustrate how and why man invites the machine into the garden: to ease the fear of what Lukács calls "the abandonment of the world by God" (97). In this sense, Cather reconsiders the mythological trope of the machine in the garden and rewrites the idea of inevitable historical progress as fiction. Rather than accept history as an objective narrative, she questions how man actually welcomes the machine into the garden and constructs his own history. Americans have become so attached to the failure of Emersonian ideals, she argues, that they have lost sight of the emblems of qualified romanticism, the novel's true Emersonian spirits: Ántonia and Lena.

VI

There is much resistance to the idea that Cather does not fully embrace Jim's vision; after all, it is Jim's narrative voice that promotes the mythic, ahistorical reading of a lost America. Hermione Lee, for example, states that "Jim's elegiac pastoral expresses Cather's deepest feelings: it would be *perverse* to argue that his reading of Ántonia is meant to be distrusted" (*Willa* 150; emphasis added). Lee contends that Jim's story is Cather's story; in many ways, it is. Cather and Jim share a similar perspective on Emersonian romance, one that links them both to the tradition of American realism. Realist literature charts the struggle of the self-reliant individual against the power of history. In these texts, the heroes and heroines are driven by Emersonian desire; they are motivated by what Henry James describes as "the value and importance of the individual, the duty of making the most of one's self, of living by one's own personal light, and carrying out one's own disposition" (*Hawthorne* 67). Yet, such desire is cast against truth: the inevitable progression of history, which increasingly favors society over the individual. Like earlier realist novels, *My Ántonia* is also about this "displaced relationship between life and essence" (Lukács 44). Jim's story examines the theme of transcendental homelessness; his narrative begins with the great Emersonian possibilities of childhood and follows his seeming inability to maintain the ideals of his youth into adulthood. As he tries to maintain his transcendental spirit, society seems to direct him repeatedly toward a divergent, more material course. His narrative, his act of remembrance, becomes his attempt to rediscover his Emersonian childhood through memory, which is seemingly the only romantic avenue left to the postbellum subject. Lee is thus right to suggest that Jim's reading of Ántonia is Cather's reading; Cather writes within Jim's realist narrative.

In *My Ántonia*, however, Cather also begins to move beyond Jim's narrative and, therefore, beyond realism. While earlier realists fictionalized the myth of Emersonian idealism and recognized its dissonance with the "facts" of reality, like Jim they failed to recognize the fiction within history itself. This is precisely why—as readers continually note—Huck Finn, Isabel Archer, and Lily Bart lack satisfying endings. In their attempts to negotiate the opposing forces of romance and realism, novels such as Mark Twain's *Adventures of Huckleberry Finn*, Henry James's *The Portrait of a Lady*, and Edith Wharton's *The House of Mirth* hit an impasse. They cannot ultimately imagine a space in postbellum America for the Emersonian subject; as a result, Huck, Isabel, and Lily all become symbolically homeless. By contrast, *My Ántonia* does imagine a spiritual "home" for its two true Emersonian heroines: Ántonia Shimerda and Lena Lingard. Their stories feel complete largely because, unlike other realist characters, they see beyond strict readings of romance and realism.

While critics therefore continually connect Cather to myth, they tend to overlook how she questions, critiques, and renegotiates myth. By rehistoricizing Cather and contextualizing *My Ántonia*, one begins to understand how the novel participates in the specific literary moment of late American realism. Mark Twain published *Adventures of Huckleberry Finn* in 1885 but set the text around forty to fifty years earlier. One can locate in Twain's novel dual layers of historical consciousness and discern how Twain—as an early realist—was writing both within and against American romance. In much the same way, Cather published *My Ántonia* in 1918 but also *set* the text decades earlier—in 1885, precisely the year that *Huck Finn* hit bookshelves. Cather's text reveals similar dialogic layers of historical consciousness and situates itself both within and against American realism. Cather becomes a central linchpin in the connection between realism and modernism by reinterpreting the romance/realism binary; *My Ántonia* begins to suggest the indeterminacy of the terms themselves. In Cather's novel, history is no longer simply the objective rendering of facts. Unlike her realist predecessors, Cather goes so far as to question the extent to which history has itself become a myth. Have the realists faced facts, or have they allowed such facts to cloud their reality? Through Jim's story, the myth of "real" history ultimately becomes, as Emerson quotes Napoleon, a "fable agreed upon." *My Ántonia* exposes the truth behind realism: that history may be just as fictional as the romance of Emerson.

Epilogue

History is the action and reaction of these two,—Nature and Thought;—
two boys pushing each other on the curbstone of the pavement.
Everything is pusher or pushed: and matter and mind are in perpetual tilt
and balance, so.

                                        —Ralph Waldo Emerson, "Fate"

Echoes of Emerson has explored a particular narrative contest in the realist
novel: between Emerson's idealistic philosophies of transcendentalism and the
sociohistorical realities of postbellum America. In tracing the echoes of Emerson in American realism, and thus examining the dialogic relationship between
two contiguous literary periods, this book raises the larger, more peripheral
issue of periodization—a critical method of dividing literature into chronological blocks of time (or "periods") differentiated by seemingly remarkable
moments in history and culture.[1] Although periodization still dominates literary studies, as a critical and pedagogical practice it has become increasingly
contested over the past several decades.[2] In *On Periodization*, Virginia Jackson
frames the current debate with the following question: "Literary periods allow
us to write literary history, but do they keep us from thinking about literary
history?" (par. 2). The question is important, as periodization remains the central structure for understanding literature. Equally important is the role periodization plays in this study of American realism. In accepting the premise
that American romanticism and realism are two distinct literary periods (separated by a specific historical event, the Civil War), my book implicitly makes
use of periodization as an underlying analytical device. *Echoes of Emerson* assumes this analytical device, however, not to "keep us from thinking about
literary history" but rather to highlight the *complexity* of that literary history.

Such complexity surfaces, in part, through the evolution of the literary
period now known as "American realism," which is not simply a construct
written into literary history by subsequent critics but is inherent in the realist
project itself.[3] In 1877, when Mark Twain directed his joke at Ralph Waldo

Emerson, Henry Wadsworth Longfellow, and Oliver Wendell Holmes during the *Atlantic Monthly* celebration, he inscribed himself into a new community of writers, one that rejected the lofty language and impractical adages of an earlier generation of romantics. In 1879, when Henry James writes in *Hawthorne* that "the Civil War marks an era in the history of the American mind" (114), he consciously closes the door on romanticism and promotes a new literary movement, one that embraces "nothing more and nothing less than the truthful treatment of material" (Howells, *Criticism* 38). By casting off the idealisms of emblematic nineteenth-century romantic writers such as Emerson and focusing instead on the objective truths of their own Gilded Age, the American realists carefully construct a new literary identity based on historical and cultural contrast.

And yet, while *Echoes of Emerson* recognizes historical contrast as something of an ontological imperative (in American realism and beyond), it relies equally on a vision of history that resists discrete beginnings and ends. Even as Mark Twain's *Adventures of Huckleberry Finn*, Henry James's *The Portrait of a Lady*, Edith Wharton's *The House of Mirth*, and Willa Cather's *My Ántonia* develop and participate in the dominant cultural discourse of American realism, they simultaneously engage in a dialogue with the residual romantic philosophies of Emerson; more specifically, these novels attempt to reconcile Emerson's idea of the self-reliant individual with the realities of postbellum history.[4] Furthermore, it is precisely through their insistence on difference that this double consciousness emerges in American realism. In the process of forging a new literary identity that distinguishes itself from American romanticism, the realists reveal their indebtedness to an earlier culture; they write both within and against their own circumscribed historical and epistemological boundaries. Periodization thus acts as what David Perkins has called a "necessary fiction," one that paradoxically allows readers to recognize the porous, penetrable, and dialogic nature of the thing—history and culture—that it seeks to contain (65).

Recent arguments against periodization claim that such divisions are outdated, marginalize women and people of color, and distort the truth. In "How Periods Erase History," for example, Gerald Graff asserts that "we are saddled in the twenty-first century with a curriculum that still reflects the positivist view of history that was in force at the founding of the departmentalized university in the late nineteenth century" (182); in *Challenging Boundaries: Gender and Periodization*, Joyce W. Warren and Margaret Dickie present a collection of essays that specifically questions the gender issues at stake in periodization; and in "Against Periodization; or, On Institutional Time," Eric Hayot brands periodization as "the enemy of clear thinking" (739) and links the practice to "a collective failure of imagination and will on the part of the literary profession" (740).

These critics all offer unique and valid claims against the practice of periodization. In outlining the problems with historical contrast, however, they also reinforce, in various ways, the concept they work to problematize. Graff, for instance, concedes that his own concerns are "not with periodization or period-centered courses as such but with the failure adequately to connect them" (178); likewise, Warren does not denounce periodization per se but rather calls for "a reconception of such divisions" in order to reinscribe women into the structure of literary periods (xix); and even Hayot, who seems most opposed to periodization itself, ultimately suggests a way to "create new periods, which would not require us to abandon periods entirely" (747). The solution, therefore, is to reconfigure rather than eradicate the paradigm.

Challenges to periodization are repeatedly linked to postmodernism—with its skepticism of such metanarratives—and most often point back to Fredric Jameson and Michel Foucault.[5] Jameson's attacks on periodization are frequently cited as a foundation for the cultural critique of historical contrast. In *The Political Unconscious*, Jameson maintains that periodization gives "the impression of a facile totalization, a seamless web of phenomena each of which, in its own way, 'expresses' some unified inner truth . . . . Yet such an impression is fatally reductive" (27). Such reductions occur, according to Jameson, on both the synchronic level—"in which everything becomes so seamlessly interrelated that we confront either a total system or an idealistic 'concept' of a period"—and the diachronic level—"in which history is seen in some 'linear' way as the succession of such periods, stages, or moments" (28).[6] In *Postmodernism, or, The Cultural Logic of Late Capitalism*, Jameson links the problem of periodization specifically back to "the loss of historicity" in the postmodern age (x). Postmodernism is, he explains, "the effort to take the temperature of the age without instruments and in a situation in which we are not even sure there is so coherent a thing as an 'age,' or zeitgeist or 'system' or 'current situation' any longer" (xi). Thus, postmodernism becomes a cultural period in history that questions the coherence of such periods; as such, periodization—the "fatally reductive" practice—ironically becomes rooted in postmodernism itself.

Connections to Foucault are equally instructive in highlighting the salient issues of this debate. In "Nietzsche, Genealogy, History," Foucault takes on periodization indirectly, by contrasting traditional readings of history with what he calls "effective history": "We want historians to confirm our belief that the present rests upon profound intentions and immutable necessities. But the true historical sense confirms our existence among countless lost events, without a landmark or point of reference" (89). Foucault emphasizes that, while "historians take unusual pains to erase the elements in their work which reveal their grounding in a particular time and place," by contrast, "effective history . . . . acknowledges its system of injustice." (90). The question remains: how do either historians or cultural critics (such as Foucault) ever escape "knowledge as perspective"? In outlining his idea of "effective history"—one that does *not* "take unusual pains to erase the elements in their work which reveal their grounding in a particular time and place"—it would seem that Foucault also grounds his argument in a particular time and place, one that takes "unusual pains" to reject more traditional readings of history.

My purpose here is not to argue against these critics but rather to emphasize the conflict inherent in their dismissal of periodization. Like the ancient symbol of the ouroboros, the serpent that eats its own tail to sustain its life, the attempts to reject periodization ironically cause it to endure. The theorist who best explains and comes to terms with this conflict is Frank Kermode, whose arguments in *The Sense of an Ending* have helped frame my book's discussion of American realism. Kermode marks historical contrast as an innate function of how humans make sense of their place in the world: "it makes little difference . . . whether you think time will have a stop or that the world is eternal; there is still a need to speak humanly of a life's importance in relation to it—a need in the moment of existence to belong, to be related to a beginning and to an end" (3–4). According to Kermode, periodization is a product of people's need for "fictive concords with origins and ends" (7), the "need to live by the pattern rather than the fact" (11).

The key word in Kermode's argument is "fictive." As discussed in chapter 4, Kermode is careful to distinguish between myth and fiction: "Myth . . . presupposes total and adequate explanations of things as they are and were. . . . Fictions are for finding things out, and they change as the needs of sense-making change" (39). Kermode adds, importantly, that fictions "can degenerate into myths whenever they are not consciously held to be fictive" (39). To explain this critical distinction, Kermode offers the following metaphor: a "fiction of the end is like infinity plus one and imaginary numbers in mathematics, something we know does not exist, but which helps us to make sense of and to move in the world" (37). Periodization, like the imaginary numbers Kermode mentions, acts as a fictional reference point, one that—precisely because it can be recognized as fiction—can work to expose rather than mask the dialogic complexities of time.

One of the realists' principal complaints against Emerson was his seeming refusal to acknowledge and engage with the vicissitudes of time. In his review of James Elliot Cabot's 1887 biography of Emerson, for example, Henry James renews his old complaints about American romanticism found earlier in *Hawthorne*: "Ralph Waldo Emerson was a man of genius, but he led for nearly eighty years a life in which the sequence of events had little of the rapidity, or the complexity, that a spectator loves" ("Ralph" 250). Emerson lived, James seems to say, a life without clear beginnings and ends, without a sense of *kairos*, a Greek word meaning "opportune time" that Kermode uses to describe "the season, a point in time filled with significance, charged with a meaning derived from its relation to the end" (47). According to James, Emerson's distance from history meant that his "eyes were thickly bandaged" against the "evil and sin of the world": "he had no great sense of wrong—a strangely limited one, indeed, for a moralist—no sense of the dark, the foul, the base. There were certain complications in life which he never suspected" ("Ralph" 269). For James, Emerson's ignorance of time helps distinguish the romantic thinker from his own cultural moment.

James's reading of Emerson's life is, in many ways, both fair and accurate. In Emerson's 1836 introduction to *Nature*, the young scholar calls on Americans to embrace the eternal present: "Why should not we have a poetry and philosophy of insight and not of tradition, and a religion by revelation to us, and not the history of theirs?" (7). By rejecting tradition and history and instead focusing on nature—which Emerson describes as those "essences unchanged by man" (8)—the individual can be free to "enjoy an original relation to the universe" (7). In 1839 Emerson addresses the issue of time more directly, writing in his journal: "I am to invite men drenched in Time to recover themselves and come out of time, and taste their native immortal air" (qtd. in Parrington 386). And he does just that when, two years later in "Self-Reliance," he instructs his readers that man "cannot be happy and strong until he too lives with nature in the present, above time" (Emerson 270). It is precisely this image of transcendentalism—promoting the spiritual timelessness of nature over social and historical reality—that the American realists contend with in their own writing.

Although Emerson became synonymous with an idea of spiritual transcendence that privileged mind over matter, his writing nonetheless reveals that he was as subject to time as the American realists themselves. More specifically, Emerson was deeply engaged with the residual, dominant, and emergent cultures of his own age. On the one hand, he helped create and shape the dominant romantic discourse of nineteenth-century transcendentalism. This is evidenced, among other places, in his position as a founding member of The Transcendental Club in 1836, which Robert D. Richardson Jr. observes was "born 'in the way of protest' on behalf of 'deeper and broader views' than obtained at present" (245). While Emerson was entrenched in the present, however, his writing also illustrates a clear indebtedness to past cultures and, in his later work, a nod to the emerging culture of American realism.

A brief examination of Emerson's early *Nature* (1836) as well as his later

Conduct of Life (1860)—two publications that might be seen as bookends to Emerson's literary career—reinforce Emerson's active dialogue with history. Emerson's cultural relationship to the past is evident in the opening lines of *Nature*: "Our age is retrospective. It builds the sepulchers of the fathers. It writes biographies, histories, and criticism. The foregoing generations beheld God and nature face to face; we through their eyes" (7). In these lines, Emerson points readers toward "new lands, new men, new thoughts," yet he does so through historical reflection (7). Even as *Nature* works to establish a new religion, "a religion by revelation to us, and not the history of theirs," it begins by examining what has come before (7). We cannot, it seems, "demand our own works and laws and worship" until we address the past, until we demarcate the now from the then, the before from the after (7).

Although the introduction opens—as Richardson writes—"by clearing the table with a broad dismissive sweep" of the past, those "foregoing generations" are deeply embedded throughout *Nature* (226). Discussions of Emerson often chart the influence of past religions, thinkers, and cultural movements on the romantic philosopher. From the Eastern religions of Buddhism and Hinduism to the Western religions of Puritanism and Unitarianism, from Greco-Roman philosophy to German Enlightenment thinkers and British Romantic poets, scholars regularly point to the residual voices present in Emerson's literature. These voices are ubiquitous in *Nature*, so much so that the book sometimes feels like a roll call—or what Lawrence Buell refers to as "an eclectic tossed salad"—of historical-cultural figures (119). Richardson underscores the book's indebtedness to the past when he states that "*Nature* is a modern Stoic handbook, Marcus Aurelius in New England. It is also a modern version of Plato, an American version of Kant" (223). Henry James sums up the duality in Emerson's writing: "Independence, the return to nature, the finding out and doing for one's self, was ever what he most highly recommended; and yet he is constantly reminding his readers of the conventional signs and consecrations—of what other men have done" ("Ralph" 262).

Emerson engages the "dry bones of the past" as a way of forging an "original relation to the universe"; as he negotiates such residual cultures in *Nature*, he simultaneously establishes the new, dominant cultural discourse of American romanticism. Joel Porte claims that Emerson "became virtually obsessed with defining his age" (6). Barbara Packer connects this claim directly to *Nature* when she asserts that the text "aims to present nothing less than a theory of the universe, of its origin, present condition, and final destiny" (728). Emerson's first major work was meant to be monumental, a manifesto that would create dramatic cultural change and mark a new period in American history. This period would challenge Americans to shed their reliance on material reality and instead embrace the immortal truths of nature. Readers are left, therefore, with something of a paradox: Emerson develops a paradigm for his time, a new cultural zeitgeist, that instructs "men drenched in Time to recover themselves and come out of time, and taste their native immortal air" (qtd. in Parrington 386). In other words, the spirit of his age is defined by the ability to transcend that age, to live with the eternal present of nature, "above time" (Emerson, "Self-Reliance" 270).

Emerson's legacy was cemented largely by the kind of philosophical idealisms espoused in *Nature*. Late-nineteenth-century writers such as Henry James took pains to point out Emerson's eternal optimism and "ripe unconsciousness of evil," but Emerson's later works, in particular his 1851 essay "Fate" published in *The Conduct of Life* (1860), reveal an epistemological shift not accounted for in James's assessment. Critics disagree about the extent to which, in "Fate," Emerson sheds his earlier optimism; but even where "Fate" may not be a radical departure from the ideas espoused in *Nature*, as Buell points out, "the later moral essays testify to Emerson's increasing attunement to pragmatic realities" (283). One such reality was the Fugitive Slave Law of 1850, which Emerson openly denounced.[7] Although Emerson is regularly criticized for not participating more openly in the abolitionist movement, his writing during this time reveals a growing awareness of the evil James insists Emerson was blind to. "Fate," in particular, becomes Emerson's attempt to negotiate his unwavering belief in individual freedom with the growing need to face what Emerson himself calls "the odious facts" (952).

"Fate" begins with a meditation on time: "It chanced during one winter, a few years ago, that our cities were bent on discussing the theory of the Age. By an odd coincidence, four or five noted men were each reading a discourse to the citizens of Boston or New York, on the Spirit of the Times" (943). Emerson's opening lines point directly back to his introduction in *Nature*: "Our age is retrospective" (7). Yet, where the opening lines of *Nature* define the "Spirit of the Times" in terms of the past, "Fate" is now entrenched in the complexities of the present. At first, "Fate" may seem like a stark contrast to the optimism of *Nature*; it initially addresses "the question of the times" in ways that are largely pessimistic—"We are incompetent to solve the times" (943). In fact, Emerson goes on to emphasize the dialectical nature of man and the world: "If we must accept Fate, we are not less compelled to reaffirm liberty, the significance of the individual, the grandeur of duty, the power of character. This is true, and that other is true" (943). While we cannot avoid the polarities of fate and liberty, there is, he maintains, "some reasonable hope of harmonizing them" (943).

Emerson seeks to establish this harmony by empowering man not to submit to fate but, rather, to trust in individual will: "Man is not order of nature, sack and sack, belly and members, link in a chain, nor any ignominious baggage, but a stupendous antagonism, a dragging together of the poles of the Universe" (953). According to Emerson, it is the "revelation of Thought [that] takes man out of servitude into freedom" (954–55). As Stanley Cavell so beautifully expresses in *Emerson's Transcendental Etudes*: "Emerson's way of confronting fate, his recoil of fate, I will now say, is his writing, in every word; for example, in every word of 'Fate,' each of which is to be a pen stroke, a common stroke of genius, because a counterstroke of fate. You make your breath words in order not to suffocate in the plenum of air" (202). Thus, Emerson's writing itself—as the "revelation of Thought"—functions as that "stupendous antagonism" of individual will.

Without reducing the important distinctions between Emerson and the American realists, I would like to suggest that the contest between individual will and "the tyrannical Circumstance" Emerson discusses in "Fate" begins to resemble the dialogic strains of thought found in American realism (949).[8] Emerson posits "history" as a dialectical relationship between the outside world and the individual: "Nature and Thought;—two boys pushing each other on the curbstone of the pavement" (964). As I have argued, the realist novel enacts this drama between man and his environment, specifically through a contest between character and plot.[9] Emerson clearly locates a more copacetic and peaceful resolution than the realists—"here they are, side by side, god and devil, mind and matter, king and conspirator, belt and spasm, riding peacefully tougher in the eye and brain of every man" (953). None of the novels discussed in my study so neatly resolve the conflict between "mind and matter, king and conspirator." That said, Mark Twain's *Adventures of Huckleberry Finn*, Henry James's *The Portrait of a Lady*, Edith Wharton's *The House of Mirth*, and Willa Cather's *My Ántonia* all seem to take up the conversation—between "the circumstance, and the life"—where Emerson leaves off (Emerson 949). Furthermore, the novels themselves become their own forms of resistance against the historic "matter" of Gilded Age America. Where "Emerson's way of confronting fate," Cavell contends, "is his writing, in every word," so the realist novel confronts history "in order not to suffocate in the plenum of air."

The ongoing dialogue between Emerson and the American realists unveils continuity within historical contrast. Both Emerson and the American realists inscribe themselves into carefully drawn periods of time defined by beginnings and ends. Emerson starts his introduction to *Nature* with two important words: "Our age." In doing so, he clears the way for those "new lands, new men, new thoughts" (7); through his writing, he helps define this new age (and, through the formation of The Transcendental Club, quite literally name it). Almost fifty years later, when the American realist Henry James writes that "the Civil War marks an era in the history of the American mind," he bears witness to a new cultural identity, one that diverges from its romantic predecessor. "The questions of those years," James insists, "are not the questions of these" ("Ralph" 233). Writers such as Emerson and James create and reinforce these fictive concords as a way to manage what Foucault describes as "our existence among countless lost events, without a landmark or a point of reference" (89). Periodization provides such a historical "landmark or . . . point of reference" and anchors us in both time and place. And yet, even as periodization cordons off, it exposes the complex dynamics of culture. As much as Emerson promotes "an original relation to the universe," as much as the realists assert that "the questions of those years are not the questions of these," the residual and emerging historical voices surface and highlight the "push and shove" in each cultural moment—"matter and mind are in perpetual tilt and balance, so."

Notes

Introduction

1. Critics, including Francis Fukuyama himself, have since noted Will's and Zakaria's references to and potential misreadings of Fukuyama's 1989 article "The End of History?" In the article, published in the *National Interest,* Fukuyama makes the following argument about historical progression: "What we may be witnessing is not just the end of the Cold War, or the passing of a particular period of postwar history, but the end of history as such: that is, the end point of mankind's ideological evolution and the universalization of Western liberal democracy as the final form of human government" (1). In an October 2001 article in the *Wall Street Journal,* Fukuyama attempts to clarify his original argument and distinguish between major historical events (such as 9/11)—which may continue to occur—and the progressive evolution of history toward liberal democracy—which, he still contends, has reached modernity. For the purposes of my argument, Will's and Zakaria's interpretations of Fukuyama's original claim are far less important than their use of such hyperbolic discourse in reacting to the events of 9/11. Their suggestions that history somehow splits, or begins and ends, highlight the effect these types of defining historical moments have had on the consciousness of the American public.

2. Connections between the Civil War and 9/11 were noted almost immediately after 9/11. In addition to the writers and politicians who continuously compared the number of deaths to Antietam (and often got these figures wrong), Governor George Pataki chose to read Abraham Lincoln's Gettysburg Address during the one-year commemoration of 9/11. The importance and relevance of Lincoln's words were announced not only in terms of eulogy but nationalism. Thus, William Safire, in a September 9, 2002, *New York Times* editorial, told readers why Pataki would repeat Lincoln's stirring words: "What makes this particular speech so relevant for repetition on

this first anniversary of the worst bloodbath on our territory since Antietam Creek's waters ran red is this: Now, as then, a national spirit rose from the ashes of destruction." Again, one notes in Safire's language the desire to make sense of tragedy by creating epochs and writing into history finite moments of what Safire calls "conception, birth, death and rebirth."

3. For an extended discussion of the consequences of the Civil War, see Louis Menand's *The Metaphysical Club*. Menand details the magnitude of the war and its connection to major economic, political, and philosophic shifts.

4. Samuel Cohen's 2009 *After the End of History*, particularly his chapter titled "History Is What Heals," offers an insightful reading of 9/11 and its historical connection to the endings of two post-9/11 novels: Jeffrey Eugenides's *Middlesex (2002)* and Jonathan Lethem's *The Fortress of Solitude (2003)*.

5. The epilogue will address the tenacity of historical contrast (or periodization) in literary studies and discuss the relevance and role it plays in this book.

6. Two additional discussions of realism might be included here, although both are tangential to my project. Eric J. Sundquist's introductory essay, "The Country of the Blue," in his 1982 *American Realism: New Essays*, for example, maintains that "romance remained a persistent force in American realism" (10). Sundquist broaches the critical question of realism's literary legacy but locates that legacy in the romantic fiction and poetry of nineteenth-century literary writers such as Hawthorne and Whitman. More recently, in *The Antinomies of Realism* (2013), Fredric Jameson takes a similarly dialectical and historical approach to realism, which he claims is "a consequence of the tension between" destiny and the eternal present, but he focuses primarily on European realism and casts his discussion in terms of the emotion/affect binary (26). Both works are, therefore, analogous but not directly related to this study.

7. There are several studies that focus on the influence of Emersonian philosophy on individual authors of the period (Andrew Taylor's *Henry James and the Father Question* and Kristin Boudreau's *Henry James' Narrative Technique* are recent examples), but these critical works do not employ Emerson's legacy as a framework for understanding the realist period itself.

8. Critics regularly note the shift in Emerson's writings and philosophy beginning with the publication of his *Essays: Second Series* (1844), which is dominated by the essay "Experience" and infused with his grief over the recent death of his son Waldo. As Robert D. Richardson Jr. explains in *Emerson: The Mind on Fire*: "Emerson's optimism, his idealism, his prospective, future-seeking point of view are still very much intact in late 1842, but they are no longer innocent, unmenaced beliefs. There is now a haunted, driven quality to his affirmations. It is as though he was never more than a step ahead of the soul-shriveling negations he so feared" (384). The epilogue in *Echoes of Emerson* will begin to address this shift in Emerson's writing, particularly as it manifests in his 1851 essay "Fate."

9. "Republic of the spirit" is a term formulated by Edith Wharton's Lawrence Selden in *The House of Mirth* (55) and one that I borrow to describe Emerson's notion of personal freedom, or what Henry James calls "living by one's own personal light" (*Hawthorne* 67).

10. In *The English Novel: From Dickens to Lawrence*, Raymond Williams makes a similar argument about the Victorian novel; specifically, he says that the Victorian writers who responded to "that disturbed and unprecedented time . . . had no unified form, no unity of tone and language, no controlling conventions, that really answered their purposes" (85).

11. Certainly, *My Ántonia* may be considered an exception here, as its place in American literary history is often contested. Chapter 4 will begin with an in-depth examination of the novel's critical history and its role as a representative realist text.

Chapter 1

1. The entire transcript of the speech can be found in *Autobiography of Mark Twain, Volume 1*.

2. Henry Nash Smith, in his 1955 article "'That Hideous Mistake of Poor Clemens's,'" and Harold K. Bush Jr., in his 1995 article "The Mythic Struggle between East and West: Mark Twain's Speech at Whittier's 70th Birthday Celebration and W. D. Howells' *A Chance Acquaintance*," both provide an overview of the editorial responses.

3. For an extensive critical history on the speech, see James E. Caron's 2010 "The Satirist Who Clowns: Mark Twain's Performance at the Whittier Birthday Celebration."

4. As Emerson was seventy-four years old in 1877 and suffered from senility, it is arguable whether his reaction stemmed as much from his mental state as from the nature of the joke itself.

5. In his article "The Mythic Struggle between East and West," Bush also notes in Twain's speech a moment of cultural conflict, what Bush refers to as a "cultural schism" (67). While Bush similarly presents this evening as a "mythic struggle" between two literary generations (70), his essay focuses primarily on "the tension pitting East and West," which he argues "found an important symbolic manifestation in the Whittier event of 1877" (63). More specifically, he suggests that both the speech and its fallout reflect Twain's and Howells's own internal struggles between the growing East/West regional and cultural extremes. He reiterates this point in his more recent *Mark Twain and the Spiritual Crisis of His Age*: "More than anything, the controversy illustrates the tensions at the center of Twain's identity of this period: easterner vs. westerner, northerner vs. southerner, genteel vs. corn pone" (95).

6. Although Twain published this essay after *Huck Finn*, the ideas espoused here match earlier sentiments and help to solidify his position on romanticism and literary culture in general.

7. Jonathan Arac's 1997 article "*Uncle Tom's Cabin* vs. *Huckleberry Finn*: The Historian and the Critics" outlines many of these critical comparisons.

8. Poirier specifically connects Huck to Emerson in order to contrast Twain's critique of society with Jane Austen's acceptance of it.

9. Baym makes this argument in her article "Melodramas of Beset Manhood," and Walker discusses the issue in her article "Reformers and Young Maidens."

10. There is some disagreement over this number, but the general consensus is that Twain wrote the novel between 1876 and 1883.

11. In her 1908 *A Motor-Flight Through France*, Edith Wharton reiterates this reading of the railroad, noting how the recent innovation of "the motor-car has restored the romance of travel. Freeing us from all the compulsions and contacts of the railway, the bondage to fixed hours and the beaten track, the approach to each town through the area of ugliness and desolation created by the railway itself, it has given us back the wonder, the adventure and the novelty which enlivened the way of our posting grandparents" (9).

12. It can, has, and should be argued that Emerson's perspective on history shifts throughout his life; my epilogue will, in fact, directly address this issue. As discussed in the introduction, however, my reading of *Huck Finn* focuses on the relationship between Twain and a specific antebellum romantic tradition, and, as a result, I refer primarily to Emerson's earlier works, those that speak to the most traditional tenets of transcendentalism and best represent what Lawrence Buell calls Emerson's role as "spokesperson for U.S. national values like 'American individualism'" (3).

13. A third voice occurs as well, emanating from the unknown context of the narrator, Huck, retelling his story. Because this context is unknown, and the connection between narrator and character appears almost seamless, the third voice is primarily silent and therefore less important.

14. This is not to say, of course, that racism is not also apparent in Southern culture. Most of the Southerners that Huck and Jim meet, for example, own slaves, and Miss Watson's as well as Pap's racism is made thoroughly apparent early in the text. It is nevertheless ironic that those characters who symbolize postbellum Northern capitalism ultimately seem most dangerous to Jim's physical and emotional welfare.

15. Hemingway reiterates this claim in a January 2, 1926, letter he writes to Ernest Walsh: "And if you will, now, read *Huckleberry Finn*, honest to God read it as I re-read it only about three months ago . . . and the last few Chapters of it were just tacked on to finish it off by Howells or somebody" (*Selected Letters* 188). While we are not meant to take Hemingway's question of authorship seriously, the passage highlights Hemingway's repeated frustration with the novel's ending.

Chapter 2

1. In *Portrait of a Novel*, Michael Gorra discusses the uncertainty surrounding the novel's inception but places it around the same time as the publication of *Hawthorne*: "He did begin the story, that much is sure, and in April 1878 offered to show some of it to Macmillan. But nobody today knows just how far he then got, or just how closely this lost ur-*Portrait* resembles the opening moments of the book we now read" (43).

2. Eric Haralson, in *Henry James and Queer Modernity*, links these terms—"modest nosegay" and "rarest and sweetest fragrance"—to James's own fear of effeminacy. The question of James's gender anxieties will be briefly discussed later in the chapter.

3. It is interesting, and even somewhat humorous, to compare James's gendered critique of the American romantic tradition with Theodore Roosevelt's jab at James in 1915: "Thus it is with the undersized man of letters, who flees his country because

he, with his delicate effeminate sensitiveness, finds the conditions of life on this side of the water crude and raw; in other words, because he finds that he cannot play a man's part among men" (qtd. in Taylor 3). While an extended discussion of such a gendered debate exceeds the scope of my project, it is worth noting the ways in which both these writers map gender onto a geographical and national landscape. 4. One also notes high praise of Emerson in several of James's other nonfiction works, most notably in his June 1883 *Century Magazine* article on Carlyle and Emerson—where he refers to Emerson as "the voice of New England" ("Ralph" 233)—and in his December 1887 *Macmillan's Magazine* review of James Elliot Cabot's *A Memoir of Ralph Waldo Emerson*—where he calls Emerson a "man of genius" ("Ralph" 250).

5. Harold Bloom outlines this theory in *The Anxiety of Influence: A Theory of Poetry*.

6. Andrew Taylor's *Henry James and the Father Question* focuses on the relationship between Henry James Sr. and Emerson and provides an in-depth consideration of how that relationship influenced the younger James's life and literature.

7. James reinforces this reading of Emerson in his December 1887 *Macmillan's Magazine* review of James Elliot Cabot's *A Memoir of Ralph Waldo Emerson* when he remembers "walking with him in the autumn of 1872 through the galleries of the Louvre and, later that winter, through those of the Vatican: his perception of the objects contained in these collections was of the most general order. I was struck with the anomaly of a man so refined and intelligent being so little spoken to by works of art" ("Ralph" 269).

8. Interestingly Madame Merle, in James's own *The Portrait of a Lady*, disparagingly describes American expatriates as "mere parasites, crawling over the surface; we haven't our feet in the soil" (171).

9. In *The Problem of American Realism*, Michael Davitt Bell ties this question of deficient masculinity specifically to the birth of American realism. He argues that in postbellum industrial America, "active participation" was associated with masculinity, and "observation" was associated with the feminine. While men were out on the battlefield, conquering the masculine world of business, or, like James's brother "Wilky" (Garth Wilkinson), moving westward in search of experience and fortune, James was left in Boston, enmeshed in the more feminine world of culture. Realism, Bell claims, was a literary movement that allowed writers of the period to "suppress worries about one's sexuality and sexual status and to proclaim oneself a man" (37).

10. Other notable texts that discuss James's conflicted gender and sexuality include: Eve Kosofsky Sedgwick's *Epistemology of the Closet*, Victoria Coulson's *Henry James, Women and Realism*, Leland S. Person's *Henry James and the Suspense of Masculinity*, Hugh Stevens's *Henry James and Sexuality*, and John R. Bradley's *Henry James and Homo-Erotic Desire*.

11. In this reading, I will be using James's 1908 New York edition, the one most widely published, read, and discussed by critics.

12. One such book is Collin Meissner's *Henry James and the Language of Experience*. In the text, Meissner reads James's literature in terms of two central questions in realist studies: how does the realist writer articulate human experience, and how does he seek to represent reality?

13. René Wellek's 1943 "Emerson and German Philosophy" provides a useful backdrop for this connection between Emerson and "German Thought."

14. For further discussion on the historical relationship between the railroad passenger and the American Indian, see T. C. McLuhan's *Dream Tracks: The Railroad and the American Indian 1890–1930*. McLuhan specifically explores how images presented to tourists by the Santa Fe Railway portrayed tribes such as the Hopi and the Navajo in terms of racial, mythic stereotypes.

15. Lyall H. Powers—in *"The Portrait of a Lady": Maiden, Woman, and Heroine*—and Richard Poirier—in *The Comic Sense of Henry James*—are two critics who have connected Goodwood's speech to *Paradise Lost*. Arnold Kettle—in *An Introduction to the English Novel*—and Sheldon M. Novick—in *Henry James: The Mature Master*—connect the novel more broadly to Milton's epic poem.

16. One notes a similar theme in Kate Chopin's *The Awakening*, in which Chopin locates Edna Pontellier's psychological awakening within her heroine's growing consciousness. In this novel, consciousness also becomes the battleground between Edna's burgeoning Emersonian spirit and historical truth (in chapter 24, as Edna figuratively awakens, she literally begins reading Emerson). I would argue, however, that the similarities largely end here. Isabel and Edna are markedly different characters, and their psychological development is quite distinct. Among other differences, Edna's awakened consciousness is primarily self-referential. Where Isabel begins to develop an awareness of the very realistic tapestry of complex, plotting characters in her world, Edna awakens to the absence of any true reality outside of her own mind. Isabel's future will entail a continued study of those "complications of existence." Edna has no future because the only external counterpart to her awakened psyche is a staid, black-and-white, thoroughly one-dimensional and artificial construction. While Isabel's awareness, therefore, involves her "trying to understand the reality that lay behind the scattered clues of the fiction," for Edna there is no "reality" behind the "fiction"; they are one and the same (Novick, *Young Master* 421).

Chapter 3

1. The two other poets she refers to are Walt Whitman and Edgar Allan Poe: "Those two, with Emerson, are the best we have—in fact, the all we have" (qtd. in Lewis, *Edith Wharton* 236).

2. While a close analysis of Wharton's library of books as well as her personal marginalia exceeds the boundaries of this study, a thorough examination of Wharton's library may shed more light on Wharton's life and literary career and even reveal compelling elements of her personality; Wharton shows a sense of irony and humor, for example, when she places parentheses around the following quote from Emerson's essay "Character": "An individual is an encloser" (Marginalia 95).

3. For further information on specific biographical references to Emerson in Wharton's life and letters, see Linda Costanzo Cahir's "Wharton and the American Romantics."

4. Wharton's ongoing interest in the image of the house was both figurative and

literal. In addition to her published works on domestic spaces, "Wharton," Hermione Lee reports, "always characterizes families and societies through the decoration of houses" (*Edith* 18).

5. Lee notes a similar theme in Wharton's short story "The Quicksand," where "an embittered mother [says] to her son's idealistic girlfriend, . . . 'How little, as the years go on, theories, ideas, abstract conceptions of life, weigh against the actual'" (*Edith* 187).

6. This argument features most prominently in both Cynthia Griffin Wolff's "Lily Bart and the Beautiful Death" and Judith Fetterley's "'The Temptation to Be a Beautiful Object': Double Standard and Double Bind in *The House of Mirth*."

7. Benjamin Anastas's 2011 *New York Times Magazine* article titled "The Foul Reign of Emerson's 'Self Reliance'" provides a humorous example of such criticism. Anastas hyperbolically links America's selfish "money fever" and corrupt political system to Emerson's "Self-Reliance," which he calls the "most pernicious piece of literature in the American canon."

8. It is important to note that Baym also acknowledges that "many books by women . . . project a version of the particular myth we are speaking of but cast the main character as a woman." She adds, however, that "instead of being read as a woman's version of the myth, such novels are read as stories of the frustration of female nature" (135). Her central complaint, therefore, is with critics whose readings of "American literature have led to the exclusion of women authors from the canon" (123).

9. This description of Lily's father closely resembles Wharton's own father, as described in Hermione Lee's biography: "Wharton's dominant memory of her father was the sight of him bent over his desk in 'desperate calculations,' in 'the vain effort to squeeze my mother's expenditure into his narrowing income'" (*Edith* 26).

10. Among other critics, Lori Merish, in "Engendering Naturalism: Narrative Form and Commodity Spectacle in U.S. Naturalist Fiction," and Despina Korovessis, in "*The House of Mirth*: Wharton's Critique of American Society," also make similar arguments. Finally, Wai-Chee Dimock offers an analogous but nuanced reading of Nettie's character, in which she locates but also critiques Nettie as "the embodiment of . . . Wharton's ideal" (389).

11. Linda Wagner-Martin, for example, argues that the novel is about "the turn-of-the-century New Woman" ("Novel of Admonition" 107).

12. Donald Pizer contends that Rosedale's religious status includes but also extends beyond his role as "outsider": "Rosedale is not merely an Outsider who wishes entrée to the small, closed world of the New York elite, as might a nouveau riche Westerner; he is also the Jew who embodies within his nature a number of threatening and undesirable characteristics that are openly attributed to him by Wharton as characteristics" of his ethnic identity (53). One might even argue that Wharton employs Rosedale's Judaism (and her own anti-Semitism) in such a way as to accentuate Selden's emotional poverty: even the "money-grubbing Jew" is more understanding and supportive.

13. As discussed in chapter 4, Wharton is not the only realist author who reserves the role of the misguided romantic for a man: a similar gender dynamic is found in

Willa Cather's *My Ántonia*. In that novel, Jim Burden plots his future—like Selden—as a lawyer in the East, but, rather than accept his choices, he blames his spiritual failings on larger, deterministic forces. In place of each of these men, in both *The House of Mirth* and *My Ántonia*, it is a woman who becomes the text's representative of spiritual heroism. Scholars who assume that the heroic role is reserved for men overlook an interesting phenomenon in Gilded Age society. During this period, Wall Street began to replace the frontier as the symbolic location of masculine virility; the male quest moved from the spiritual to the material realm. Thus, while Lawrence Selden's and Jim Burden's gender and class allow them to profess their spiritual leanings blithely, they hide behind ideas of determinism to validate their participation in mainstream culture and justify their complacency. Lily Bart and Ántonia Shimerda lack this privilege; as women, they must address the spiritual inconsistencies that Selden and Burden continually avoid. Their plots become both difficult and tortuous, but their inability to play an "amphibious" role ultimately renders them stronger proponents of spiritual romanticism and Emersonian heroism.

Chapter 4

1. Stout's use of contradictory and qualifying adjectives—"romantic realist" and "minimalist modernist"—accentuates the conflicting nature of these critical accounts.

2. Joan Acocella—in both her 1995 *New Yorker* article "Cather and the Academy" and her 2002 book *Willa Cather and the Politics of Criticism*—has been quite vocal about her distaste for academic readings that tie Cather to feminist and queer studies. Acocella says of Judith Butler's chapter on Cather in *Bodies that Matter*, for example, that "it is not a chapter on Cather; it is an essay on politics, in which Cather's text lies bound and gagged" (72).

3. As I will discuss, Cather was not necessarily a fan of William Dean Howells's writing, but I would argue that his literary ideas make their way into her writing nonetheless.

4. Regarding Cather's interest in Edith Wharton's writing, Hermione Lee points out that Cather had "reservations towards other women writers" and "did not meet, or admit much interest in, the other great women writers of her time, Edith Wharton or Ellen Glasgow or Gertrude Stein" (*Willa* 14).

5. Norris specifically lamented the minuteness of realism, which he sarcastically described as "the drama of a broken teacup, the tragedy of a walk down the block, the excitement of an afternoon call, the adventure of an invitation to dinner" (278).

6. An exception to this argument can be found in the Winter 2001 edition of *American Literary Realism*, which seeks—in the words of Susan J. Rosowski—to "trace Willa Cather's life-long engagement with issues of representation identified with the literary school of realism" (95). While these articles certainly work toward making an important connection between Cather and the realists, interestingly none of the articles offer an extended treatment of *My Ántonia*. In addition, there remains the occasional tendency to qualify Cather's relationship to the literary movement by insisting on her overwhelmingly slippery, indefinable qualities. Janis P. Stout writes, for example: "If

literary labeling is risky with regard to Willa Cather, it is especially so when the label being applied is that of realism. Indeed, the elusiveness of the term 'realism' might well be seen as parallel to the elusiveness of Cather herself" (169).

7. See chapter 1 for a brief discussion of Howells's famous grasshopper reference.

8. In her biography *Willa Cather: Double Lives*, Hermione Lee also employs this quote in her discussion of Cather's literary themes. That said, Lee and I read its relevance to Cather in different ways. She argues that—through the "wholehearted use of pastoral"—Cather is able to "find a way of negotiating the fundamental opposition between myth and fiction" (95). I suggest that, in *My Ántonia*, Cather actually warns against the dangers of myth itself.

9. I will be using the original 1918 version of the introduction, found in the Library of America edition. In 1926, at the urging of her Houghton Mifflin editor, Ferris Greenslet, Cather revised and shortened her introduction. In the revision, Cather focuses less on Jim's current failures and makes Jim responsible for the idea to write a manuscript about Ántonia.

Although many critics choose to read the revised edition, I have chosen the original text for one central reason: as I am interested in the text as a work of American realism, it makes sense to accept the earlier 1918 version. Much happened in American history, in Cather's life, and to her writing style between 1918 and 1926. To read the 1926 version of the introduction, therefore, would be to mix Cather's literary styles and motivations.

The big issue in the 1918 introduction is the admission by the frame narrator that Jim's manuscript is "substantially as he brought it to me" (714). Sharon O'Brien and other critics point out that the "word 'substantially' . . . changes our reading experience completely," as it makes this narrator an editor and makes the reliability of the manuscript suspect (16). In the revision, though, Cather does not simply remove the word "substantially" but takes out the whole sentence. I would argue, therefore, that the reliability of the text in this later edition is just as suspect; where the first edition reveals that the manuscript is "substantially" as Jim wrote it, the second edition leaves the veracity of the manuscript completely ambiguous.

10. As I will discuss, readers are also meant to distrust Jim's role as narrator. Such a reading begins to present itself as early as the introduction, where three fundamental clues point to his unreliability. First, Jim's story is told in the first person, which highlights his subjective perspective (his use of the first-person possessive in his title, "My Ántonia," accentuates this subjectivity). Second, the frame narrator's portrait of Jim—as a capitalist lawyer in a sterile marriage and as a developer of the land he once loved—makes readers question his subsequent narrative vision. Finally, in the case of any framed narrative, readers will be asked to compare the worldview of these competing, layered narratives to locate the true values of the text.

11. That these words are inscribed on Willa Cather's tombstone emphasizes their significance in the text and accentuates the importance of Emerson's philosophy in Cather's life.

12. John J. Murphy, in My Ántonia: *The Road Home*, is another critic who reads Lena as Ántonia's foil.

13. This reading counters early criticism of the novel's form. Some complaints held that book 3, which is primarily about Lena Lingard, diverges from the focus of the book (Ántonia) and creates a loose and disjointed plot. I would argue that the section on Lena makes complete formal sense, as it illustrates that Ántonia's path is not the only one supported by the text. Through Lena, Cather suggests that it is possible to maintain spiritual integrity even outside of nature. By contrast, Jim's own path signifies a turn away not only from nature but also from the very Emersonian vision that both Ántonia and Lena embody.

14. There has been much debate over whether or not Jim and Lena become lovers. There is no clear evidence either way, and the question seems insignificant, particularly to this argument. The central point is that Jim clearly admires and even desires Lena; comments such as "I could sit idle all though a Sunday morning and look at her" make issues of consummation largely moot (887).

15. Judith Fetterley is one critic who makes this connection—in her article "*My Ántonia*, Jim Burden and the Dilemma of the Lesbian Writer."

16. Calling this moment an "epiphany" is, in itself, problematic. When Jim says "now I understood" (as opposed to the present tense, "now I understand"), one can assume that the "epiphany" is experienced by the character and not the narrator. In fact, Jim announces in the introduction that his narrative is a remembrance of things past; he says, "I didn't arrange or rearrange. I simply wrote down what of herself and myself and other people Ántonia's name recalls to me" (713–14). As such, he makes it quite clear that the text is based on memory, filtered through and greatly affected by his subsequent failures. Any epiphanies are therefore realistically those of the narrator, who "now understands" in the present. As I will discuss, Jim's seeming epiphany is simply one final attempt to rewrite history.

17. In "The Forgotten Reaping-Hook: Sex in *My Ántonia*," Blanche H. Gelfant connects Ántonia to this goddess figure.

18. Joan Acocella claims that *My Ántonia* and *One of Ours* offer "sentimental endings" ("Cather and the Academy" 62). This type of reading is precisely what is at stake, however, in reading Jim's narrative purely as Cather's own: we miss Cather's actual critique of his "sentimental ending."

19. In *Tomboys: A Literary and Cultural History*, Michelle Ann Abate argues that Ántonia is depicted not only in terms of national but also racial difference: "groups that we would now consider different white ethnicities—such as Poles, Syrians, Greeks, Armenians and Sicilians—were seen as different races during this era. Echoing this attitude, the native-born narrator in *My Ántonia* identifies his Bohemian neighbor as a marginally white person at best" (108).

20. This newfound strength of the immigrant over the traditional American may account, in part, for Cather's 1924 comment denouncing "this passion for Americanizing everything and everybody" (qtd. in Reynolds, *Willa Cather in Context* 73).

Epilogue

1. In *Why Literary Periods Mattered*, Ted Underwood outlines the critical history of periodization.

2. The December 2001 edition of *Modern Language Quarterly*, for example, is dedicated to a discussion of periodization.

3. Critics have since broadened the term to include most writers who published between the Civil War and World War I. The realists, however, actively initiated, delineated, and promoted a distinct period known as "American realism."

4. As I have argued, *My Ántonia* begins to engage emerging cultural ideas. One might also locate such emerging voices in the other three texts discussed in this book (particularly in James's *Portrait*), although I would suggest that these voices are not as palpable as they are in Cather's novel.

5. Lawrence Besserman, in *The Challenge of Periodization,* is one critic who frames this discussion as "the postmodern debate about periodization" (3); he offers a thorough reading, in particular, of Jameson's and Foucault's connections to the debate.

6. Jameson himself seems to qualify his own dismissal of periodization, as when he says in *The Political Unconscious* that "the problem of periodization and its categories . . . would seem to be as indispensable as they are unsatisfactory for any kind of work in cultural study" (28).

7. Emerson's May 1851 "Fugitive Slave Law Address" clearly reveals his growing anger over the issue of slavery. And, although they seem to disagree over whether "Fate" was composed in late 1850 or 1851, both Stanley Cavell (194) and Robert D. Richardson Jr. (500) link the essay to that important historical event.

8. One might argue that Emerson's essay "Fate" is closer to the ideas of American naturalism than realism. Certainly, the naturalists focus more on the power of nature and fate than the realists. Naturalism, however, tends to take individual will, that essence so central to the concerns of realists, out of the equation. Emerson's essay, much like realism itself, seeks some possible harmony between man and his environment.

9. Among other differences, the realists seem to conceptualize the word "history" in different terms than the romantic philosopher. In *Hawthorne,* for example, Henry James writes that "it takes a great deal of history to produce a little literature, that it needs a complex social machinery to set a writer in motion" (2). In this sense, history is not a product of man's relationship with his environment but is a fundamental component of that environment. Furthermore, in James's rendering it is culture that is produced by man's interaction with the "complex social machinery" of life. That dialogic contest between mind and matter, nevertheless, exists in both instances.

Works Cited

Abate, Michelle Ann. *Tomboys: A Literary and Cultural History*. Philadelphia: Temple UP, 2008.

Acocella, Joan. "Cather and the Academy." *New Yorker* 27 Nov. 1995: 56–71.

———. *Willa Cather and the Politics of Criticism*. Lincoln: U of Nebraska P, 2000.

Ammons, Elizabeth. *Edith Wharton's Argument with America*. Athens: U of Georgia P, 1980.

Anastas, Benjamin. "The Foul Reign of Emerson's 'Self-Reliance.'" *New York Times Magazine* 2 Dec. 2011. Web. 15 Apr. 2015. www.nytimes.com/2011/12/04/magazine/riff-ralph-waldo-emerson.html?_r=0

Arac, Jonathan. "Nationalism, Hypercanonization, and *Huckleberry Finn*." *Boundary 2* 19.1 (Spring 1992): 14–33.

———. "*Uncle Tom's Cabin* vs. *Huckleberry Finn*: The Historians and the Critics." *Boundary 2* 24:2 (Summer 1997): 79–100.

Bakhtin, M. M. *The Dialogic Imagination: Four Essays*. Translated by Caryl Emerson and Michael Holquist. Austin: U of Texas P, 1981.

Bauer, Dale M. *Feminist Dialogics: A Theory of Failed Community*. Albany: SUNY P, 1988.

Baym, Nina. "Melodramas of Beset Manhood: How Theories of American Fiction Exclude Women Authors." *American Quarterly* 33.2 (Summer 1981): 123–39.

Bell, Michael Davitt. *The Problem of American Realism: Studies in the Cultural History of a Literary Idea*. Chicago: U of Chicago P, 1993.

Bell, Millicent. *Meaning in Henry James*. Cambridge: Harvard UP, 1991.

Benert, Annette L. "The Geography of Gender in *The House of Mirth*." *Studies in the Novel* 22.1 (Spring 1990): 26–42.

Berman, Russell A. "Politics: Divide and Rule." *Modern Language Quarterly* 62.4 (Dec. 2001): 317–30.

Berthoff, Warner. *The Ferment of Realism: American Literature, 1884–1919*. Cambridge: Cambridge UP, 1965.

Besserman, Lawrence, editor. *The Challenge of Periodization: Old Paradigms and New Perspectives*. New York: Garland Publishing, 1996.

Blair, Walter. *Mark Twain and Huck Finn*. Berkeley: U of California P, 1960.

Bloom, Harold. *The Anxiety of Influence: A Theory of Poetry*. Oxford: Oxford UP, 1973.

———. Introduction. *Major Literary Characters: Ántonia*. Edited by Harold Bloom. New York: Chelsea House Publishers, 1991. 1–3.

Boudreau, Kristin. *Henry James' Narrative Technique: Consciousness, Perception, and Cognition*. New York: Palgrave Macmillan, 2010.

Bowden, Edwin T. "The Frontier Isolation." Excerpt from *The Dungeon of the Heart: Human Isolation and the American Novel*. New York: Macmillan, 1961. 46–54. Reprinted in *Major Literary Characters: Ántonia*. Edited by Harold Bloom. New York: Chelsea House Publishers, 1991. 14–18.

Bradley, John R. *Henry James and Homo-Erotic Desire*. New York: St. Martin's Press, 1999.

Brodhead, Richard H. *The School of Hawthorne*. New York: Oxford UP, 1986.

Brooks, Peter. *Reading for the Plot: Design and Intention in Narrative*. Cambridge: Harvard UP, 1984.

Brown, Lee Rust. *The Emerson Museum: Practical Romanticism and the Pursuit of the Whole*. Cambridge: Harvard UP, 1997.

Budd, Louis J. Introduction. *New Essays on "Adventures of Huckleberry Finn."* Edited by Louis J. Budd. Cambridge: Cambridge UP, 1985.

Buell, Lawrence. *Emerson*. Cambridge: Belknap-Harvard UP, 2003.

Bush, Harold K., Jr. *Mark Twain and the Spiritual Crisis of His Age*. Tuscaloosa: U of Alabama P, 2007.

———. "The Mythic Struggle Between East and West: Mark Twain's Speech at Whittier's 70th Birthday Celebration and W. D. Howells' *A Chance Acquaintance*." *American Literary Realism* 27.2 (Winter 1995): 53–73.

Cady, Edwin H. "Realism Reflects a Common Vision of Everyday Life." Excerpt from *The Light of Common Day: Realism in American Fiction*. Bloomington: Indiana UP, 1971. Reprinted in *American Realism*. Edited by Christopher Smith. San Diego: Greenhaven Press, 2000. 56–67.

Cahir, Linda Costanzo. "Wharton and the American Romantics." *Edith Wharton in Context*. Edited by Laura Rattray. Cambridge: Cambridge UP, 2012. 335–43.

Caramello, Charles. *Henry James, Gertrude Stein, and the Biographical Act*. Chapel Hill: U of North Carolina P, 1996.

Carden, Mary Paniccia. "Creative Fertility and the National Romance in Willa Cather's *O Pioneers!* and *My Ántonia*." *Modern Fiction Studies* 45:2 (Summer 1999): 275–302.

———. *Sons and Daughters of Self-Made Men: Improvising Gender, Place, and Nation in American Literature*. Lewisburg, PA: Bucknell UP, 2010.

Cargill, Oscar. "*The Portrait of a Lady*." Excerpt from *The Novels of Henry James*. New York: Macmillan, 1961. 78–119. Reprinted in *Perspectives on James's "The Portrait of a Lady": A Collection of Critical Essays*. Edited by William T. Stafford. New York: New York UP, 1967. 256–96.

Caron, James E. "The Satirist Who Clowns: Mark Twain's Performance at the Whittier Birthday Celebration." *Texas Studies in Literature and Language* 52.4 (Winter 2010): 433–66.

Carter, Bill and Jim Rutenberg. "After the Attacks: Television; Viewers Again Return to Traditional Networks." *New York Times* 15 Sept. 2001. Web. 25 May 2016. www.nytimes.com/2001/09/15/us/after-the-attacks-television-viewers-again-return-to-traditional.html?pagewanted=print

Cavell, Stanley. *Emerson's Transcendental Etudes.* Edited by David Justin Hodge. Stanford: Stanford UP, 2003.

Cather, Willa. *My Ántonia. Cather: Novels & Stories 1905–1918.* New York: Library of America, 1999. 707–937.

———. "The Novel Démeublé." *On Writing: Critical Studies on Writing as an Art.* New York: Alfred A. Knopf, 1949. 33–43.

Chandler, Marilyn R. *Dwelling in the Text: Houses in American Fiction.* Berkeley: U of California P, 1991.

Chase, Richard. *The American Novel and Its Tradition.* Baltimore: Johns Hopkins UP, 1957.

Chopin, Kate. *The Awakening.* Edited by Margo Culley. 2nd ed. New York: W. W. Norton, 1994.

Cohen, Samuel. *After the End of History: American Fiction in the 1990s.* Iowa City: U of Iowa P: 2009.

Coulson, Victoria. *Henry James, Women and Realism.* Cambridge: Cambridge UP, 2007.

Cox, James M. "Remarks on the Sad Initiation of Huckleberry Finn." *Sewanee Review* 62 (July-Sept. 1954): 389–405. Reprinted in *Huck Finn Among the Critics: A Centennial Selection.* Edited by M. Thomas Inge. Frederick, MD: University Publications of America, 1985. 141–55.

Crowley, John W. "*The Portrait of a Lady* and *The Rise of Silas Lapham*: The Company They Kept." *American Realism and Naturalism.* Edited by Donald Pizer. Cambridge: Cambridge UP, 1985. 117–37.

Cummings, Sherwood. "Mark Twain's 'Hideous Mistake,' How It Nearly Did *Huckleberry Finn* In, and How He Finally Overcame It." Fullerton: Patrons of the Library-California State U, 1985.

Cunliffe, Marcus. "The Two or More Worlds of Willa Cather." *The Art of Willa Cather.* Edited by Bernice Slote and Virginia Faulkner. Lincoln: U of Nebraska P, 1974. 21–42.

Davidson, Rob. *The Master and the Dean: The Literary Criticism of Henry James and William Dean Howells.* Columbia: U of Missouri P, 2005.

Davis, Rebecca Harding. *Rebecca Harding Davis: Writing Cultural Autobiography.* Edited by Janice Milner Lasseter and Sharon M. Harris. Nashville: Vanderbilt UP, 2001.

"The Day the World Changed." *Economist* 15 Sept. 2001: 13–14.

DeVoto, Bernard. "The Artist as American." Excerpt from *Mark Twain's America.* Boston: Little, Brown and Company, 1932. 310–20. Reprinted in *Twentieth Century Interpretations of "Adventures of Huckleberry Finn."* Edited by Claude M. Simpson. Englewood Cliffs, NJ: Prentice-Hall, 1968. 7–15.

Dimock, Wai-Chee. "Debasing Exchange: Edith Wharton's *The House of Mirth*." Reprinted in *The House of Mirth*. By Edith Wharton. Edited by Shari Benstock. Boston: Bedford Books, 1994. 375–90.

Eakin, Paul John. *The New England Girl: Cultural Ideals in Hawthorne, Stowe, Howells and James*. Athens: U of Georgia P, 1976.

Edel, Leon. *Henry James: A Life*. New York: Harper & Row, 1985.

Ellison, Ralph. *Going to the Territory*. New York: Random House, 1986.

Emerson, Everett. *Mark Twain: A Literary Life*. Philadelphia: U of Pennsylvania P, 2000.

Emerson, Ralph Waldo. *Essays and Lectures*. Edited by Joel Porte. New York: Library of America, 1983. (All Emerson quotations and references cite this edition.)

Erlich, Gloria C. *The Sexual Education of Edith Wharton*. Berkeley: U of California P, 1992.

Fabi, M. Giulia. "The Reluctant Patriarch: A Study of *The Portrait of a Lady*, *The Bostonians*, and *The Awkward Age*." *The Henry James Review* 13:1 (Winter 1992): 1–18.

Fetterley, Judith. "*My Ántonia*, Jim Burden, and the Dilemma of the Lesbian Writer." *Gender Studies: New Directions in Feminist Criticism*. Edited by Judith Spector. Bowling Green, OH: Bowling Green State University Popular Press, 1986. 43–59. Reprinted in *Major Literary Characters: Ántonia*. Edited by Harold Bloom. New York: Chelsea House Publishers, 1991. 132–47.

———. "'The Temptation to Be a Beautiful Object': Double Standard and Double Bind in *The House of Mirth*." *Studies in American Fiction* 5.2 (Autumn 1977): 199–211.

Fitzgerald, F. Scott. *The Great Gatsby*. New York: Scribner, 1925.

Foucault, Michel. "Nietzsche, Genealogy, History." *The Foucault Reader*. Edited by Paul Rabinow. New York: Pantheon Books, 1984. 76–100.

Fraser, Gordon. "The Anxiety of Audience: Economies of Readership in James's *Hawthorne*." *The Henry James Review* 34 (2013): 1–15.

Fukuyama, Francis. "The End of History?" *National Interest* 16 (Summer 1989): 1–18.

———. "History Is Still Going Our Way." *Wall Street Journal* 5 Oct. 2001. Web. 26 May 2016. www.wsj.com/articles/SB1002238464542684520

Gates, Henry Louis, Jr. *The Signifying Monkey: A Theory of African-American Literary Criticism*. New York: Oxford UP, 1988.

Geismar, Maxwell. "Nostalgic Poison." Excerpt from *Henry James and the Jacobites*. Boston: Houghton Mifflin, 1962. 40–47. Reprinted in *Twentieth Century Interpretations of "The Portrait of a Lady."* Edited by Peter Buitenhuis. Englewood Cliffs, NJ: Prentice-Hall, 1968. 45–50.

Gelfant, Blanche H. "The Forgotten Reaping-Hook: Sex in *My Ántonia*." *American Literature* 43:1 (Mar. 1971): 60–82.

Giannone, Richard. "*My Ántonia*." Excerpt from *Music in Willa Cather's Fiction*. Lincoln: U of Nebraska P, 1968. 107–23. Reprinted in *Major Literary Characters: Ántonia*. Edited by Harold Bloom. New York: Chelsea House Publishers, 1991. 83–96.

Gorman, Michael. "Jim Burden and the White Man's Burden: *My Ántonia* and Empire." *Cather Studies, Volume 6: History, Memory, and War*. Edited by Steven Trout. Lincoln: U of Nebraska P, 2006. 28–57.

Gorra, Michael. *Portrait of a Novel*. New York: Liveright, 2012.

Graff, Gerald. "How Periods Erase History." *Common Knowledge* 21.2 (2015): 177–83.

Haralson, Eric. *Henry James and Queer Modernity*. Cambridge: Cambridge UP, 2003.

Hayot, Eric. "Against Periodization; or, On Institutional Time." *New Literary History* 42.4 (2011): 739–56.

Helmick, Evelyn. "The Mysteries of Ántonia." *The Midwest Quarterly* 17.2 (Jan. 1976): 173–85. Reprinted in *Willa Cather's "My Ántonia."* Edited by Harold Bloom. New York: Chelsea House Publishers, 1987. 109–17.

Hemingway, Ernest. *Green Hills of Africa*. New York: Charles Scribner's Sons, 1935.

———. *Selected Letters 1917–1961*. Edited by Carlos Baker. New York: Scribner, 1981.

Hertzberg, Hendrik. "Tuesday, and After." *New Yorker* 24 Sept. 2001: 27–28.

Hicks, Granville. "The Case Against Willa Cather." *English Journal* 22.9 (Nov. 1933): 703–10.

Hinton, Laura. *The Perverse Gaze of Sympathy: Sadomasochistic Sentiments from* Clarissa *to* Rescue 911. Albany: SUNY P, 1999.

Holman, C. Hugh. "The Bildungsroman, American Style." Excerpt from *Windows on the World: Essays on American Social Fiction*. Knoxville: U of Tennessee P, 1979. 183–85. Reprinted in *Major Literary Characters: Ántonia*. Edited by Harold Bloom. New York: Chelsea House Publishers, 1991. 34–35.

Holmes, Catherine D. "Jim Burden's Lost Worlds: Exile in *My Ántonia*." *Twentieth Century Literature* 45.3 (Fall 1999): 336–46.

The Holy Bible: King James Version. Nashville: Thomas Nelson, 1989.

Homestead, Melissa J. and Guy J. Reynolds. Introduction. *Cather Studies, Volume 9: Willa Cather and Modern Cultures*. Edited by Melissa J. Homestead and Guy J. Reynolds. Lincoln: U of Nebraska P, 2011. ix–xx.

Howe, Irving. "A Reading of *The House of Mirth*." Excerpt from Introduction. *The House of Mirth*. By Edith Wharton. New York: Holt, Rinehart & Winston, 1962. Reprinted in *Edith Wharton: A Collection of Critical Essays*. Edited by Irving Howe. Englewood Cliffs, NJ: Prentice-Hall, 1962. 119–29.

Howells, William Dean. *Criticism and Fiction and Other Essays*. Edited by Clara Marburg Kirk and Rudolf Kirk. New York: New York UP, 1965.

———. *My Mark Twain: Reminiscences and Criticisms*. Edited by Marilyn Austin Baldwin. Baton Rouge: Louisiana State UP, 1967.

———. Review of *Hawthorne*. By Henry James. *Atlantic Monthly* 45 (Feb. 1880): 282–85. Reprinted in *Letters, Fictions, Lives: Henry James and William Dean Howells*. Edited by Michael Anesko. New York: Oxford UP, 1997. 143–46.

Jackson, Virginia. *On Periodization: Selected Essays from the English Institute*. Cambridge, MA: English Institute in Collaboration with the American Council of Learned Societies, 2010. *MLA International Bibliography*. Web. 27 July 2016. http://quod.lib.umich.edu/cgi/t/text/text-idx?c=acls;idno=heb90047

Jacobs, John. "From the World to the Wilderness: Renewal in Thoreau and Cather." *Teaching Cather* 3.2 (Spring 2003): 12–16.

James, Henry. "The Art of Fiction." *Literary Criticism: Volume One*. New York: Library of America, 1984. 44–65.

———. "Ralph Waldo Emerson." *Literary Criticism: Volume One*. New York: Library of America, 1984. 233–71.

———. *Hawthorne*. Ithaca: Cornell UP, 1997.

———. *Notes of a Son and Brother*. London: Macmillan, 1914.

———. Preface to the New York Edition (1908). *The Portrait of a Lady*. Edited by Robert D. Bamberg. 2nd ed. New York: W. W. Norton, 1995. 3–15.

———. *The Portrait of a Lady*. Edited by Robert D. Bamberg. 2nd ed. New York: W. W. Norton, 1995.

Jameson, Fredric. *The Antinomies of Realism*. London: Verso, 2015.

———. *The Political Unconscious: Narrative as a Socially Symbolic Act*. Ithaca: Cornell UP, 1981.

———. *Postmodernism, or, The Cultural Logic of Late Capitalism*. Durham, NC: Duke UP, 1991.

Jones, Gavin. *American Hungers: The Problem of Poverty in U.S. Literature, 1840–1945*. Princeton: Princeton UP, 2008.

Joyce, James. *A Portrait of the Artist as a Young Man*. Mineola, NY: Dover Publications, 1994.

Kaplan, Amy. *The Social Construction of American Realism*. Chicago: U of Chicago P, 1988.

Kaplan, Fred. *Henry James: The Imagination of Genius*. Baltimore: Johns Hopkins UP, 1992.

Kaplan, Justin. "Born to Trouble: One Hundred Years of *Huckleberry Finn*." Florida Center for the Book. Broward County Library, Fort Lauderdale. 11 Sept. 1984. Lecture. Reprinted in *"Adventures of Huckleberry Finn": A Case Study in Critical Controversy*. Edited by Gerald Graff and James Phelan. Boston: Bedford Books, 1995. 348–59.

Kassanoff, Jennie A. "Extinction, Taxidermy, Tableaux Vivants: Staging Race and Class in *The House of Mirth*." *PMLA* 115 (Jan. 2000): 60–74. Reprinted in *Edith Wharton's "The House of Mirth": A Casebook*. Edited by Carol J. Singley. New York: Oxford UP, 2003. 299–330.

Kaston, Carren. *Imagination and Desire in the Novels of Henry James*. New Brunswick, NJ: Rutgers UP, 1984.

Kazin, Alfred. *On Native Grounds: An Interpretation of Modern American Prose Literature*. San Diego: Harvest, 1995.

Keats, John. *Selected Letters*. Edited by Robert Gittings. Oxford: Oxford UP, 2002.

Kermode, Frank. *The Sense of an Ending: Studies in the Theory of Fiction*. London: Oxford UP, 1968.

Kettle, Arnold. *An Introduction to the English Novel: Volume II*. 2nd ed. London: Hutchinson University Library, 1974.

Korovessis, Despina. "*The House of Mirth*: Edith Wharton's Critique of Society." *Seers and Judges: American Literature as Political Philosophy*. Edited by Christina Dunn Henderson. Lanham, MD: Lexington Books, 2002. 49–72.

Kress, Jill M. *The Figure of Consciousness: William James, Henry James, and Edith Wharton*. New York: Routledge, 2002.

Lears, T. J. Jackson. *No Place of Grace: Antimodernism and the Transformation of American Culture, 1880–1920.* Chicago: U of Chicago P, 1994.

Lee, Hermione. *Edith Wharton.* New York: Vintage Books, 2008.

———. *Willa Cather: Double Lives.* New York: Vintage Books, 1989.

Lewis, R. W. B. *The American Adam: Innocence, Tragedy, and Tradition in the Nineteenth Century.* Chicago: U of Chicago P, 1955.

———. *Edith Wharton.* New York: Fromm, 1985.

Lowry, Richard S. *"Littery Man": Mark Twain and Modern Authorship.* New York: Oxford UP, 1996.

Lubin, David M. "Act of Portrayal." Excerpt from *Act of Portrayal: Eakins, Sargent, James.* New Haven: Yale UP, 1985. Reprinted in *Henry James's "The Portrait of a Lady."* Edited by Harold Bloom. New York: Chelsea House Publishers, 1987. 99–115.

Lukács, Georg. *The Theory of the Novel.* Translated by Anna Bostock. Cambridge: MIT P, 1971.

Marx, Leo. *The Machine in the Garden: Technology and the Pastoral Ideal in America.* New York: Oxford UP, 1964.

———. "Mr. Eliot, Mr. Trilling, and *Huckleberry Finn.*" *American Scholar* 22.4 (1953): 423–40. Reprinted in *"Adventures of Huckleberry Finn": A Case Study in Critical Controversy.* Edited by Gerald Graff and James Phelan. Boston: Bedford Books, 1995. 290–305.

Matthews, Brander. Review of *Adventures of Huckleberry Finn,* by Mark Twain. *Saturday Review* [London] 31 Jan. 1885: 153. Reprinted in *Adventures of Huckleberry Finn.* By Mark Twain. Edited by Thomas Cooley. 3rd ed. New York: W. W. Norton, 1999. 330–33.

Matthiessen, F. O. "The Painter's Sponge and Varnish Bottle." Excerpt from *Henry James: The Major Phase.* Edited by F. O. Matthiessen. Oxford: Oxford UP, 1944. Reprinted in *The Portrait of a Lady.* By Henry James. Edited by Robert D. Bamberg. 2nd ed. New York: W. W. Norton, 1995. 577–97.

Maynard, W. Barksdale. *Walden Pond: A History.* New York: Oxford UP, 2004.

Mazzella, Anthony J. "The New Isabel." *The Portrait of a Lady.* By Henry James. Edited by Robert D. Bamberg. 2nd ed. New York: W. W. Norton, 1995. 597–619.

McCall, Dan. Foreword. *Hawthorne.* By Henry James. Ithaca: Cornell UP, 1997. vii–xvii.

McLuhan, T. C. *Dream Tracks: The Railroad and the American Indian 1890–1930.* New York: Abrams, 1985.

McMahan, Elizabeth E. "The Money Motif: Economic Implications in *Huckleberry Finn.*" *Mark Twain Journal* 15.4 (Summer 1971): 5–10.

Meissner, Collin. *Henry James and the Language of Experience.* Cambridge: Cambridge UP, 1999.

Menand, Louis. *The Metaphysical Club: A Story of Ideas in America.* New York: Farrar, Straus and Giroux, 2001.

Merish, Lori. "Engendering Naturalism: Narrative Form and Commodity Spectacle in U.S. Naturalist Fiction." *Novel: A Forum on Fiction* 29 (Spring 1996): 319-45. Reprinted in *Edith Wharton's "The House of Mirth": A Casebook.* Edited by Carol J. Singley. New York: Oxford UP, 2003. 229–70.

Miller, James E., Jr. "*My Ántonia* and the American Dream." *Prairie Schooner* 48:2 (Summer 1974): 112–23.

Milton, John. *Paradise Lost. John Milton: A Critical Edition of the Major Works.* Edited by Stephen Orgel and Jonathan Goldberg. Oxford: Oxford UP, 1991. 355–618.

Mitchell, Charles E. *Individualism and Its Discontents: Appropriations of Emerson, 1880–1950.* Amherst: U of Massachusetts P, 1997.

Monteiro, George. "'The Items of High Civilization': Hawthorne, Henry James, and George Parsons Lathrop." *Nathaniel Hawthorne Journal* (1975): 146–55.

Montgomery, Judith H. "The American Galatea." *College English* 32:8 (May 1971): 890–99.

Murphy, John J. Introduction. *Critical Essays on Willa Cather.* Edited by John J. Murphy. Boston: G.K. Hall & Co., 1984. 1–28.

———. *"My Ántonia": The Road Home.* Boston: Twayne Publishers, 1989.

Nettles, Elsa. "What Happens to Criticism When the Artist Becomes an Icon?" *Cather Studies, Volume 7: Willa Cather as Cultural Icon.* Edited by Guy Reynolds. Lincoln: U of Nebraska P, 2007. 3–12.

Nevius, Blake. *Edith Wharton: A Study of Her Fiction.* Berkeley: U of California P, 1953.

Niemtzow, Annette. "Marriage and the New Woman in *The Portrait of a Lady.*" *American Literature* 47.3 (Nov. 1975): 377–95.

Norris, Frank. "A Plea for Romantic Fiction." *Boston Evening Transcript* 18 Dec. 1901: 14. Reprinted in *McTeague.* By Frank Norris. Edited by Donald Pizer. 2nd ed. New York: W. W. Norton, 1997. 277–80.

Novick, Sheldon M. *Henry James: The Mature Master.* New York: Random House, 2007.

———. *Henry James: The Young Master.* New York: Random House, 1996.

O'Brien, Sharon. Introduction. *New Essays on "My Ántonia."* Edited by Sharon O'Brien. New York: Cambridge UP, 1999. 1–29.

Olin-Ammentorp, Julie and Ann Ryan. "Undine Spragg and the Transcendental I." *Edith Wharton Review* 17.1 (Spring 2001): 1–9.

Orvell, Miles. "Time, Change, and the Burden of Revision in *My Ántonia.*" *New Essays on "My Ántonia."* Edited by Sharon O'Brien. New York: Cambridge UP, 1999. 31–56.

Packer, Barbara. "Ralph Waldo Emerson." *The Columbia Literary History of the United States.* Edited by Emory Elliot. New York: Columbia UP, 1988: 381-98. Reprinted in *Emerson's Prose and Poetry.* Edited by Joel Porte and Saundra Morris. New York: W. W. Norton, 2001. 725–38.

Parrington, Vernon Louis. *Main Currents in American Thought: The Romantic Revolution in America, 1800–1860.* Vol. 2. Norman: U of Oklahoma P, 1987.

Peck, Demaree C. *The Imaginative Claims of the Artist in Willa Cather's Fiction: "Possession Granted by a Different Lease."* Selinsgrove, PA: Susquehanna UP, 1996.

Perkins, David. *Is Literary History Possible?* Baltimore: Johns Hopkins UP, 1992.

Person, Leland S. *Henry James and the Suspense of Masculinity.* Philadelphia: U of Pennsylvania P, 2003.

Peters, Matthew. "Henry James's *Hawthorne.*" *The Cambridge Quarterly* 42.4 (2013): 305–17.

Pizer, Donald. *American Naturalism and the Jews: Garland, Norris, Dreiser, Wharton, and Cather*. Urbana: U of Illinois P, 2008.

Poirier, Richard. *The Comic Sense of Henry James: A Study of the Early Novels*. New York: Oxford UP, 1967.

———. *A World Elsewhere: The Place of Style in American Literature*. Madison: U of Wisconsin P, 1985.

Porte, Joel. "Introduction: Representing America—the Emerson Legacy." *The Cambridge Companion to Ralph Waldo Emerson*. Edited by Joel Porte and Saundra Morris. Cambridge: Cambridge UP, 1999. 1–12.

Powers, Lyall H. *"The Portrait of a Lady": Maiden, Woman, and Heroine*. Boston: Twayne Publishers, 1991.

Powers, Ron. *Mark Twain: A Life*. New York: Free Press, 2005.

Rahv, Philip. "The Heiress of All the Ages." Excerpt from *Image and Idea*. Norfolk, CT: New Directions, 1957. 51–52, 62–70. Reprinted in *Perspectives on James's "The Portrait of a Lady": A Collection of Critical Essays*. Edited by William T. Stafford. New York: New York UP, 1967. 139–47.

Railton, Benjamin A. *Contesting the Past, Reconstructing the Nation: American Literature and Culture in the Gilded Age, 1876–1893*. Tuscaloosa: U of Alabama P, 2008.

Reif, Rita. "Twain Manuscript Resolves Huck Finn Mysteries." *New York Times* 26 Feb. 1991. Web. 2 June 2016. www.nytimes.com/1991/02/26/books/twain-manuscript -resolves-huck-finn-mysteries.html

Restuccia, Frances L. "The Name of the Lily: Edith Wharton's Feminism(s)." *The House of Mirth*. By Edith Wharton. Edited by Shari Benstock. Boston: Bedford Books, 1994. 404–18.

Reynolds, Guy. Introduction. *Cather Studies, Volume 7: Willa Cather as Cultural Icon*. Edited by Guy Reynolds. Lincoln: U of Nebraska P, 2007. ix–xi.

———. *Willa Cather in Context: Progress, Race, Empire*. New York: St. Martin's Press, 1996.

Richardson, Robert D., Jr. *Emerson: The Mind on Fire*. Berkeley: U of California P, 1995.

Rosenblatt, Roger. "The Age of Irony Comes to an End." *Time* 24 Sept. 2001: 79.

Rosowski, Susan J. "Introduction: Willa Cather and American Literary Realism." *American Literary Realism* 33:2 (Winter 2001): 95–98.

———. "Prospects for the Study of Willa Cather." *Resources for American Literary Study* 22.2 (1996): 147–65.

———. *The Voyage Perilous: Willa Cather's Romanticism*. Lincoln: U of Nebraska P, 1986.

Rovit, Earl. "James and Emerson: The Lesson of the Master." *American Scholar* 33.3 (Summer 1964): 434–40.

Rubin, Larry. "Aspects of Naturalism in Four Novels by Edith Wharton." *Twentieth Century Literature* 2.4 (January 1957): 182–92.

Ruland, Richard. "Beyond Harsh Inquiry: The Hawthorne of Henry James." *ESQ* 25 (1979): 95–117.

Sabiston, Elizabeth Jean. *The Prison of Womanhood: Four Provincial Heroines in Nineteenth-Century Fiction*. London: Macmillan, 1987.

Safire, William. "A Spirit Reborn." *New York Times* 9 Sept. 2002: A23.

Salomon, Roger B. "Realism as Disinheritance: Twain, Howells and James." *American Quarterly* 16:4 (Winter 1964): 531–44.

Sawicki, Joseph. "Authority/Author-ity: Representation and Fictionality in *Huckleberry Finn.*" *Modern Fiction Studies* 31.4 (Winter 1985): 691–702.

Scholes, Robert E. "Hope and Memory in *My Ántonia.*" *Shenandoah* 14.1 (Autumn 1962): 24-29. Reprinted in *Major Literary Characters: Ántonia.* Edited by Harold Bloom. New York: Chelsea House Publishers, 1991. 18–22.

Scholes, Robert, James Phelan, and Robert Kellogg. *The Nature of Narrative.* Fortieth Anniversary Edition. New York: Oxford UP, 2006.

Sedgwick, Eve Kosofsky. *Epistemology of the Closet.* Berkeley: U of California P, 1990.

Shi, David E. *Facing Facts: Realism in American Thought and Culture, 1850–1920.* New York: Oxford UP, 1995.

Showalter, Elaine. "The Death of the Lady (Novelist): Wharton's *House of Mirth.*" *Representations* 9 (Winter 1985): 133–49. Reprinted in *The House of Mirth.* By Edith Wharton. Edited by Elizabeth Ammons. New York: W. W. Norton, 1990. 357–72.

Simon, Roger. "Innocence Lost Forever on 9/11." *U.S. News & World Report* 14 Sept. 2001. Web. 25 May 2016. www.usnews.com/news/articles/2001/09/14/innocence -lost-forever-on-911

Singley, Carol J. Introduction. *Edith Wharton's "The House of Mirth": A Casebook.* Edited by Carol J. Singley. New York: Oxford UP, 2003. 3–25.

Smith, Henry Nash. "'That Hideous Mistake of Poor Clemens's.'" *Harvard Library Bulletin* 9.2 (Spring 1955): 145–80.

Stevens, Hugh. *Henry James and Sexuality.* Cambridge: Cambridge UP, 1988.

Stineback, David C. *Shifting World: Social Change and Nostalgia in the American Novel.* Lewisburg, PA: Bucknell UP, 1976.

Stokes, Claudia. *Writers in Retrospect: The Rise of American Literary History, 1875–1910.* Chapel Hill: U of North Carolina P, 2006.

Stone, Donald David. *Novelists in a Changing World: Meredith, James, and the Transformation of English Fiction in the 1880's.* Cambridge: Harvard UP, 1972.

Stouck, David. "Willa Cather and the Impressionist Novel." *Critical Essays on Willa Cather.* Edited by John J. Murphy. Boston: G. K. Hall & Co., 1984. 48–66.

Stout, Janis P. "Seeing and Believing: Willa Cather's Realism." *American Literary Realism* 33:2 (Winter 2001): 168–80.

Sundquist, Eric J. "The Country of the Blue." *American Realism: New Essays.* Edited by Eric J. Sundquist. Baltimore: Johns Hopkins UP, 1982. 3–24.

Taylor, Andrew. *Henry James and the Father Question.* Cambridge: Cambridge UP, 2002.

Thoreau, Henry David. *Walden; or, Life in the Woods. A Week, Walden, The Maine Woods, Cape Cod.* Edited by Robert F. Sayre. New York: Library of America, 1985. 321–587.

Trout, Steven. Introduction. *Cather Studies, Volume 6: History, Memory, and War.* Edited by Steven Trout. Lincoln: U of Nebraska P, 2006. xi–xxv.

Turner, Frederick Jackson. *The Frontier in American History.* New York: Henry Holt, 1921.

Twain, Mark. *Adventures of Huckleberry Finn*. Edited by Thomas Cooley. 3rd ed. New York: W. W. Norton, 1999.

———. *Autobiography of Mark Twain, Volume 1*. Edited by Harriet Elinor Smith et al. Berkeley: U of California P, 2010.

———. "Fenimore Cooper's Literary Offences." *Huck Finn; Pudd'nhead Wilson; No. 44, The Mysterious Stranger; and Other Writings*. New York: Library of America, 2000. 669–81.

———. *Life on the Mississippi*. New York: Oxford UP, 1990.

Underwood, Ted. *Why Literary Periods Mattered: Historical Contrast and the Prestige of English Studies*. Stanford: Stanford UP, 2013.

Veblen, Thorstein. *The Theory of the Leisure Class*. Amherst, NY: Prometheus Books, 1998.

Wagner-Martin, Linda. "*The House of Mirth*: A Novel of Admonition." Excerpt from *"The House of Mirth": A Novel of Admonition*. Twayne's Masterwork Studies. Boston: G.K. Hall, 1990. 1–11, 30–40. Reprinted in *Edith Wharton's "The House of Mirth": A Casebook*. Edited by Carol J. Singley. New York: Oxford UP, 2003. 107–30.

———. *The Modern American Novel 1914–1945: A Critical History*. Boston: Twayne, 1990.

Walcutt, Charles Child. *American Literary Naturalism, A Divided Stream*. Minneapolis: U of Minnesota P, 1956.

Walker, Nancy A. "Reformers and Young Maidens: Women and Virtue in *Adventures of Huckleberry Finn*." *One Hundred Years of "Huckleberry Finn."* Edited by Robert Sattelmeyer and J. Donald Crowley. Columbia: U of Missouri P, 1985. 171–85. Reprinted in *"Adventures of Huckleberry Finn": A Case Study in Critical Controversy*. Edited by Gerald Graff and James Phelan. Boston: Bedford Books, 1995. 485–504.

"The War Against America: An Unfathomable Attack." Editorial. *New York Times* 12 Sept. 2001: A26.

Warren, Joyce W. "The Challenge of Women's Periods." *Challenging Boundaries: Gender and Periodization*. Edited by Joyce W. Warren and Margaret Dickie. Athens: U of Georgia P, 2000. ix–xxiv.

Wellek, René. "Emerson and German Philosophy." *New England Quarterly* 16.1 (Mar. 1943): 41–62.

Welty, Eudora. "The House of Willa Cather." *The Art of Willa Cather*. Edited Bernice Slote and Virginia Faulkner. Lincoln: U of Nebraska P, 1974. 3–20.

West, Rebecca. *Henry James*. New York: Henry Holt, 1916.

Wharton, Edith. *A Backward Glance*. New York: Simon & Schuster, 1998.

———. *The House of Mirth*. Edited by Elizabeth Ammons. New York: W. W. Norton, 1990.

———. Marginalia. *Essays: Second Series*. By Ralph Waldo Emerson. Boston: Houghton, Mifflin and Company, 1884. Personal collection of Edith Wharton. Lenox, MA: Library at The Mount: Edith Wharton's Home.

———. *A Motor-Flight through France*. New York: Atlas, 2008.

Whitley, John S. "Kid's Stuff: Mark Twain's Boys." Excerpt from *Mark Twain: A Sumptuous Variety*. Edited by Robert Giddings. New York: Barnes & Noble, 1985. 60–

61, 64–76. Reprinted in *Major Literary Characters: Huck Finn*. Edited by Harold Bloom. New York: Chelsea House Publishers, 1990. 155–63.

Will, George F. "The Paradox of Terrorism." *Washington Post Online* 11 Sept. 2001. Web. 25 May 2016. www.washingtonpost.com/wp-srv/nation/articles/will11.htm

Williams, Raymond. *The English Novel: From Dickens to Lawrence*. New York: Oxford UP, 1970.

———. *Marxism and Literature*. Oxford: Oxford UP, 1977.

Woodress, James. *Willa Cather: A Literary Life*. Lincoln: U of Nebraska P, 1987.

Wolff, Cynthia Griffin. "Lily Bart and the Beautiful Death." *American Literature* 46.1 (1974): 16-40. Reprinted in *The House of Mirth*. By Edith Wharton. Edited by Elizabeth Ammons. New York: W. W. Norton, 1990. 320–39.

———. "Lily Bart and the Drama of Femininity." *American Literary History* 6.1 (Spring 1994): 71–87. Reprinted in *Edith Wharton's "The House of Mirth": A Casebook*. Edited by Carol J. Singley. New York: Oxford UP, 2003. 209–28.

Zakaria, Fareed. "The End of the End of History." *Newsweek* 24 Sept. 2001: 70.

Index